Terri

From:

[signature]

Date:

6/29/09

Once Broken, Now Blessed:

A Testimony of Trials and Triumphs

Shaundale Hornes Johnson
JOURNEY TO JOURNAL PUBLISHNG, LLC
http://www.shaundalejohnson.com
shj@shaundalejohnson.com

This publication is designed to provide accurate and authoritative information in regard to the subject matter covered. It is sold with the understanding that the publisher is not engaged in rendering any legal, medical, accounting, or other professional service. If legal, medical, financial, or other expert assistance is required, the services of a competent, professional person should be sought. This publication is also a testimony of my own life and a testament to my own faith. The circumstances of certain events, the names of certain individuals, and the locations of certain places mentioned have all been changed to protect the privacy of the persons and/or establishments involved.

This book, or parts thereof, may not be reproduced in any form, stored in a retrieval system, or transmitted in any form by any means—electronic, mechanical, photocopy, recording, or otherwise—without prior written permission of the publisher, except as provided by United States of America copyright law.

Unless otherwise indicated, all scripture quotations are taken from the New International Version® of the Holy Bible, Copyright ©1973, 1978, and 1984 by International Bible Society. Used by permission of Zondervan Publishing House. All rights reserved.

The "NIV" and "New International Version" trademarks are registered in the United States Patent and Trademark Office by International Bible Society. Use of either trademark requires the permission of International Bible Society.

Scripture quotations marked "Amplified" are from the Amplified Bible. Old Testament copyright ©1965, 1987 by the Zondervan Corporation. The Amplified New Testament copyright ©1954, 1958, 1987 by the Lockman Foundation. Used by permission.

Scripture quotations marked "KJV" are from the King James Version of the Bible ©1970 The National Publishing Company.

Johnson, Shaundale Hornes
Once Broken, Now Blessed: A Testimony of Trials and Triumphs / Shaundale Hornes Johnson / Inspiration / Motivation / Non-fiction / Autobiographical / Christian Living

ISBN: 978-0-9777245-0-5

Copyright ©2009 Shaundale Hornes Johnson. All rights reserved.

Printed in the United States

Photography/Cover Design by Sean Love (*http://www.the-lovegroup.com*)

"[While on your **JOURNEY**] *Write thee all the words that I have spoken un***TO** *thee in a book* [**JOURNAL**]." Jeremiah 30:2 *(Inserts and emphasis added.)*

DEDICATIONS

Emahn and Eian,

You are my daily accountability. It is because of you that I strive to walk worthy of the name Christian, holy and acceptable before the Lord. I know that you are on loan to me from God, and it is my spiritual responsibility to send you back just like you came forth: knowing His voice, obeying His commands, and praising His name. May you find your own purpose, follow your own path, and fulfill your own dreams... *to the glory of the Most High God!*

Dreaming big and expecting much,
Mom

In Loving Memory,
Dr. E. K. Bailey, Founding Pastor
Concord Missionary Baptist Church - Dallas, Texas

Mrs. Mittie Milo Hornes
September 17, 1919 – June 19, 2007

AUTHOR APPRECIATIONS

To my Father who tore me down to build me up,

Thank You for granting me the peace I needed, the wisdom I sought, and the faith I'll forever exemplify.

To my husband and my friend,

You have supported me when I've spun "seemingly" out of control, loved me when I have lashed out, and encouraged me when the last thing I wanted to do was endure. Because you believed in me, even when I stopped believing in you, I now know what faith looks like. Although this is my story, it is our journey to happily ever after. *Once upon a time... in a land far away...*

To my peers with sincere gratitude,

From the answering of questions to simply lending a listening ear, each of you contributed to the success of this project. Thank you Lois Snell, Francis Ray,

ReShonda Tate Billingsley, Vivi Monroe Congress, Charitta Danley, Nea Anna Simone, Victoria Christopher Murray, Marc Lacy, Elaine Flowers, Michelle Stimpson, Chris Howell, Pastor Daryl Tate, Sheila M. Goss, Vincent Alexandria, Kendra Bellamy-Norman, W. Eric Croomes, Mark D. Crutcher, Electa Rome Parks, and Eric Jerome Dickey for all of your patience. I am grateful for your accessibility and your time.

To my faithful "no limit" friends who need no recognition,

Thank you for your encouragement and protection of who you know I am, have always been, and will continue to be. You remind me that "the more things change, the more they remain the same."

Special thanks to Rhonda Russell and Dr. Corinne S. Pearson, DDS. You ladies are definitely my Aaron and Hur. When my arms got tired, you held them up. When I cried, you dried my tears. When I felt like dying, you spoke life. When I whined that God had forsaken me, you kept me from forsaking Him. I am forever indebted to your strength. Thanks for making me sit down somewhere, while you kept me up on the mountain and out of the battle below. You two are the best!

Acknowledgements

Remembering the stories I was told surrounding my birth, I chuckle. I was born two months early and, having gone through this new rebirth experience, I can truly say thanks to all of you who assisted me in this process of spiritual growth.

Having heard I weighed only four pounds and three ounces, I was kept in an incubator until I was able to go home. To those who kept me safe and warm, thank you for *helping* me to grow by listening, advising, and praying.

Born incredibly small, I was carried around on a pillow for cushion and support. To those who were my comfort and strength, thank you for *enabling* me to grow by embracing membership, expecting maturity, and making a difference.

With little need for space, I slept in the top dresser drawer until I was ready for a crib. To the ones who gave me security, thank you for steadying, preparing, and *encouraging* me to grow by sowing into that which God has birthed in me.

INTRODUCTION

*T**his is the day the Lord has made! I will rejoice and be glad in it.* (Psalm 118:24) Now, I didn't just say this because we've recently celebrated our first anniversary, or on today we closed on our first house. No, today is the first day of the beginning of our lives!

I come from a small town in central Louisiana. I'm the eldest of two daughters; the one who was constantly told she dreamed too big and wanted too much. So, I never grasped the concept of my dreams being tied to my destiny, nor being a gift from God. I'm also the one who, through a painful journey of God's unfailing love, discovers He has a purpose and a plan for my life—and has all along—as He tells me "what shall become of my dreams."

Derrick and I were married in November of 1998 and received a letter, one month later, regarding employee stock options from his employer. The options were to be awarded and begin vesting in December of the following year. God definitely had His hands on us, or so we thought.

I began to talk with Derrick about my desires to become a foster/adoptive parent early in our marriage. I had no idea why I felt this burden to become a foster and/or adoptive parent at some point in my life, but I did—awfully bad. Slowly, I started to gather information online, and when we found out we were having our first child I thought that would be the end of my foster/adoptive parent longings.

We later moved into our newly built home on January 21, 2000 and life was good. In fact, life was great because the stock market was soaring. I definitely thought we had arrived and that was where God apparently wanted us in this life. By now I had a child of my own, but my longings to adopt/foster had returned—at an increased rate. When I decided to look into foster parenting again, I later learned we were expecting our second child and thought surely God was against the idea of me becoming an adoptive/foster mom. After all, both times I'd given serious thought to the matter, we'd conceived.

Accepting this as the fate of our family, I tried to silence the desires within me. Then, when a series of winds began to blow that would not only test our family—but our faith, marriage, and finances as well—I had to not only learn the severity of how to lean and depend on God, but to listen to and follow His voice, too. He'd blessed us, but by this time I'd practically cursed Him with my self-proclaimed "success."

Standing in front of the bathroom mirror, I looked around and took in all we'd accomplished: our marriage, our family, our money, and our possessions. With my chest stuck out and my nose held high, I recalled all of the promises I'd made myself as a child. I'd gone to college and done well. I'd accepted one of four job offers and graduated (the way I saw it, having to find a job defeated the purpose of graduating). I'd married by 25. And, I'd become a millionaire by 30. *You did it,* I thought. *Look at all you've done.* Then, I proudly shouted at the reflection in the mirror, "Look at all I've done. Look at all *I've* done." That's when I felt it. Something left me. I knew what it was immediately and gasped.

My heart became heavy and I held my hand in place over it. "Lord, I'm sorry," I whispered. *"Please,* forgive me!" I screamed. But, there was no one there. I lowered my hand and bowed my head. As I turned and dragged my feet out of the bathroom, I reached for the light switch and suddenly the room became as cold and as dark as the spirit of gloom hovering over me. My anointing was gone. The favor of God had left me and I didn't know what to do about it, or how to get it back. He'd heard me cry out. I knew He cared. He *had* to, I convinced myself. Otherwise, His Word wouldn't be true and that would make Him... "A liar," I sighed.

"Is God a liar?" I asked myself. After all, He said He'd never leave me or forsake me. Now, He was gone. Had He abandoned me? *Had* he left? I became *angry.* I was so sad and at such a loss... a loss for words and a loss for emotion, a loss for what was true and who could be trusted. Surely, not God; *He* couldn't be trusted. I was lost, hurt, and confused, but what had I done? I'd *forsaken* Him. I'd *disowned* Him. I'd disconnected myself from who He was as Jehovah-Jireh (My Provider) and I believe He'd had just about enough of me. Do you ever feel like that as a mom or dad? As a sibling or child? Perhaps, maybe even as a friend or employer/employee? Have you ever just had enough? *I have.*

Well, God knew He had to do something. He had to get my attention. Would that be a whipping? A "time-out?" Withholding a privilege or grounding? Maybe I needed a flat-out, old-school beating. Well, what I got was the scolding of a lifetime and all my stuff taken away [until I could act like I had the good sense He gave me]. God knew the best way to get my attention was to take it all back—everything He'd ever given me. I thought I'd earned it all with my degree, based on my experience, or the people I knew. *Whatever!* He needed to show me that without Him I am capable of nothing—doing nothing, acquiring nothing, and being nothing. And, He did. In His own way, He stripped me of everything and left me with nothing. Then, He called me by my name—the one He gave me, not the one I'd created—and He wrapped His loving arms around me and held me close.

When the wind is howling and the rain is pouring, God doesn't scream, nor does He shout. He simply opens the Door and calls out. This book is my answer. Out of the overflow may my brokenness be a blessing unto you, and may you and I dwell together in the house of the Lord—forever broken and eternally blessed.

Once Broken: The Trials

*The Lord is my shepherd;
I shall not want.
He maketh me to lie down in green pastures;
He leadedth me beside the still waters.
(Psalm 23:1-2, KJV)*

"Sorrow is better than laughter,
because a sad face is good for the heart." Ecclesiastes 7:3

"The sacrifices of God are a broken spirit;
a broken and contrite heart, O God, you will not despise."
Psalm 51:17

"A man's pride brings him low,
but a man of lowly spirit gains honor." Proverbs 29:23

"Blessed are the poor in spirit,
for theirs is the kingdom of heaven." Matthew 5:3

"For with much wisdom comes much sorrow;
the more knowledge, the more grief." Ecclesiastes 1:18

"Blessed are those who mourn,
for they will be comforted." Matthew 5:4

"The righteous cry out, and the Lord hears them;
he delivers them from all their troubles." Psalm 34:17

"The Lord is close to the brokenhearted
and saves those who are crushed in spirit." Psalm 34:18

"The salvation of the righteous comes from the Lord;
he is their stronghold in time of trouble." Psalm 37:39

"The brother in humble circumstances ought to take pride in his
high position. The Lord sustains the humble."
Psalm 147:6; James 1:9

I Did Neither

1 Whew! New marriage, new millennium, new baby, new house, *and* new life! January 2000 was certainly special to the Johnson family. Derrick and I had definitely arrived. *Whatever that meant.*

We'd sold approximately 600 shares of vested stock options and received an automatic deposit of around $187,000.00 from his employee investment plan. Construction on our home had been completed one week prior to Super Bowl Sunday, and we closed on Friday, January 21, 2000. I remember it like it was yesterday. We went to the bank, requested a cashier's check for approximately $124,000.00, and glanced at each other when the bank teller looked at us strangely. Having waited patiently for her to get approval from the manager (which seemed to take forever), I smirked when the cashier's fee of $3.00 was waived, thinking it was funny, *knowing* she would have charged us if we didn't have any money.

After leaving the bank, we headed to the builder's office. There, we handed over the cashier's check for the full amount of the house, signed some forms, and walked out with the title and deed in our possession. We began to move into our newly built, four bedroom, two bath, two car garage home that same evening. Several people commented on our age, while others mentioned how good it must have felt to purchase a house outright. A week passed, and the following Sunday was Super Bowl XXXIV. Derrick and I invited our Bible study group, of which we had been members for only a few months, to come and perform a house blessing after church. When the ceremony ended, everyone hung around until evening, being joined later by a few more friends and family who were coming to attend the football festivities. We officially hosted our very first gathering, a Super Bowl Fellowship. With God, Christian friends, and family, we made the transition smoothly into our new status as homeowners.

We used the first portion of our investment to purchase and furnish the house, and had a little over $18,000.00 left to pay tithes. With barely enough to start a savings account separate of the stock portfolio, we already knew we would give God what He was due because we tithed off of our salaries and this was no different. *Or, was it?*

We realized it was actually very easy to write a check for a couple of hundred or maybe even a few thousand dollars, but $18,000.00 was a lot of money and, truth be told, we were in the early stages of our spiritual development. We hadn't actively begun to mature yet.

Derrick and I started to discuss whether to tithe, then how much to tithe, followed by *when* to tithe. One person even said, "Y'all are not going to give *the Church* $20,000! If y'all give that church $20,000, then y'all are crazy." I guess we started believing we just might *not* be after all, because we didn't. Besides, what regular*, working-class* people give a church almost $20,000.00 in lump sum anyway?

Well, lo and behold, Derrick and I started to converse about what would happen to the money. You know, if we actually gave it to our church. Having been members for only a short while, we determined those people were not going to do right with it. *Boy! Does that sound stupid now? As if we would do better.*

At any rate, we took the money and bought a much-needed sports utility vehicle (SUV), a Mitsubishi Montero Sport to be exact, for approximately $18,700.00. It was almost to the penny of what our tithes were supposed to be alone. Yes, I felt a little guilty, but I convinced myself we'd made a good *intellectual* choice. Never mind the spiritual repercussions of it. Besides, we'd given something. *Right?*

The New Year had come and gone and, with no problems of our own, life was good for Derrick and me. January ended peacefully, and February began just as typically as any other month. It was quiet and my soul was singing. When the phone rang during the middle of the afternoon, it could only be one person.

"Hello, my love," I said in my usual voice. Then I heard, "You will not believe this," coming from the receiving end of the telephone. "We're being sued!" Derrick said. Thinking aloud, I responded, "Sued? For what? By whom?" Then, my husband proceeded to tell me he had been served a legal notice from an officer of the court. It read, "Greetings, you are being sued." *Greetings? What the heck?*

How could you greet someone and follow it with "you" and "sue" in the *same* sentence? Derrick then told me he would give me all the details when we saw each other that evening, and we said our good-byes. Part of me was a nervous wreck. I thought about court, jail, lawyers—the whole nine yards. Although, other parts of me wondered, *Lord, what could this be about?* Quite naturally, I had butterflies the remainder of the day until my husband and I met to discuss the specifics.

The first thing Derrick said, after he walked into the house and we embraced one another, was that someone was suing us for $500,000.00. I repeated out loud, "*$500,000.00?*" as if I didn't hear him say it correctly the first time. Derrick then handed me the papers as I questioned in my head, *Where did this come from?* Sure enough, in bold black lettering it read, "Greetings, you are being sued."

Upon reading the document *thoroughly,* I threw a holy hissy-fit right there in the kitchen. Although it may have been considered extreme, by some, I jumped up and down while stomping my feet and shouting at the top of my voice, "You have to get out of here devil! This is *my* house. No weapon formed against me shall prosper. (Isaiah 54:17, KJV) I will not have that up'n here! Get out! Get out! *Get out!*" By the time I calmed down, I admit even if I felt much better, I was still nervous about the entire situation. I didn't know if I still had God's protection, so maybe *every* weapon formed would prosper. I was shocked at that revelation and confused by it, but I was especially angry.

Having never been sued before, neither Derrick nor I had any idea of what was to come. What could this *really* be about? I mean, this could not possibly be from God. *Or, could it be?* Well, whatever it was, Derrick didn't hesitate to respond. He immediately picked up the telephone to call one of his uncles who is an attorney. Without any hesitation, he took the case and prepared us for the upcoming hearing which had already been set. Derrick and I prayed together and began to fast, as well.

In the beginning, it was definitely about money. I would be a liar if I said it wasn't. I just could not perceive giving *anyone* half a million dollars without a shove (a nudge just wouldn't do it) from the Holy Ghost. Also, because Derrick's employee stock option plan only allowed us to touch a certain amount of those shares during specific times of the year, as they vested, we simply did not have $500,000.00 in cash lying around under a mattress, buried in the backyard, stuffed in a cookie jar, hidden in the freezer, or in domestic or foreign accounts someplace.

As the court date neared, the butterflies in my stomach worsened. I would love to say I let go and let God, but it wasn't quite that easy for me then. I prayed day in and day out, for months, about the lawsuit. Around that same time, oddly enough, we began to hear Fred Hammond's song "No Weapon" randomly played on one of the local gospel stations day in and day out, too. When it wasn't playing on the radio, we heard it in Sunday morning worship service. Interestingly enough, Donnie McClurkin's song "Stand" always followed Fred's. For us, those two songs became an umbrella in the storm. Little did we know they would become our raincoat and goulashes, too.

We continued to hear those same two songs play on the radio before we went to court in the fall of 2000. It was almost as if God Himself was shielding us from something. He was because, after approximately 15 minutes of legal deliberations, we won! The judge based her decision solely on a document our attorney had submitted into evidence, relieving us of any financial obligation to the matter-at-hand. What God had for us was ours and that was that. *Or, was it?*

After the conclusion of the court hearing, life was grand again. It was the middle of a beautiful summer, and Derrick and I had grown closer to each other, and to God, through our first marital attack. We had defeated the devil, and it was all good. *God is definitely with us,* I thought, as we continued to live our lives to His glory.

We enjoyed attending our church where we had been members for two years at the time. The only problem was Derrick's original work schedule during the early months of our marriage. He worked on Sundays from 6:00 a.m. – 3:00 p.m. We began to pray about his schedule when we were first married, because we really wanted to attend church services and worship together.

To accommodate for the scheduling conflict, we began attending a Tuesday night Bible study growth group. We also started going to Wednesday night prayer service at the church. I would pick Derrick up from work, in downtown Dallas, and head straight toward what we affectionately came to know as "The Cord" in Oak Cliff.

On most occasions, we skipped dinner on Wednesdays because we fasted all day. It was something we'd become accustomed to during the time of the trial. Derrick and I continued this for eleven months until God answered our prayer regarding a schedule change. He allowed him to make a lateral move on his job, and his hours changed to Monday through Friday, 9:00 a.m. – 6:00 p.m. After adjusting to the new schedule, our lifestyle changed a lot.

Because we were striving to grow spiritually, Derrick and I attended Sunday morning worship service and Sunday evening Concord Center for Biblical Studies (CCBS) courses. We were also still attending Tuesday evening Bible study sessions, as well as Wednesday night prayer meetings. I don't recall ever being tired, only excited about this newfound desire I had for the knowledge of Christ.

Concord later adopted the motto "Sunday is not enough," and I knew why. If we were going to stay spiritually strong enough to last all week, and our marriage strong enough to endure forever, then we needed to refuel *regularly*. I had already experienced the consequences of my spirit man running on empty when I was single, and I wasn't interested in that lifestyle anymore *ever*—married or single.

Shortly after joining Concord, the late Dr. E. K. Bailey (our founding pastor and one of the finest expository preachers in the country of his time) began several sermon series. One, in particular, was "Breaking the Cycle," which dealt with stopping generational curses. Another was "The Jabez Series," taken from 1 Chronicles 4:9-10.

Derrick and I began to pray off family curses of divorce, adultery, drug abuse, alcoholism, homosexuality, and poverty to name a few. Anything we visibly saw on either side of our families, detrimental to our spiritual maturity, was covered in those prayers during the early stages of our marriage as God brought them to our attention.

As I watched a local Christian television network one day while pregnant with Emahn, our firstborn, a televangelist out of Ohio was preaching on the same topic of generational curses. Something got my attention that afternoon in our apartment, and I felt an arrest in my spirit.

Home alone, it was as if I couldn't move. As I sat in a chair, seemingly immobilized, I submitted my will and placed my hands on my stomach. Crying out to the Lord on behalf of my child, I prayed for my unborn baby with tears streaming down my face.

It was my thinking that if I could spare my child from even *half* of the mess I went through, hands down, *I would*. Not the typical life-changing, character-developing issues necessary for our development, but *curses* that were never intended to be part of our existence. I'm talking about things like "The Deadly D's" of divorce, depression, and drugs. So, since prayer—to me—had become synonymous with talking to God about *His* best possible outcome, I began to pray the prayer of Jabez over our lives, too.

I'd read Bruce Wilkinson's book "The Prayer of

Jabez" and accepted his challenge to make it a habit to pray the prayer daily. I did it prior to stepping out of bed each morning as a girlfriend, Monique Rodgers, had suggested. However, if she would have also informed me that seeking God's best hurt so much, I may have opted to leave well enough alone.

We were now in our new house for almost a year, with no additional drama. Then, at exactly the same time twelve months later, we received another lawsuit notice. This one, dated exactly a year to the date of the first, did not begin with the former "Greetings, you are being sued." It was, however, from the same people.

This time Derrick and I decided to seek the assistance of a different attorney. I can't even tell you why, because I don't know. I just picked up the phone and called one of our Bible study members—that "Jabez-praying" girlfriend of mine, Monique. Mo would know what to do. She wasn't just a lawyer; she was a *practicing* Christian! In fact, I didn't even know what kind of lawyer she was at the time. I just called her.

To my surprise, I handled this incident totally different than the first. Although we never saw it coming, we still had to deal with it because it was here. So, sobbing into the phone, I sat at my desk with the lawsuit notice in my hand saying, "Monique, this is Shaundale, and *girl* let me tell you what has been going on."

For that entire year only close friends and a few family members knew about our legal situation, but no one—not even us—knew we were at spiritual warfare. We were attending church, Bible study, prayer meeting, etc. but we were dealing with all of this together, yet alone. I had no idea what was up, but calling Mo was the first time I'd followed the leading of the Holy Spirit, in this matter, and reached out. Monique already knew both Derrick and I socially and spiritually, and now she was getting ready to know us on a professional level. So, I shared with her the previous year's drama which led to our current situation.

After hanging up the telephone with Monique, I stormed into our master bedroom closet. With tears streaming down both cheeks, like a waterfall, I cried out to the Lord. I can see myself now as if having an out-of-body experience—all bowed down and weeping—as I began to reflect back to the very first biblical studies course Derrick and I ever enrolled in at Concord together. It was "The Hour that Changes the World," a course on designing a practical plan for personal prayer. The class was based on the book by Dick Eastman, and it was taught by Elder H. Rick Jordan.

As I began to go through the A.C.T.S. of Prayer (Adoration, Confession, Thanksgiving, and Supplication), as regarded in the book, I praised God for whatever this new storm was going to bring. Yes, I could have gone through the "Why me, how could You let this happen?" bit, but as *embarrassed* and upset as I was, I referred to my Heavenly Father by every name I knew to call Him at the time. I'd learned praise is what you do in order to get God's attention, which was exactly what I wanted *and* needed. Now, it was time to put it into effect.

It had been so long since I felt I'd had intimacy with God. I was still dealing with the mental and emotional scars of what had taken place in the bathroom over a year prior when He withdrew His provision. I still hadn't felt His hand the way I wanted to, but at least I saw it. I knew there was a lot God had prevented from happening despite everything going on. For starters, He could have let us lose the first lawsuit. Also, He could've just called me on home and let Derrick and Emahn enjoy the life we'd built. I didn't complain when I thought about the Sovereignty of that. So, although I didn't feel Him gently rubbing my back, He was there standing beside me—even if His arms were folded because He'd taken His hands off of me. I had His presence and His protection from what I could gather, but His provision was limited and His power was *off* limits.

I lowered my head and sobbed. *The devil is a liar,* I thought. *He wants me to sit and sulk, but the Bible says, "I will bless the Lord at all times and His praises shall continually be in my mouth (Psalm 34:1)."* Then, I opened my mouth and confessed what I already knew: how wrong I was. I said, "Lord, I'm sorry. I am *so* sorry. *Please*, forgive me." Suddenly, I felt lighter. It was as if a burden had been lifted. Had He heard me because, this time, I'd confessed? I tried to gather my thoughts. The first time I'd simply screamed, "Please, forgive me!" I hadn't even asked. But, there was nothing. I felt alone and empty in that cold, dark bathroom. It was well-lit, but I couldn't tell. Now, I felt light again. There was something different about this experience. I'd repented with a sincere heart and He had responded.

Amazed at my growth, more scriptures began to run through my mind and I went with them as they came. I had passed the praise test and it worked. I had gotten His attention! I remembered saying specifically, "Lord, You said, *'No weapon formed against me will prosper (Isaiah 54:17).'*" "You said, *'Having done all, to stand (Ephesians 6:13).'*" "You said, *'The effectual fervent prayer of a righteous man availeth much (James 5:16, KJV); that all I have to do is ask, and it shall be given; seek, and I shall find; knock, and it shall be opened unto me (Matthew 7:7).'*" "You said, *'Delight myself also in You, and You will give me the desires of my heart (Psalm 37:4); that whatsoever I ask in Your name, You will do (John 14:14).'*" "In the name of Jesus, anoint me, Lord! Make this place a holy place." "You said, *'I don't have to be anxious for anything, but in all things by prayer of thanksgiving with supplication to make my requests known unto You (Philippians 4:6).'*" "You said... You said... *You said!!!"* Then something happened that changed my life. He did it... *all of it!* Something broke in the heavens and I felt it. The closet became holy ground! Immediately, I went into worship. Without any warning at all, my whole attitude and demeanor changed. Instead of sitting on my knees, hunched over, with my hands clasped I was up on my knees with my arms and head raised. Praise may have been what I needed to get God's attention, but worship was going to keep it!

With tears still streaming, my voice was loud as I began to shout at the top of my lungs in exaltation. In all of that anger and all of that sorrow—snot, tears, and all—I felt the full presence of God again, with all of His power! It was as if, even though my flesh was going off, my spirit was in check and recognized someone as Holy who had inhabited the space and was worthy of honor. My spirit told my flesh to be quiet, so it could shout!

In hindsight, this was not the first time I had experienced the presence of God. However, it was the first time I had encountered Him at this magnitude. It felt like I had pushed through a huge door and, once it opened, God Himself just started pouring out. He was filling my cup, right there! He had anointed me, and I was flooded with all kinds of emotions. God was with me in that closet, and I sensed the outpouring of warmth and love, but more importantly... *I felt the overflow.*

I knew with everything in me that I had broken through and began to pray all over again. I wanted everything I had missed out on during the past year and wasn't going to stop until I got it all back. *"Bless me indeed and enlarge my territory. Keep Your hands upon me and keep me from evil that it will not grieve me* (1 Chronicles 4:10)*,"* I prayed. In essence, I was going to hold onto Him and not let go until He blessed me *again.*

What happened next, I was not prepared for. I often say, "God be trippin'," and yes, I meant to say that.

Although I may have thought I was not ready, He certainly knew otherwise. I began to pray a prayer of blessing over the plaintiffs and their families, as well. I simply said thereafter, "Fix this. I'm sick of going to court. I know *now* what You have for me is mine, but that which You've given we can't even enjoy. Just fix it." When I came out of that closet, there was so much peace. It wasn't just within me; it was all around. I didn't know what exactly had happened, but I did know *something* had been done.

I later read a book entitled "How to Claim the Abrahamic Covenant" by Jay Snell. He referenced a verse in Proverbs 10:22 (KJV) that says, *"Not only does the blessing of the Lord make rich, but He addeth no sorrow to it."* I then started to question the circumstances under which our "blessings" had come, and wondered why we had gone through so much if that scripture was true. No, my attitude wasn't right, but I was supposed to be happy. So, the jury was out on that one for a while, but praying blessings over my enemies was one of the best things I had done *ever*.

Having had my closet experience, I began to look at things from a new perspective. Like Jabez, I believed God had heard and granted my requests. The next few months after He did were smooth sailing, too. I was living each day as it came, and God gave me an absolute spirit of peace; one He knew I would need in the next few months to come.

The second lawsuit notice stated that we had approximately 30 days from the date of delivery to comply with the rules which had been set forth. We then immediately faxed a copy to Derrick's uncle, who had previously worked on the case. We later faxed a second copy to Monique, who was now new to the case.

Derrick and I were still praying and, because Emahn had been weaned, we also began to fast together again.

The second lawsuit mentioned that we needed to submit some form of documentation, but we did not have to be present. Therefore, we left the paperwork to our attorneys. What Derrick and I didn't know was that we were expected to reappear in court around that 30-day period. Because we didn't show up, we received another letter that stated we had not complied with the second lawsuit, and the plaintiffs were granted their petition *by default*. I was more hurt than angry.

Frantic, I called Monique, and she told me Derrick's uncle had sent in the proper paperwork prior to the judgment, and there must have been some confusion. Not exactly sure of what had taken place, a new court date was set one month later. Although Derrick and I did not have to appear, our attorney, the plaintiffs, and their counsel were all present—and so were we. Derrick and I showed up as spectators.

Between court cases, Monique did some digging and informed us that the original documents submitted by Derrick's uncle had been misplaced. The devil was being flat-out ugly. For the first time, during the entire legal process, I actually saw Derrick become angry. Me? On the other hand, let's just say my neck started rolling and my fingers went to snapping. I mean, to lose legal documentation to a lawsuit, the defendant's documents matter-of-fact, was outright irresponsible to me. Didn't anyone other than us have a clue that our livelihood was at stake, or did no one else care?

At the request of opposing counsel, the court asked us to turn in all of our financial information from the preceding year. I was a stay-at-home mom during that time, so we gathered up all of Derrick's pay stubs, W-2 forms, our checking account statements, and so on. *On paper* we were worth $1.2 million. I emphasize that, because the account documented the unvested shares of stock, which did not represent our liquid assets.

The opposing attorney was still trying to figure out a way to receive a percentage of those unvested shares (which we couldn't touch *ourselves* until they were fully vested) for his clients, and it was now a year later. He wasn't even taking into consideration the fact that none of the figures they were calculating from the stock options even counted towards Derrick's actual income. They were only interested in what they *thought* we had, not in what they *knew* was actual. Which is why when the opposing counsel asked his clients how they came about the knowledge of the shares, I was floored. To hear, in court, that someone actually heard our testimony and shared it for personal gain was outlandish! Do you laugh because *naturally* the whole point of the testimony was missed, or do you cry because *spiritually* what the devil intended for evil, God meant for good?

Derrick and I left the courthouse that day with a list of documents to fax to Monique. The default ruling, which had been wrongfully augmented in the first place, was then over-turned and our hearing was scheduled to continue one month later. However, before we could proceed with our attorney, we had to pay $500.00 to the plaintiffs' lawyer in order to reverse the ruling. *How shady was that?*

Our documents were misplaced, the plaintiffs' attorney wrongfully filed a default judgment against *us* because of it, and *we* had to pay for it factually, figuratively, and financially. God had our backs, though. He heard and He answered my prayer about being tired of having to go to court and wanting to be left alone, so when Monique phoned later to tell me not to come and not to worry, I did neither.

STRAIGHT TRIPPIN'

2

Having been assured there was no reason to return to court, nor a reason to worry about it, I did neither. Surprisingly enough though, the choir sang *No Weapon* during worship service that following Sunday after the cancelled court date, and even more interesting the Pastor of Worship and Fine Arts sang *Stand* for the Invitational Hymn. Naturally, Derrick and I glanced at one another, because we had learned those two songs were God's way of preparing us for an upcoming storm. We knew every time we heard those particular songs played or sang consecutively, it was as if God Himself had called our names and we would stand at attention. Yet, I continued to wake daily praying the prayer of Jabez. Thus, came another day I shall never forget.

Our family was preparing to leave for Bunkie, Louisiana in order to visit my relatives over the Easter holiday weekend of 2001. It was the afternoon of Good Friday when I left the house with our daughter, Emahn, headed to pick up my sister and nephew. Already prepared to make the five-hour drive home, Derrick had previously loaded the Montero before work that morning. All I needed to do was pick him up after we left my sister's.

En route to Arlington, I first made my way to Dallas to run errands. That's when it happened. I looked both to the right and left, and seeing no sign or vehicle, I preceded forward, hit the brake, and saw everything that happened from that moment on in slow motion. After hearing a resounding boom, I realized I had hit a car. I was in an accident! The truck would not stop! Both vehicles skid up the road and there was a white, smoke-like blur quickly surrounding me.

I screamed constantly for Emahn, whose car seat was in the driver-side, rear section. I saw people gather around as I felt my bottom lip growing and my right forearm stinging. Then, I saw a lady in front of me get out of a car while holding her left leg. I had hit the driver-side of a white Grand AM. To my right, I saw another lady on a cellular phone and heard her say, "There's a lady with a baby in the car." As I tried to unbuckle my seatbelt, a white cloud continued to fill the vehicle. I then heard a third lady constantly yelling, "Get out of the truck!" I jumped out, only to realize a second later Emahn was still inside and hurried back in.

From the outside I had attempted to open the driver-side, rear door to get my daughter out of her car seat, but the door would not open. I could hear people telling me to stay out, but I saw smoke filling the entire area. I then said, unsure if I was speaking aloud or thinking to myself, "I'm not getting out of this truck without my baby." I had climbed back into the driver seat, turned around, reached back, and unbuckled her car seat. I then pulled Emahn over the driver's seat and jumped out with her in my arms. She was approximately twenty-one months old at this time.

Once on the street, I looked at the red Mitsubishi

Montero I had once enjoyed. Overcome with both fear and grief, I was in the middle of the street praising the Lord in my spirit. I felt a "Thank You, Jesus" all in my stomach and began to shout. My Montero had just been destroyed, but I was able to stand and testify that I'd walked out of it with only a burn on my right forearm, which isn't even a visible scar, and my child unharmed.

The smoke I saw was from the airbags inflating. In addition to that, the entire windshield shattered. The front bumper also hung off, while the engine fell down. To make matters worse, the front driver-side door would not open totally, but the back driver-side door wouldn't open at all. The dashboard sat only inches from my lap. I walked to the curb and sat there. I cried, because we were okay. I cried, because we were alive. I cried because, in my opinion, there was no way I should have walked out of that vehicle without at least a temporary limp.

The paramedics came and left. My bottom lip felt as if it was swelling, because it had grown numb from the sting of the impact from the driver-side airbag inflating against it. The same was true of my right forearm which also stung. However, Emahn was in perfect health.

When the police arrived on the scene, the first question one of them asked was, "What happened?" I answered honestly and said, "I looked to my right, then to my left and, seeing no stop sign, I continued forward." The other driver, who was riding alone, was asked the same question. She answered that since she did not have a stop sign, she drove forward as well.

Unfamiliar with the area, neighborhood onlookers told us a stop sign was supposed to have been on my side of the intersection. However, it was allegedly stolen and reported to local authorities, but never replaced. The policeman put that information in his report and called tow trucks for both of us. As I sat waiting for family to arrive, I continued to cry. I believe I held Emahn as tightly as I had when she was born. *What was with all of this?*

When my tow truck arrived, I signed a form for the driver and had the Montero delivered to our house. Because we could not ride with the driver, Emahn and I continued to wait. Later, two sets of cars came. One of my brothers-in-law and his family were in one, and my husband and mother-in-law were in the other. It was then I cried the most. I mentioned to another family member I felt like I was constantly under attack. I mean, from the former lawsuits to the current auto wreck, what could possibly happen next?

After that, I realized the devil had tried to kill me. Not only that, he'd attempted to destroy my seed! Satan had sense enough to know if I got it right, then I'd teach her to *do* it right. Afterwards, I heard a still, quiet voice whisper within, *"This battle is not yours."* It was amazing how just when I thought I couldn't take anymore, God always had a Word for my soul.

Heading home from the accident, I began to lighten up, although I was in no mood to travel to Louisiana. Besides, I had just wrecked my Montero. I was happy to be alive; however, I was *not* happy. Obviously, I still had some maturing to do.

Since I never made it to my sister's apartment to pick her and my nephew up for our trip to Bunkie, they came over on their own and awaited our arrival. The Montero was left out front by the tow truck driver and the neighbors, having seen it, had either visited or called. From looking at the truck, they'd asked my sister if Emahn and I were at the hospital. Arriving shortly afterwards, I was very happy to announce I had only been burned on the forearm, and the baby was just fine.

The luggage was still packed, and everyone was ready to travel except me. Derrick, having been in an automobile accident years prior to our meeting, understood my anxiety. Although I was not excited about the drive, I knew I wasn't going to allow the enemy to paralyze me with fear. It was as if he had switched courses. Instead of coming after our finances, he was now after our lives. After further discussion about what our options were at this point, my sister decided she still wanted to go and rented a car.

Making the drive home was not as comfortable to me as it had once been. I kept hearing that loud boom in my head, and I could not sleep like I once did. It was possibly one of the worst trips I had ever taken nerve-wise, but it was Resurrection Sunday weekend and God had given me a testimony! In fact, He had given me several. We spent the next two days in Louisiana, with my family, and returned to our home late Sunday evening.

The next week began no differently than any other, with the exception that the Montero sat out front, as opposed to inside the garage. We still had the rental car, because we never needed two cars before the accident; although, at that time, we simply needed backup transportation. Derrick and I did everything and went everywhere together, outside of work, during the earlier years of our marriage. I know having only one car seemed strange to most, but when we explained that we are not in the "keeping up with the Joneses" clique the conversation quickly went away.

There were days when a second car would have helped, but there were more days when the upkeep would have only been an added expense. It wasn't about how much money we made. It was about how much money we saved. Besides, we'd paid cash for the Montero and knew if we really needed a second mode of transportation, God would supply it. In all honesty though, remember we paid our tithes and offering for it. Thus, we found ourselves in our current predicament.

"Believe you, me," as the folks back home would say, "God will get His in the end." *Believe that!* We owed Him approximately $18,700.00 in tithes, and He took $18,700.00 in transportation! Nevertheless, rumors of a corporate-wide lay-off surfaced at Derrick's office. Wednesday following that previous Sunday's car wreck, I received a phone call. Because it was during the middle of the day, I answered in my usual "Hello Honey" voice. I heard the words "Come and get me," followed by laughter and looked at the telephone receiver. With a raised eyebrow, I asked, "Are you serious?" I thought, *you must be kidding*. Then, as if he had read my mind, I heard Derrick say, "No. Come and get me from work. I'll explain when you get here."

Shaking my head, I loaded Emahn into the rental car and drove to Deep Ellum where his office was located. Upon my arrival, I parked the car and Derrick walked towards me with a box in his hands and a smile on his face. His entire department, including management, was amongst the first round of approximately 50 local corporate employees to be laid off.

When Derrick climbed into the car, we looked at each other and fell out laughing. I mean, *we laughed.* It was still April, and in a few short days we had faced a plethora of spiritual floods: the second lawsuit, the car wreck, and then the lay-off. I finally understood the analogy "When it rains, it pours." I just had to ask "What else could possibly happen?" To top all that off, the remaining shares of stock (which were not fully vested yet) all went back to the company. *So, what now?* I told God to fix it, and fix it is exactly what He did.

Derrick and I had major plans for those unvested shares; they were our retirement money. We'd decided we were going to move to the Carolinas and make a nice home in one of the newly urbanized Cliffs Communities in five years. By then, every share would have been completely vested and cashed out.

My husband left his job with approximately 10,000 unvested shares of stock options, and nine months to go before another window of opportunity to cash out would have come. However, by that time, the stock market had also begun to decline. Yet, those shares were still worth something to us, especially then. There we were with an inoperable vehicle, savings that would last about 90 days, and no future income. What was God doing? In fact, was He doing anything after all?

We rationalized that either God was extremely angry *with us*, or He had major plans *for us*. I knew I was the culprit, but couldn't bring myself to tell my husband. It was almost like the people in the Old Testament when somebody stole something and tried to hide it from God. Then, He shed light on it and told the others to kill them, bury them under their tent, and burn it down—the guilty and the unknowing alike all received the same punishment. Regardless, that night I prayed for something Derrick and I could do together, from home, which would support our family. I asked God for whatever it was to be confirmed through my husband, so I would know. I guess part of me felt like although He had heard me in the closet, He still might not be talking to me just yet. Especially, after what had just taken place.

Days later, Derrick mentioned a great business idea to me. It was multi-media streaming. Because of our combined backgrounds in Computer Information Systems and Radio/Television, we were already toying around with this idea and servicing others in our area with it free of charge. We had been providing this service approximately six months or so, simply as a means to discover new and sharpen existing skills. We believed God was definitely calling us into a business that would utilize both our professional experience, so trusting our instincts we put forth an even greater effort to make it work.

Derrick and I felt we'd been chosen to do Internet streaming for Christian-based organizations. We were so excited that we began to share our ideas with others. One day, while sitting around the house entertaining guests, we started talking about our new plans. It was mentioned that this would be a great investment opportunity for others. As Derrick looked at me, I looked at him. He then asked me what I thought. I toyed with the idea mentally and motioned that it just might work.

Having made the decision to join forces, we later began holding meetings to gather information and compare research. We were making plans for this, that, and the other when God dropped the words "You never prayed for partners" into my spirit. *Oh, my goodness!* He was talking to me again. God and I were back in fellowship and I was elated. I shared what the Lord had told me with Derrick, but we kept on going, assuming it would all be okay. *Wrong!* I was excited, but I should've been listening to hear and not just hearing. We assumed God would bless any business we were a part of, but everybody knows "God don't bless no mess!"

During those meetings, things began to come out I never thought I would witness. For starters, I felt like a scene out of *Waiting to Exhale* had taken place. All of those hours—all the work we had already invested before there was ever any mention of a business to anyone else—and suddenly there were people around us saying, in a sense, "Scratch all that; we're doing this. And, we can do it without you."

Derrick and I never had indecisions about *any* business we would start together. We counted on everyone coming into the plans we were already working on, in the form of a ministry. Also, living through lawsuits at the time, I didn't want us to "add fuel to the fire" later on. So, my husband and I previously agreed that in place of his name, mine would go on every contract as a representative of our family.

Man! You would have thought someone bombed the kitchen! Opinions and attitudes all began to fly back and forth across the room. Everyone then turned and looked at Derrick as if to ask whether he meant what he'd said, or if in fact he'd even said it. When he agreed, the next thing I knew, everyone was puffing. Little ol' "look-for-the-good-in-everybody" me had no clue why my name being on forms would cause such a riot. So, I asked. The answers I received, I will *never* forget. I realized then I was not part of our circle of influence, but was simply expected to be influenced by the circle.

People started "what-iffing" about issues my husband and I never entertained. For instance, "What if y'all get a divorce, and then she owns a percentage of *our* business?" *Our? Divorced? What the heck?*

When the conversation shifted to devising severance packages in the event of a marital split, I knew what God meant when He said, "You never prayed for partners." So, realizing and accepting that as truth, I decided to just hush up about it until Derrick and I could talk more in private. Then, we moved on to the next item of discussion.

Derrick and I knew from the start, since before the start actually, that we would only service other Christian-based organizations and some corporate businesses. Well, that wasn't in everyone else's plans. When the group started to discuss our target market, some of everything and everybody came out *literally*.

There were people yelling out every religion available. Not *denominations* like Baptist, Pentecostal, Methodist, etc. (all who have some form of *Jesus* somewhere in there). I mean *religions* like Christians, Muslims, Jews, Buddhist, etc. (where there is clearly a distinction of the "haves" and the "have-nots"). Derrick and I were like, "What? We are not streaming the message of anybody who is non-Christian." Argument number two quickly went into play. Everyone turned to us and wanted to know why not. *Why not?*

I'm sure you can imagine the other things that went through my mind, but years ago I learned a scripture that says to speak the truth in love. It's found in Ephesians 4:12-16, and references us coming into the *same* knowledge of the Son of God, which *clearly* we all had not. If we all had, then there would not have been any uncertainty about whether all other faiths were even up for discussion. Keep in mind, I did not say we weren't all saved; we just weren't all in the same knowledge of the *inner workings* of Christ.

Just as simply as one may know Jesus *is* Lord, doesn't necessarily mean they know Him *as* Lord. So until that distinction has been *personally* made in one's life, there could be no knowledge or application made either. That's when I learned a tough lesson on being unequally yoked, and why I was experiencing the consequences of not praying to God about partners. I felt guilty, because we had not. Look where it got us; but, oh, the things I learned.

Once we were alone, Derrick and I discussed the previous events. I went to bed that night in tears. You cannot imagine the disappointment I felt. The phone kept ringing. It was apparent that my feelings were hurt, and a few people called back. Later that evening, I shared with my husband that I would not have any parts of it. What God put together, let no man separate (see Mark 10:9). This obviously was not the case, because God hadn't put any of us together. I saw that *clearly* naturally and spiritually.

Derrick and I were concerned with streaming the Gospel in an effort to reach the masses and save souls, first and foremost. Naturally, we wanted a successful business. Just not at the expense of sending people to hell because they opted to hear the message of Islam, or stumbled upon the message of a Buddhist aired in a time slot divinely digitized (I made that up) for Christians.

The next morning we called the church and scheduled a meeting with Dr. E. K. Bailey, our founding pastor. We scheduled the meeting just to be doing so, truthfully. What else did we have to do? We were both unemployed, both seeking God about some things, and both at the church so much people probably thought we were on staff anyway. Concord was our safe haven; even though, it seemed the more I prayed to God for good things, bad things happened.

I ended up asking Pastor Bailey how someone could keep his or her personal and professional life separate from their faith. I just wanted to know, because Derrick had asked another minister (from a different church) for his opinion of our partnership dilemma. When he said, "Business is business," we were hurt because it seemed to us your Christian walk is your Christian walk. You didn't just decide to *not* be a Christian in your business for the sake of a dollar, and then become one again when the invoice was paid.

We were later asked, "Who are we to judge?" I didn't feel like we were judging at all. I just wanted to keep in line with not causing a brother or sister to fall. Besides, the Bible doesn't say, "Judge not," with a period. It says, "Do not judge, or you too will be judged." (Matthew 7:1-2) For example, if you tell someone their child is bad, then yours acts a fool, don't get defensive when it gets back to you. Whatever we are bold enough to speak over someone else's life *always* has the potential to come right back around to ours, and I didn't have any problems with someone questioning my loyalty to Christ. In fact, questions were welcomed. Either they would prove I was right where I should be, or I would be convicted to get where I needed to be. Anyway, that's beside the point. I just wondered, *Shouldn't every decision a believer makes, especially in business, be reflective of their spiritual beliefs?* That's when I learned a new phrase. Pastor Bailey said, "Don't prostitute your principles!" *At least he knew I had some*, I thought.

We were later called E.K. Bailey followers. I laughed because ignorance didn't deserve a remark. Pastor Bailey didn't have a thing to do with the equation; it was the *principle* of the matter and where it lined up with Kingdom purposes. Solomon said in Proverbs 22:1, *"A good name is more desirable than great riches; to be esteemed is better than silver or gold."* Now, don't get me wrong, I wanted another financial blessing, too. It just wasn't at the top of my list.

Pastor Bailey then asked us in what areas did we serve at the church. We told him we had been part of a Bible study growth group for nearly three years, and we enjoyed it. He asked us why didn't we lead our own and we answered, "What for?" I mean, we were happy. We were members of one of the North Dallas/Richardson Growth Groups that was just like family and, in some instances, better. Then he asked us, "Don't you think it's fair that other new members have the same opportunity to experience what you have?" So, with that you should know we prayed and began the process to lead our own in-home Bible study growth group, which remained active four years. At first I asked, "God, why didn't You just say, 'Lead a Bible study?' We didn't have to go through all this to become growth group leaders, did we?" It was then apparent that God often takes the long, scenic route.

After that discussion, Pastor Bailey asked us about children. I told him we had one child, a little girl named Emahn. With that, we figured the meeting was over. *Not!*

He asked us whether we were finished having babies, and bright-eyed and bushy-tailed I answered, "Yes!" So, mimicking my enthusiasm he asked, "Well, would the child feel like an orphan if something happened to both of you?" Okay, he had me there. "I'll think about it," was all I could say.

After praying and making the decision not to follow through with the joint business venture, I began to redirect my interests. I had stopped working on my own business endeavors in order to join my husband with this new project, but it was time to get my own ball rolling again. I had previously started a small technical support business, which God later expanded to include web design. I was still primarily a stay-at-home mom, but because Emahn was growing fast I wanted to use this time to transition back into my career. This was my goal for once she turned three years old and had started preschool.

Having met with Pastor Bailey and feeling better equipped to make a spiritually sound decision Derrick agreed to move forward in the partnership, once boundaries were established. Although I still had reservations, it was agreed that he would handle all Christian clientele. Somewhat satisfied and supportive, I began to really work my business while he worked the joint venture.

All of the work I received resulted from word-of-mouth referrals. I started my business with a laptop, a few other office supplies and equipment, and the knowledge I had gained over the years from past experience. God was definitely working this thing for my good, and the company was blessed. I began to get phone calls and people were even stopping me at church. The income from my company alone supported us during this time. Our savings were depleted, and the severance package Derrick had received after the lay-off was gone.

After the Enron incident, we were happy to have even gotten one.

As I persistently worked my business separately from my husband's partnership, I continued to watch them get a potential client, only to be turned down for their services in the end. Gradually, my business grew as the partnership withered. It got to a point where only Derrick and a couple of others were doing all of the work originally intended for approximately eight or so others. In time, it all dwindled.

I was later reminded of the song "Only What You Do for Christ Will Last." I knew God had His hands on me and expected more. That was why I wasn't comfortable compromising by beliefs. The devil had done the fool and switched lanes *again*. He had moved from my finances, to my life, to my peers. He was straight trippin'!

SAVE THE CHILDREN

3 Until the point of the attempted joint business endeavor, we were singing "happy-happy, joy-joy," if you will. The year 2001 was coming to an end, and we had not been back to court at all—not even for the car accident. However, the devil was still *straight trippin'*. I received two phone calls from the other driver's attorney and said, "Lord, You know I don't need this." I later called my attorney-friend, Monique, and she told me if they sued us, then we'd sue the city for that missing stop sign. Oddly enough, the phone calls stopped and the accident isn't even on my driving record. Things began to finally look brighter, and Derrick and I were hopeful of this storm passing.

It was the beginning of 2002, and my company was growing by the month. We finally had balance and, as I continued to work my business, Derrick persistently looked for a job in his field. People continued to be laid off in our circle of friends, while others in our extended circle who were self-employed continued to lose business. The economy was definitely headed into a downward spiral. Oh, how we longed for the days of old when we would go online just to view our financial portfolio.

We began to do less and less together due to a lack of finances. I was busy trying to build my business in order to take care of the family, and everything was going to either household or business expenses. My company may have been Potiphar's house, but I was definitely headed for prison. It was during this time when I fell into a deep depression. I was mommy or honey; there was no Shaundale. I was building the business and taking care of the house and family, but what about me? I had always been career-driven and goal-oriented. There were still days when I awoke and said, "I can't believe I'm a wife," or "I can't believe I'm somebody's mama."

Despite my hesitancy, the Bible study was going very well. We met at our house on Thursdays, because we still wanted to attend our original group meetings held on Tuesday evenings. In addition, I started to attend a women's Bible study on Tuesday mornings. God was trying to tell me something, and I was determined to find out what.

The job lay-off was seriously starting to get to me, by this point. Doors were not opening for Derrick at all, and I just wanted to scream. It was during this time that I also began to get out more. I started hanging out with some of my old girlfriends, who are now strong Christians. This ended up being a good move because, although we only met monthly to have dinner, we were able to *really* talk. We shared testimonies, experiences, jokes, etc. Hanging out together became something we each looked forward to. It was also when I began to grow the most, I believe.

To my remembrance, the first time I heard God speak to me audibly was during the time when I took another Concord Center for Biblical Studies (CCBS) course. It was a class entitled "How to Listen to God," based on the book by Charles Stanley. This lesson was taught by one of the elders of our church, Jon Edmonds, and opened the door to many mega-spiritual experiences of my immediate lifetime.

Thinking back to another trip we'd made home to Bunkie, I was reminded of Mother's Day weekend in 2002. It was Derrick's 31st birthday, so I decided to throw him a surprise party while we were there. Most of my family was home for the holiday, so the timing was good.

On that particular trip home, one of my cousins referred to Derrick as my boyfriend. I was giving the party that Saturday before Mother's Day, on his actual birthday, and asked my older male cousins to take him somewhere briefly. Upon returning, one of my younger female cousins came in yelling that my boyfriend was back. Naturally, I didn't respond—for obvious reasons. Then she called me by my name, and I looked at her with my eyebrows raised, as if to ask "B*oyfriend?*" So she said, "Yes. Your boyfriend is back."

At that point, I had no idea some of the people back home thought I had been co-habitating and pro-creating, or shacking up and having babies to put it bluntly, for the past four years of my life. I questioned myself about why they didn't remember me getting married, then about why they'd assumed I wasn't. However, what I *really* wanted to know was whether I was walking in the Light before them. I felt if I had been, then *clearly* there would not have been any speculation to the fact that I was married with a child.

I could only assume the main reason my cousin had responded the way she did was because I live in Dallas, and she had no clue about my life. So, although I continued to walk *in* the Light, now I wondered whether my light just wasn't shining through. Oh yeah, it was on *inside*, but what about *outside*?

Derrick and I were married in Cancun, Mexico, so

many of them who did not make the trip probably just forgot. God sure did have me thinking, though. I hadn't even done anything and was convicted. I wasn't living in sin, but I wasn't witnessing about my deliverance from it either. The people in Dallas who were getting to know me *now* knew "saved and sanctified" Shaundale. The people back home who knew me *then* remembered "saved and sinning" Shaundale. There was a divinely, distinct difference between the two. *Trust me!*

To top off having to explain that Derrick is my legal, legitimate husband after almost four years of marriage, the next day was Mother's Day. I had to prepare myself to attend Sunday morning service. I said "prepare" because that is the only way to explain it.

There was a time when I would go home and wrestle with whether to attend church, and which one. At that point in my life, I was searching so badly to grow, little seemed to satisfy my hunger away from Concord. Now, I will admit that at "The Cord" we are spoiled. I don't care who gets up to do what, it's going to be off-the-hook from Praise and Worship to the Benediction. However, visiting anyone else's church was oftentimes very uncomfortable for me.

For starters, if there was no time set aside for Praise and Worship at the beginning of a service, I would have a silent fit. *That's just me.* It's because I'd come to church excited about the week I'd had all by myself with Lord and was hungry for corporate worship. Yes, I'd been having myself a ball at home, but now was the time to fellowship "in worship" with other believers. Not just when a good selection was sang, but when a medley of Praise and Worship songs continued. When I wasn't given a *specific* opportunity to celebrate God in the beginning of a church service, I felt awkward.

Having also learned that praise and worship aren't *for us*, but *for Him*, I noted that chips and salsa at your local

Mexican restaurant aren't really for us either. They met an immediate need of quenching our appetites, but in actuality they bought the wait staff and chefs more time. That's why they're free and come whether you order an appetizer or not.

So, the praise and worship portion of the service was us giving God *His time* to do what was needed *behind the scenes*. It was *extremely* necessary to me in a church service, because I wanted to give God all the time He needed. The remainder of the service was then for me. It was about listening, giving, and waiting—all forms of worship. Now, you can read on to fully understand the rest. This is the original series of e-mails sent to and from various Bible study members. I shared these experiences after a series of supernatural incidents began to occur as a result of the heaviness in my heart over whether I was being a light.

This took place after it was assumed that I was living in a continual state of sin, and no one even bothered to tell me it wasn't acceptable. It hurt more that everyone was okay with it if I was, than it did to be assumed I did. I thought, *well, just let me die and burn then why don't you?* Then, it dawned on me that was exactly what I was doing myself, by not sharing my Light with everyone else.

```
-----Original Message-----
From: Shaundale Johnson
To: Undisclosed Recipients
Sent: September 12, 2002 4:14PM
Subject: Something to Shout About
```

Hey y'all,

When we went home for Mother's Day, my heart bled for my hometown in Louisiana. I came home to Dallas very down because of some of the things I witnessed there. Some of the people closest to me are living in total darkness. On the whole trip home (a five-hour drive), my heart was heavy and I was crying over the reality of some of them just not getting it, or reaching their full spiritual potential, yet.

That night I was having trouble sleeping when Emahn woke up and walked into our bedroom. Usually, when she comes down there I'm half asleep, so I just let her climb in the bed with us. That night I couldn't sleep though, so I walked her back to her own bed. When I kneeled over her and prayed as she went back to sleep, I cried out from way down in my heart, "Lord, what am I going to do about my loved ones in Bunkie?" My heart was heavy and I was crying, "Lord, how can I save them?" As clearly as bell, I audibly heard with my own ears, "If you want to save them, save their children." I heard it, and I know I heard it. NOBODY can tell me that I did not.

I just started praising God, because I was the only person up in the house. To have heard somebody talking to me it HAD to be God. So I said, "Okay, Lord, I think I know what You're saying, but You're gonna have to help me with this one." Then the words *"Suffer not the little children who come unto me"* went through my mind. AMAZING! I was outdone. So, I immediately knew my highest calling has to do with children.

Now, over the past three years or so, I've been praying for a revival in Bunkie. Because I can see the destruction that's headed there, I've just been seeking God for that place. Like Jeremiah, I can see what God is getting ready to do to those who don't confess their sins to Him and repent. So after that conversation with God, I really started studying my Bible. I began with all of the verses that pertain to children. Well, I remember mentioning that if God is preparing to move me back home, I'll go.

Derrick is still unemployed a year and a half after his lay-off. He has had the bomb job opportunities, interviews, and so on, but for some reason doors are still not opening for him to walk through. The other day, after a position that would have highlighted his career was not made available to him, I sat back with a heavy heart and asked, "Lord, what am I to do? I don't understand. What are we supposed to be doing? What am *I* supposed to be doing?"

Well, I finished reading the book of Acts about two months ago. I decided to read it again, just to do so. That very next morning, I picked up my Bible and started reading. I stopped at Acts 2:36-41, I believe. It speaks of the events that happened on the day of Pentecost when Peter and the other apostles were asked, "Brothers, what shall we do?" Then, Peter answered, "Repent and be baptized." I read on, and it mentioned receiving something that would be for them and their children, as well as others afar off whom God will call. It also mentioned, a little further down, that they should save themselves from this corrupt generation. My loved ones in Bunkie ran through my mind, only because I thought of the children.

I'm on my toes when I read the words "children" or "generations" in the Bible now, because I know those are rhema words for me. So, that evening I prayed a prayer. It was simple as in, "Lord, I'm available to You. If You can use anything, use me. I'm here for Your glory." It's because I hear Him loud and clear when He speaks to me now. It also helps that last session during Fall Inclusion I enrolled in a CCBS course entitled "How to Listen to God." I never knew the class would impact me like this though, and I attribute it to all of my current experiences.

Well, after that "Lord, what am I supposed to be doing?" prayer, I laid down to sleep. I had a dream that was later confirmed as a vision. These were the events as I recalled them. Tune in.

My sister, my mom, my daughter, two of my closest girlfriends, and I are in Bunkie at their parents' home. The doors are locked, and the alarm has been activated. We are talking, or something, when my mom questions, "Did y'all see that?" We are like, "See what?" She tells us that it is a ghost and we are like, "Yeah right. There's no ghost in here." Then we resume our conversation and suddenly we all start screaming. We all see it! It is a fluffy, white cloud about 3-feet above the ground, moving through the house. It is as if it's being controlled or led. It's not just aimlessly wandering or floating. It moves like it actually knows where to go.

Immediately, one of my girlfriends runs to the door, and my daughter walks toward the cloud. It starts heading down the hallway and she follows. I look at her and ask, "Where is she going?" Then, as it turns the corner, I snatch her because I don't want her to follow it anymore. Instantly, after snatching her up in my arms, out of the corner of my eyes I can see the little brass vases (fireplace accessories) shaking as they fall over at the fireplace. When I look, the fireplace utensils are hanging from their holder and shaking as the vibration increases from whatever is coming down the chimney. I'm in awe because it is brick, and I can actually see the ripples of the blocks as whatever it is continues to fall. A dreadful, eerie noise then comes out of the fireplace.

One of the ladies and I instantaneously turn to each other, back to back with our palms up and out, going around in circles and screaming, "I rebuke you in the name of Jesus. I rebuke you in the name of Jesus," about three times. While we are doing that, something flies out of the fireplace at us and blows up like a big ball of fire. Bits and pieces of ash are falling all around us. After that, we all run to the door screaming. By then, the white, floating object has returned to the room with us. The first girlfriend opens the door and the alarm sounds. I scream, "The noise! The noise! Turn it off! Turn it off!" She slams the door and responds, "I'm trying. I'm trying." I then say, "No, let it stay on. It will signal help. It will call the police." After that, she opens the door.

Well, catty-corner to where we were when we opened the door, on the outside is a police officer running towards us with his gun pointed at the house. Out of nowhere, in a split second, a black cloud comes up and sucks his uniform off with the gun. The man stands there in his boxer shorts, with his hands up, and does not move. The other cops show up to our right, and it is like a scene out of a movie. You know, when they have somebody surrounded in a house and they say, "Come out with your hands up. We have you surrounded." It is like that outside, only to the right though. We then walk out of the house easily.

We head to the left of the yard, both away from the stripped policeman and the other cops. I ask my girlfriends if they saw the cop get stripped, as well as *whom and what was that about. One of them comments that it looks like their uncle and says, "He's not a real cop anyway." In my head, I question, What?*

I then turn around to look at the house we had just come out of. My mouth flies open and my heart sinks, as I see a child in the doorway looking at me. His face and hands are pressed into the screen door as children do. He is looking at me as if to ask "Why did you leave me? Why did you run away?" I say aloud, "Look! Look! Do y'all see that?" However, nobody is there. I am the only one who has seen it. Although, I look around and notice that the stripped cop should have been able to see from his location.

That was it. It was not a nightmare. I did not wake up afraid, panting, sweating, or anything like that. The same morning, I spoke with one of our pastoral staff members. I shared with him this entire experience dating back to the trip in Bunkie, and he gave me his interpretation. Now, I'd shared this vision with Derrick when he awoke, and his explanation was good too. Following is what he and the pastor collectively agreed on:

It happened in my girlfriends' home because, as a child, that was the family which appeared to be the most ideal of what a Spirit-led family should look like. We're not sure why those particular people were involved; however, we do know of those present, the second girlfriend and I were the most spiritually mature. This is because we were the only ones who recognized the power within us to rebuke the evil we discerned coming down the chimney.

My daughter following the spirit showed that she was comfortable, or it was familiar. Now, it could have been trying to lead her out of the house, or simply out of the room, because it knew something evil was getting ready to come in through the fireplace. It knew something was about to happen and was trying to protect her, and possibly us too, if we had simply followed.

The fireplace, being that the alarm was set and the doors were locked, was the only unsecured access to the inside, from the outside. The minister said the environment sounded like that on the day of Pentecost... they were upstairs, the doors were locked, etc. (He didn't even know I'd just read about that day.)

The fact that we were locked in shows that we were being protected from whatever was outside, is what Derrick said. It was night to me, but it was later revealed that it wasn't necessarily night, just dark (evil).

Girlfriend number one running to the door first, shows she isn't as rooted in her faith. My mom being the first to have seen the spirit could have meant she was on her guard about something going on in her own life that has her uneasy. Oh, the fact that girlfriend number two and I were back-to-back in the middle of the floor, going around in circles, is how God fights according to the minister. It represents having an angel over each shoulder, and the objective is to get to the nearest wall in order to fight shoulder-to-shoulder. The fact that we were going around in circles shows that there was evil all around us. Derrick and Pastor

Rod's exact words were, "You're going into battle."

After that statement, my heart dropped to my stomach and it's still there. I honestly have not been the same since that meeting. Oh, the alarm sounded because it warned others. It got the "good cops" on their way. When we opened the door but didn't go out, it meant we were still protected inside the house when the evil dark cloud came to strip the fake cop of his authority.

Now, the cops represent ministers, and that's when this got even heavier for me. The fake cop was coming to help us when he didn't particularly have the authority to do so. *Deep! Huh?* Now, when the other cops (ministers) showed up, we all left the house, meaning we felt comfortable or secure enough to go on to safety, because our real help had come. That symbolized there will be others to join us in the battle. Real soldiers will come to assist us.

Me turning around was symbolic of looking back and being concerned enough to care. The child who was watching me through the door was a little blonde-haired, Caucasian boy around the age of three or four years old. He had the biggest, roundest, most beautiful eyes. He was the floating object. Although he never spoke a word, his spirit represented the children when his face questioned "Why did you leave me? Why did you run away?" The children are crying out to me, I was told.

Now, I figured if you want help, you just cry out for help. "Why me?" is my question, but that's a flesh issue I have to take up with the Lord, as my husband so eloquently put it. Nobody else with me saw the little boy, because it was only intended for me to see him. Although, there's a possibility that the fake cop (stripped minister) saw it as I walked away.

Now the minister says he definitely sees a calling, definitely sees an anointing, and it was definitely a vision. He said he wouldn't even be surprised if I was called to be a children's pastor.

The white cloud, because it gave light was good; however, the black cloud, because it consumed light was evil. When I told Derrick the part about that black cloud at the house, the first thing he said was, "Uh, that black thing... that ain't good."

I've been praying and preaching myself through for days now. "Fear is not of the Lord," I say as to remind myself that God will never tempt me beyond what I can bear (see 1 Corinthians 10:13, KJV). Then, I speak that we wrestle not against flesh and blood, but against principalities, against powers, against the rulers of the darkness of this world, and against spiritual wickedness in high places. (Ephesians 6:12, KJV) I mean, the Word just keeps on coming. I didn't even know I had all of this in me. It's like something in my stomach is just trying to burst forth.

I can't even begin to tell you guys the joy, but concerns I have. I'm getting excited simply thinking and typing. I feel like the prophet Jeremiah. *"It's like fire!"* The minister advised me to read that book. He says if this is to come true and we are to eventually move back to

Bunkie, then God focusing on generations with me is like Jeremiah's message not being for the people of old, but for the people of today. My message will not be for the parents or grandparents, but for the children. They said it's like Noah preaching "It's Gonna Rain" for *years*. I'm being called to break tradition of religion and start one of relationship. *Powerful stuff, huh?*

So, that's where we are. Derrick is now seeking employment in the cities surrounding Bunkie. It's hard to believe that just over a year ago I couldn't see past a declined stock market, lawsuits, a car wreck, and a lay-off. I even remember mentioning to Monique that the devil tried to kill me. Now, I know why. I have received, acknowledged, and accepted my call to the ministry!!! My mind took me back to when a friend said I'd make a great motivational speaker, as she listened intently to me tell another testimony, and I smiled. PLEASE, PRAY FOR MY FAMILY!

Something to shout about,
Shaundale

    I awoke the next morning singing. I later realized I had rebuked Emahn from following the cloud of light in the dream, because I didn't understand her following it as she did. All I saw in the natural was a ghost and screamed, but my child's *spirit* connected with the *Spirit* and she surrendered, or followed. Not only had I hindered her walk, but I had also blocked her blessings. It was trying to save her and the rest of us as well, if only we had followed.

    As a parent, that was eye-opening. The Word of God

says, "The children will lead them." Who's them? *Us.* The children will lead *us.* When I got that, I shouted. Every time an adult hindered their child's walk, *both* their spiritual blessings were blocked. *That's* why my heart was so heavy from the beginning. Because, I could see in the natural what was being done to the children, in the spirit, *by the adults.* Through the vision God wanted *me* to see the little boy asking with his eyes, the windows to his soul, "Why did you leave me?" I didn't have an answer, but I had to be ready to stand in faith because God wanted me to save the children.

Home

4 Even after all of the other experiences God had recently taken me through, from telling me to save the children to allowing me to dream dreams and have visions, I still found I needed to trust Him more, especially in the little things. Because I had grown accustomed to bells and whistles whenever the Lord shared anything with me, I started to overlook Him in simple ways. I often took for granted that He was speaking to me even in the slightest situation, so I ended up missing out on some vital information even when He just wanted to share something with me. I ignored Him twice in one day all because I felt the items were trivial.

It was now August, and due to our current circumstances we had to finance our house. There was little income to be expected or budgeted for, so we had to do what was necessary. Taking out a mortgage on our home after paying for it out-right really hurt, but God blessed us to use a portion of the home equity to purchase a 1998 Jaguar XJ8, which cost less than half the price of the Montero as a replacement for it.

Well, one day while driving home from The Parks

Mall in Arlington (more than likely window-shopping), God told me to turn right at a stop sign. As stiff-necked as the Israelites (see Exodus 32:9) I went straight and sat in traffic that seemed to come out of nowhere. The only reason I continued straight when I *know* God told me to turn was because I didn't think it was Him. I made the comment to myself, "Why would God be interested in me turning right? I know He has bigger issues going on somewhere else." *Duh! That would be me.* I was the bigger issue! Getting me to trust Him was one of His *biggest* interests.

Within an instant, I saw a flash of my sister and me as children waiting outside of our childhood home for the school bus to arrive. We had a friend named Lil' Lawrence. Some mornings, on his way to his grandparent's home before he went to school, Lil' Lawrence would play this shouting game with my sister. Because she and I were in elementary school at the time, we rode the school bus. Lil' Lawrence was in junior high school, so he walked.

As soon as he would get in front of our house, *every morning* my sister would start yelling, "Ol' bad Lil' Lawrence." In retaliation he'd yell back, "Ol' bad Evette." This would go on and on, all the way down the street and around the corner. When he turned the corner they would still be yelling, just not as frequently. It was as if there was a delay. Evette would yell and wait, and then Lil' Lawrence would respond. He'd then listen, wait, and respond again. This would continue on until they were no longer in earshot of each other. It lasted about five minutes and was interesting just to listen to Lil' Lawrence's voice drift farther and farther away.

God spoke to my spirit that day in the traffic jam and said, "I keep talking to you… sometimes yelling until you're out of earshot. Sometimes you just can't hear Me, because you're too far away." I accepted then that on some days God *is* still shouting in my life. For instance, on days when He told me to do simple things like stop and I went. *Go figure.*

Not even realizing it, I had allowed the hustle and bustle of the day, circumstances, and/or events to pull me out of fellowship with God. So, while sitting there in the car, I asked God to forgive me for being disobedient and keeping straight. It wasn't just for then. That was for *every* time He'd told me to do something simple, and I let it pass because I didn't think it was Him. I decided to learn my lesson then. It was time for me to listen up, so I asked God to test me again in the area of yielding to Him even in the slightest things, because that gut feeling was Him too.

Weeks passed before my next trial. I had driven to Arlington to run errands and decided to stop at a girlfriend's apartment for a short visit. Because I didn't have her phone number with me to call, I chanced it. When I approached the entrance gate to her apartment complex, I buzzed her. When I entered the security code, her voice mail picked up. In my mind I heard a voice telling me to go on in after the car ahead and knock, because she was there. Thinking to myself, *I just heard the machine pick up and it was obvious she wasn't there,* I drove away, headed for home. Then, in my stomach, I felt a quickening. Ignorantly, I shook it off.

My head was saying to go home, but my gut was telling me to go through. What did I do? I made the logical, *stiff-necked* choice to drive home. When I made it back to the house, my girlfriend had left a message stating she was there and I should have knocked. I could've kicked myself. *I probably did.*

I apologized to the Holy Spirit and once again sucked up the disappointment I'd caused *and felt* for being disobedient. Days later I was tested in a more severe manner. God was tightening the rope, and I *had* to get it this time; otherwise, it might have turned into hours later. This next one got my attention really well, because the car overheated after the Holy Spirit told me to slow it down. I was headed home from taking my nephew to the doctor in Arlington when the car started running strangely. It was almost comical that every time God had tested me regarding "yielding," it involved me being in the car headed to or away from Arlington, Texas.

While driving, I looked at the dash as the needle began drifting to the far right side where the heat indicator is located. As I slowed the car to below the speed limit and put on my hazard lights, I began to pray I'd make it home safely. All I wanted was to get there, so Derrick could take care of getting the car to the auto mechanic. With that, I decided to pull over in order to check the water. I at least knew that much, so I made sure it was full and sat waiting for a while, giving the engine time to cool off. Afterwards, I got back on the road and things went well. I didn't take the normal route home on FM 1382 that day because of the car trouble, though. Just in case I had to make another emergency stop, I wanted to do so safely. I preferred not to be stranded along some wooded highway, as opposed to in some established parking area.

As I was merging from I-20 East onto Highway 67 South, I took my foot off the gas and intended to let the car cruise around the exit loop. Well, in my gut I felt I should slow the car down, but it was cruising along fine so I did nothing. Instead of pushing the brake, I let the car glide around the loop and, as soon as I made it, something happened. I didn't know what, but I felt it as soon as it occurred... *something broke*. There was black smoke, a horrible burnt smell, and a lot of "putt-putting." I took the first exit, and the car literally died in the parking lot of Jack-in-the-Box. I was maybe ten minutes from our house, at most. I just wanted to scream.

I was always looking for something big, so God gave me something *really* big. I had to strike out three times to get it, but guess what. I did! I later realized why it was so imperative that God got my attention even in the most minute situations. It was because He didn't just need me to *hear* Him; He needed me to *see* Him.

Feeling the responsibility of my call, I became afraid to the point where butterflies took up permanent residence in my stomach. Then, one day while sitting in my favorite chair, preparing to study the Word, I felt something I had never experienced before in my life. It was warmth like that which I had only encountered in my closet. I felt love and peace, and I relaxed and enjoyed it. I could not have been more comfortable in anyone else's arms.

I looked around behind me and saw Derrick coming up the hallway, headed into the master bedroom. Emahn was napping, and I knew with everything in me that Jesus was holding me. He was standing behind me, right there in our den, with his arms wrapped around me from behind. I could feel Him from shoulder-to-shoulder, and I rested in all that He was. For, at that time, He was Jehovah-Shalom (my Peace), Jehovah-Shammah (my Present), and He was certainly Yahweh (the Self-Existing One). I praised God for that experience most of all, because He was exactly what I needed Him to be *when* I needed Him to be it. *Amen.*

God had begun to give me fire and brimstone messages. I thought immediately about how I would create adversaries and said, "Lord, You cannot send me home to make enemies." It was hard enough for me that I was going home telling folks I had been called into the ministry, but God told me His promises are for His people. I thought about my loved ones in Bunkie once more and felt an incredible weight on my shoulders. I said, "Lord, some of those people are old enough to be my grandparents. How do I go back down there and tell them all the things You've given me to share?" Why, oh why, did I ever ask that question?

One morning, I received a phone call from one of the computer students I had befriended at our church. He was an older gentleman who was a member of our senior center. I met him when he enrolled in my Beginner's Computer Class, which was restricted to senior citizens. He had phoned to invite me to join him for Bible study at his church. I immediately passed on my own Tuesday morning women's Bible study, because I knew there was something I was supposed to get out of going to church with him. I just knew there was a blessing waiting for me; otherwise, God would not have let him invite me.

The morning of Tuesday, September 17, 2002 (my grandmother's 83rd birthday), he came and picked me up from home. Our car was still in the shop, because it had overheated during the previous week. As we drove to his church, I recalled being open to whatever the Spirit had in store for me. What I got when I arrived there, I never expected. There was a lady present who I later discovered was the Assistant Pastor of the church. She was an older woman, whom I could tell simply from listening to her God uses mightily. I didn't know why, but I felt something tugging at me to get acquainted with this woman of God. It was as if I was being drawn to her for some reason that was beyond me.

As the lesson began, the instructor started to speak of babes in Christ. The lesson came from Hebrews 5. I thought that was strange considering all I knew God was dealing with me on, but had no clue as to how they knew it too. Naturally, I zeroed in on verses 12-14 which reads, *"In fact, though by this time you ought to be teachers, you need someone to teach you the elementary truths of God's word all over again. You need milk, not solid food! Anyone who lives on milk, being still an infant, is* not acquainted with the teaching about righteousness. *But solid food is for the mature, who by constant use have trained themselves to distinguish good from evil.*" I sat up and began to pay even closer attention. God was *definitely* in on this one. The only person I knew in the entire class was the gentleman who had invited me, and I had not yet shared any of my experiences with him. How could *this* be happening?

As I continued to listen to the instructor, the Assistant Pastor interrupted the class with something she said she felt led to share. She had already gained my respect earlier; however, what happened next made the hairs on the back of my neck stand at attention. The Assistant Pastor began to read from the book of Ezekiel in the 33rd chapter. She prefaced it by saying, "God has given somebody a testimony, and He expects you to share it." My heart sank to my stomach, and all I remember hearing were the words "blood being on your hands if you don't share what thus said the Lord." I started to cry uncontrollably. I knew everyone in that room, by then, probably thought I was crazy, but I could do nothing aside from sitting there sobbing.

The Assistant Pastor then called for the class's attention. I heard her say there was a situation upfront and immediately all eyes were on me. I sat there and poured my heart out concerning the vision and of how afraid I was to have to go back home and tell people, especially some of my elders, what thus said the Lord concerning their fate in that city. After hearing my testimony, the people there were so encouraging that I left feeling empowered to do nothing but the will of God at all costs. When God said to go, I would. He did, and I went. Approximately three days later, we drove back to Louisiana—not because I *wanted* to, but because I *had* to. A few days prior to this trip, I had another vision. Tune in.

A train appears before me. When it comes to a halt, I'm actually sitting in a seat beside Derrick and Emahn. I can see people all around. I look out of the window to my right and people are lined up for miles over the hills. To my left, I see people with tears streaming down their faces as they walk away with their heads hanging low. This really disturbs me, and I begin to get restless.

I look straight ahead and see the other cities coming up over the hills. I look out of the window to the right at all of the people who still have to get on the train and grow even more agitated. Not because of all the people waiting to board, but because of all the people who are being turned away. I don't know it immediately, but I soon figure out we are heaven-bound. There is a man standing at the doors to the train, dressed in a white robe. Although I cannot see His face, I know it is Jesus. (Don't ask me how, I just know.)

One thing, in particular, that bothers me about the ride is the lady who is sitting in front of me. I continue to look out of the window to the left at all of the sad faces walking away. I become more disturbed with each one. I then notice the lady in front of me making herself comfortable and getting all settled in. She has on a nice suit with a huge hat. I mention something about the others and she comments with, "Well, I'm on the train." I don't become angry, just disappointed. I lean over to tell Derrick something and whisper that I will be right back. When he asks where I'm going, I tell him that I already have my seat, to watch Emahn, and I'll be back. This became stranger by the minute.

As I stand, I can see farther over the hills before us. I don't know where we are, but I continue to see masses of people to the right getting on the train, with some here and there being turned away to the left. The closer I walk to the front of the train, the farther ahead I can see. Bunkie is up ahead. I say, "Master, can I go? There's still time. We're not there yet."

I know from experience it only takes five hours to make the drive from my home in Texas, but not knowing where we are or where the train is headed next I have no clue how long the trip will be from this point. I just know with all of those people still waiting to get on, or to be turned away, I have to at least try to warn others. Unlike the lady who sits in front of me with that big ol' hat on, I am willing to give up my comfort just long enough to run ahead and warn the people in Bunkie that the train is coming... Jesus is on His way! *I say once more, "I'll go. I've already got my seat. I'll go and warn them that You're on Your way." With His approval, I jet off the train in the direction of the hills that are before me.*

For me, this vision was confirmation of my call. Jesus wanted me to see with my own eyes that He *is* the Doorkeeper. No one could board the train without coming by Him. Likewise, no one will get to heaven without going *through* Him. He even said Himself, "No man cometh unto the Father, *but by Me.*" (John 14:6, KJV *(Italics added)*) He didn't care if you knew the bus driver, the mechanic, or the baggage claim person. You had to walk through *the Door* with your own nametag on. Either you *knew* a child of God (left), or you *were* a child of God (right). Regardless, the bus was moving on even if you weren't on it, and I just couldn't bring myself to enjoy the ride knowing some people were going to be left behind due to a lack of knowledge.

Having arrived in Bunkie just three days after the incident regarding the testimony and the Associate Pastor's prophecy, I had decided I wasn't saying *anything*—and that meant *nuthin'*—outside the will of God. I was so sensitive to the Spirit that I didn't even hold idle conversation on that visit, and on Sunday morning I was sick. Yep, the devil tried to get me. I knew exactly what it was. It was the Word and the responsibility of it boiling over in my belly. By the time I made it to church, all I knew was that I was either going to spit it out, or God was going to make me cough it up. As the service began, the pastor made his way to me during the welcome portion of the program. When he greeted me, I whispered to him that I had something to say. At least I had gotten that part out, but I knew then my chances of backing out were over and that no matter what I was fighting against, it was going to lose. Whatever had to be heard, God was going to ensure it be said. The pastor then went to the microphone and called for the testimony period. *Oh Lord, please not now,* I thought. I knew I was supposed to go, but I was so nervous that I continued to sit.

Nearing the end of the service, my stomach worsened. I couldn't even explain it. Whether it was the conviction in my gut, the weight of my heart as it sank into my stomach, or just breakfast, I didn't know. Whatever it was though, it did not feel good. The Word was coming forth, and I could do nothing to stop it. I sat through the remainder of the church service on pins and needles. Then, right after they closed *the Door* to the Church, but before the Benediction, I rushed to the altar. I knew it was then or never. As I closed my eyes and opened my mouth, the Spirit spoke.

After that, as the Lord continued to tell me more things I knew would not be well received, I continued to pray. I talked with the minister from Concord whom I'd originally shared my first vision with, and he mentioned that it is the responsibility of a minister to take what God says, dissect it, and share it with others. "Rarely does God give a harsh Word and say leave it as it is. It happens, but it's rare," he said. I shook my head and left his office thinking, *I would be in the rare number.*

I knew that since I had re-dedicated my life to Christ,

I had also reverted back to my old soft-spoken and timid ways. So, to have me be the one to preach "fire and brimstone" messages simply made no sense to me at all. I learned quickly when walking in the Spirit, God often does things out of the ordinary. I remembered telling two of my closest girlfriends, "You know, I asked God 'Why can't I have peace and prosperity messages? Why do I have to give the "God's going to get you" type of messages?'" *Did they laugh at me?* I got that answer soon enough, though. I had been given a ministry of deliverance. God wanted us to prosper *as our souls prospered* (see Proverbs 19:8). It wasn't about peace and prosperity alone. I realized then it has never been, nor will it ever be.

After this revelation, I accepted that I had been given the responsibility of telling and/or writing it like it was, but *in love*. Because, regardless of who or where we are in this life, God wanted someone to ensure that we understood the train *is* coming. In fact, it has already left the station, and Jesus is already *the Door! And, that's the truth!* However, the question I needed to ask *in love* was, "Are you on the left, or are you on the right?"

This level of understanding came after I heard the words "choke them" in my spirit. I repeated them to myself as if to ask a question, "Choke them?" Then, I heard, "Yes, choke them." Immediately, I thought this conversation was of the devil, because I couldn't visualize God choking anyone. But, do you want to know what the Spirit said? He gave *all* of us free will to either choose, or not to choose, salvation... but aha! He gave *none* of us a choice in choosing righteousness. He expected it upon our choosing salvation! 1 Peter 1:14-16 says, "*As obedient children [of the Light], do not conform to the evil desires you had when you lived in ignorance [of the dark]. [But] Just as he who called you is holy, so be [you] holy in all you do; for it is written:*

Be holy, because I am holy." (Inserts added.) The aforementioned was not suggested; it was commanded.

By this time, I'd grabbed a piece of paper and a pen. I did not have my journal with me, but I had learned to write everything as it happened, or as I heard it. During this process, I quickly learned that God was bringing discipline to my writing. I'd gotten into the habit of carrying a notebook everywhere I went. I eventually even traded my purse for a backpack, which most of the time consists of a journal, notebook, Bible and pens, at minimum.

Having grabbed a few things to write with, I continued to put into writing what the Spirit was whispering to me concerning this choking thing. "God's promises are for God's people" had begun echoing in the back of my mind almost all of the time. However, this was later interpreted as "God's promises are for *Godly* people." At that point, I equated my every experience to home.

BECOMING NEW

5 Having finally learned the importance of listening to God, in specific detail, I was more in-tune to Him than I believe I had ever been before. I mean, He just kept pouring out His Spirit, so I kept receiving Him and writing. This was personal now; it was about home.

Daily, I was having experiences where I knew someone was talking to me. I also knew if I didn't get what I was being told, at that time, the conversation would be lost for good. It seemed as though I had tapped into something and was being elevated into another realm.

On October 5, 2002, I sat down to write one of my loved ones a letter, which I never mailed. I couldn't bring myself to send it, because the contents weighed heavily on my heart. It was addressed to an older relative on my maternal side of the family tree.

Thinking more about the contents of the letter, God revealed to me that although I was concerned with lost souls, I was definitely more troubled over lazy ones. After closing the letter, I remembered looking at Derrick and asking, "If we were in a boat and saw a ship that started to sink, would we throw one the lifesaver we have and watch the others drown, or would we try to save them too?" Derrick just looked at me and smiled. Then, he replied, "Shaundale, some of them can swim. They simply choose not to." *Man! How profound*, I thought. He didn't even know I was struggling over the issue of helping those who *chose* not to swim. One week later, after praying consistently for the resolution of specific issues noted in the letter I had written, I experienced another dream.

In this particular vision, Derrick, Emahn, and I were in Bunkie again, but this time it was different. The sky was bright, sunny, and clear. It was like a day out of *Home and Garden Magazine*. I say that because, in mostly all of the other dreams, there was a heavy, dark cloud that seemed to hover over the entire city. I instantly recognized the difference in this one. Tune in.

My grandmother, Muh (as in Madear), and I were standing in her front yard when she said, "I have something I want you to see. Let me show you what they've written about so-and-so." The local church had written a poem honoring the very person I had written the letter to. Muh then handed me a bookmark of some sort that read: "A Woman after God's Own Heart." I got excited! I looked at her and she said, "They wrote that about her." She was talking about the local church.

I saw the entire poem before someone started to shake me by my left shoulder, as they tried to get my attention. I attempted to push them away, because I was talking to my grandmother and wanted to read the poem in detail. I could feel the shaking, but could not see a face. I turned around in the dream, but in actuality I awoke.

Although I could not see who was shaking me in the

vision, in the natural it was Emahn needing to go "potty" between three and four in the morning. I was slightly angered, because I only had a chance to read these words:

> *"A Woman after God's Own Heart"*
>
> *You are a woman after God's own heart.*
> *No other woman...*

After waking up, I lost the remainder of the poem. At first, I could see it as plainly as if someone had given me a hand-written note. I took Emahn to the bathroom and thought about journaling right then. I decided not to only because I was hoping I would fall asleep again, continuing the dream where it left off, and be able to see the entire poem. It never reappeared, but I had peace in knowing my prayers of intercession were answered.

It later dawned on me, as I skimmed through my journal and noticed dates, that dream had occurred exactly seven days after I wrote the letter and prayed once more. It was as if writing it was a point of release for me. I let go of the things concerning me and gave them totally and unyieldingly to the Lord. Never mind I didn't mail the letter, God heard my heart and I believe He replied with that dream. I knew then I had a promise to hold onto regarding a specific prayer request, concerning a specific person.

About a week later, another one of my girlfriends called. She told me she had been thinking about me during the last week and again the day before, so she called and left a message because we were out. When I hadn't called her right back, she mentioned she'd thought about me once more and decided to call again. This time, I answered. Immediately, I could hear in her voice that she was searching for something. Overall, she's doing well, but I sensed she was probing for something in the

Spirit.

My girlfriend then shared with me that she'd bumped into a stranger who had informed her that she would have a successful career. The stranger had also told her she should begin to pray over her marriage. Upon hearing those words, I shared with her that during the week before she'd flashed through my mind, while I was dusting, and I felt a need to pray for her. I told her immediately I'd stopped and done so, right then.

Once I began to pray for her, the Spirit automatically led me to pray for her husband and their marriage. I didn't know why; it just turned out that way. In sharing that experience with her, she began to cry. After talking a little longer, she expressed that she and her husband had begun to have problems only a week ago... right around the day I had prayed for her. Had I not been where I should be spiritually, I could have easily allowed the devil to convince me that it was me. However, I knew God was definitely telling me that He was still with me, listening to and guiding me, so I prayed with her over the telephone and let it go. I continued that day in a spirit of joy. Having fasted three days, I realized my life had been grand since I had finally learned how to listen to and abide in Christ.

For whatever reason, Pastor Bailey later crossed my mind. Immediately, I stopped and said a prayer for him as well. I had no idea four days later, during Sunday morning worship service, he'd announce he had been diagnosed with another type of cancer *for a third time*. Shocked and in tears, that was when I needed to remind myself that God would not put more on me than what I could bear *again*.

I caught one of my favorite female televangelists twice on television later that same evening. She was on both of the local Christian television stations, and both messages hit home. In one sermon, I recalled her saying,

"You don't want it badly enough!" As though I heard a voice echoing, I asked, "Huh?" The voice was referring to me not getting out of bed when God woke me in the early mornings. I shivered with multiple chills.

God had been waking me up *consistently* every morning for the past two weeks at 5:45 a.m. I knew it was Him, but turned over and went right back to sleep. At one time I even said, "Lord, but it's so cold in here. If You would just let the heat kick on in a few minutes..." *Don't laugh.* I learned from sharing this experience, I was not alone. *Boy! Was I convicted?*

To think some of the people closest to me were possibly on the verge of getting breakthroughs if only I would have made myself get up at dawn and pray for them when God awakened me to do so, was disheartening. It's not that He wasn't listening during the other hours of the day; He just initiated the conversations during the dawn of each new morning. That meant He had something He wanted to share with me. I knew then obedience was better than sacrifice. It was better for me to get up and pray, as opposed to sacrificing my loved ones' well-being for my own comfort and sleep.

Now, the televangelist's second message was about being in the fire. She mentioned something about if you're in the fire, then that's where God needs you to be in order to bless you. You have to go through the fire *first.* I thought, *Lord, I* must *be in the fire then.*

I realized after that I had become a Christian television junkie. I watched it faithfully from sun-up to sun-down. I flipped from one channel to another with the remote control recall button. In fact, I knew the daily lineup of one station in particular. Christian television had become my soap opera channel. I was addicted to the Word. All I knew was I needed It, and if God was trying to tell me something, then I was trying my best to hear Him.

Doors were not opening for Derrick in his career, and we were at a financial standstill. He would apply for positions and get telephone interviews, and according to the employers everything was fine, they were impressed, yadda, yadda, yadda, but it always came down to them not being ready or able to relocate for a particular position. We had long since given up on staying in Dallas. So, convinced that we were obviously doing something wrong, I began to feel anger, resentment, bitterness, and abandonment. I told God all of that when I locked myself in the bathroom one morning. Well, in actuality, I was soaking in the bathtub and didn't want to be bothered. So, I told Derrick I was taking a bath, and that meant nobody had better call me for *nuthin'*.

Once in the tub, I sank into the water with tears streaming down my face in outrage. I told God everything I thought or felt at that moment, and then I wished I could just sink under the water and wake up on the other side. I sat there and cried, and cried, and cried. When I finally stepped out of the tub, the television was still on. I listened to the man of God speaking as I dressed. I didn't recognize who he was; just that he immediately got my attention with the words: God says that those of you who feel abandoned are not alone. I froze, with the exception of the pounding of my heart.

When I finally turned to look at the television, the man continued to say, "God says He is here. Wait on Him to bless you. It may take a lifetime, but you're in His presence and He will give you strength." With tears once again rolling down my cheeks, I continued to listen to, "God has something waiting especially for you, but you started depending on man to bring you out."

I started to think about how consumed I had become with relocating. All I could think was that if we could leave this place, then things would be better somewhere else. I had become obsessed with Derrick finding a job in another state and with doing something, almost *anything* else for myself. Then, the man of God said, "God wants you to wait on Him, for He knows the plans He has. Wait on Him. You may ask Him why, but don't give up faith. Ask Him why, but don't cross the line and give up on God. He will come through."

I began to praise and worship the Lord right there in the bedroom. I knew, without a doubt, that message was for me. How could that man have known what I had just talked to God about? How could he have had so timely a message? Oh, how I pleaded for forgiveness over the things I had previously felt and thought about a God who had shown me so much favor in the past.

The strangest thing was that *same* man of God was on that *same* channel earlier that *same* morning, but I didn't want to watch him then. First off, I didn't know who he was; and secondly, I had too much going on already to just be still. *Imagine that.* I could have prevented the entire breakdown had I just been still and listened. *There's a message in there.*

Just when I thought I'd almost had enough of "The Rise and Fall of Derrick and Shaundale Johnson," God got my attention. It turned out the man of God on the television is the son of another prominent televangelist. I enjoy listening to his father, but had never seen nor heard of this son. I was so glad I had finally listened to him on that day, because God used him to bless me. He also used another prominent televangelist in the Atlanta area immediately afterwards who spoke, "I don't care where you are now, it's not where you will end up." So, at that moment with my spirit full, I was able to go on.

Later, my emotions continued to fluctuate. One day I was up; the next day I was down. Still, I continued on. By this time, I had begun to look for work. I was ready to let my company go for a more stable income with benefits. I took a part-time job, but that began to get the best of me whenever I would leave home in the evenings and Emahn would cry. I was working at a local department store and began to feel even more resentment. It was one of those "Is this what I gave up my career to do?" situations. I thought, *How unfair?* I had been out of work for approximately three and a half years while staying home and raising our daughter. Derrick and I had agreed that I would return to my career when Emahn turned three years old. God granted the success of my business, which was temporarily satisfying. However, when we needed additional income and doors were still not being opened for my husband, as a wife and mother, I began to panic in fear.

The next Tuesday morning, I dragged myself to my women's Bible study meeting at the church. God was so timely. When I arrived, the group had just begun reading and discussing a new book entitled "When Your Rope Breaks" by Steve Brown. Those ladies' comments were right on- time. I really needed their words of encouragement, because my rope had broken long ago. I left there knowing God still loves me and He cares. That was good too, because I was so tired of everything that I wanted to give up to the point where I had decided it made no difference whether I tithed or prayed anymore.

I talked to Derrick one night about my feelings and he said, "God doesn't need you to hype Him up." He told me that, because I had mentioned to him I partially prayed out of habit. You know, pray in the morning and again at night. It was a routine I had grown up with, but I didn't feel like doing it anymore.

There were times during the day when I would feel the need or simply the desire to pray, and would *fervently* talk to God aloud or enter into my closet in private (which were my most intimate and sincere moments). Then, when I laid down for bed at night, I would have to force myself to pray out of habit, because I thought I was supposed to. I had been feeling that way for about a week or so, and I decided not to do it anymore. If I didn't really want to talk to God at that time, why was I going to continue to act like I did? As if He didn't already know anyway.

I finally realized my heart had not been right, and as a result my prayers weren't getting through during those times anyhow. It amazed me how I could pray for others throughout the day and rejoice, but when nightfall came I was so fed up with the day's events that I didn't really want to pray for myself. So, I stopped doing it.

One week later, I had a new, fresh desire to talk to God. I guessed I must have been doing something right, since I'd actually missed Him. It was a good thing too, because I caught my favorite female televangelist on Christian television another day shortly after that, and she was referring to the three Hebrew boys in the fire. I didn't know what was up with the fire messages, but could definitely relate. She said, "No more complaining. Come out of, or go through, the fire. This is for your deliverance that God might be glorified." So, I decided then to stop complaining that God might be glorified in my "fiery furnace" fiasco.

I then thought back to how from time-to-time God would place people on my heart. I had no idea why, but even when I was in college and someone would cross my mind, I would pick up the telephone to call them. Immediately after hearing my voice they would speak into the phone, "Shaundale, you always call when I need someone to talk to." That happened on numerous occasions. However, since I had finally learned that God was speaking to me even during those minute times, I also realized He was transitioning me. Instead of calling the person when they crossed my mind, I learned to call *on Him* concerning the person who had crossed my mind. Thus, was the case on this particular day.

Derrick and I were sitting in our home office one evening when I thought about an old acquaintance I had met approximately five years prior. I had no idea why, but I began to pray for him, his wife, children, extended family, etc. Then, for some strange reason, I began to search online for any contact information on this person. During my search, his personal website appeared in the search results window and I was shocked.

Remembering why he and I had discontinued our friendship in the first place, I clicked the contact button on the site and began typing an e-mail to him. It was brief and read along the lines of a simple greeting. When I clicked the "Send" button Derrick was sitting behind me, looking over my shoulder. We don't have any issues along the lines of male/female friendships, and he remembered my stories about that drama from when I was single. In fact, as I began to tell him about the last time I had e-mailed Payton, he stopped me because he already knew the rest of the story. So, I looked at him and asked, "I wonder if *she'll* get it?"

Based on past experience, I tried not to think about the response I may or may not receive from that e-mail. In fact, I turned the lights off and we headed for bed. As I lay down, thoughts filled my head. I wondered what would happen, this time, if the man's wife intercepted my e-mail. The next afternoon, as I sat down to the computer, my nerves rattled.

When I used to e-mail my friend in the past, I would always send him jokes. I was told his wife would read them, laugh, and say, "Whoever that person is sending these jokes is crazy. She ain't got *no* sense." They were funny, if I must say so myself.

At any rate, this was during my pre- "I'm living for Jesus *for real"* days. During this time, the guy and I had a mutual female friend named. One day, I made the mistake of referencing her a little too casually in an e-mail to him, and that's when the grits hit the pan... *talk about steam*. The next day I received an e-mail from his wife. I'll never forget the Subject line "Guess Who?" and the words "Do not send anymore e-mails to this address." Respecting her wishes, I never did.

To make a long story short, as a result of that e-mail, along with other things, I learned their marriage began to suffer even more, and the camaraderie we once shared was strained. Although it was all innocent, his wife didn't see him "chit-chatting" with other women above suspicion. He was my friend, and so was the other person. The way I saw it, we were all friends. The problem was, in hindsight, that unbeknownst to his wife were these *friendships*.

I never understood, as a single person, the severity and complexity of that situation. When I finally got it, I felt like it was my fault for years. However, as my husband and I still laugh now about some of the *many* things I've blurted out, I thought that was just like me to say something. In *my* head, having cross-gender friendships meant nothing, but to the person who mattered most, it *definitely* meant something. Besides, who was I to question her judgment where it concerned *her* marriage? Everyone sets different boundaries and, to her, theirs had been crossed. Thinking back, she could care less about what I thought anyway.

Oddly enough, it was during this time (prior to my marriage) when God began to deal with me the most. I had been up and down, in and out. Depression had been something I'd secretly battled with since middle school, and now it seemed to have set in for what appeared to be the long-haul. I was not happy; I didn't even know why. From the outside, looking in, I was told it appeared I had it "going on." I had a great career in Information Technology, drove a nice white Nissan Maxima, and lived in a very comfortable and spacious three-bedroom townhouse apartment with my cute little dog, a Pomeranian named Vanity Shay. I was aggressive, professional, and goal-oriented.

I kept a rotation of weekly dates prior to dating my guy friend's cousin, which was how he and I had actually met. I would meet someone for lunch Monday afternoon, and then someone else would take me to dinner Monday evening. Wednesday afternoon I would have another lunch date, and Saturday another person would take me someplace else. Although most of these people were just male friends or simply male co-workers, it didn't appear that way to on-lookers. Besides, I loved the attention and having variety. It only worked because for everything I liked to do, there was a specific person who enjoyed the same. It was all about timing. There was just one thing missing, although I could not figure out what it was.

This was around the time in my life when God started messing with me. Even with the hustle and bustle of the day I had nothing of value to do, not even my work. With all of the people I was constantly around or who were constantly around me, I still came home lonely. This went on for months. My life was so empty; I would lie in bed at night and just cry. Then, I would wake up to face another day, and do the same thing all over again.

By that time, I couldn't wait until I left work on Fridays because I was headed away from Dallas, to Houston or Shreveport, where one or two of my oldest and dearest friends would be waiting for me almost every other weekend. Even with my best friends, I didn't release and let them know what was going on with me exactly. Notice I said, "I didn't," not that I couldn't. This was primarily because I was clueless about what was happening. All I knew was that I was headed into an emotional downward spiral.

To make matters worse both of my roommates, my sister and a college friend, felt as though I was starting to hide myself from them. Truthfully, I hid myself from me. I didn't want to be around anyone who connected me to this life. I wanted to live another existence… a life in a world where everything was perfect. A life where when I was home over the weekend, I wouldn't go downstairs into the kitchen, look out the window, and sob. Then, it happened.

The better things appeared to be on the outside, the worse they were on the inside. I felt like I was losing my mind. How could I have gone from having it professionally altogether, to falling emotionally apart? Looking at me, you would have thought I really did have it "going on." Instead, something had me going, and it was either getting ready to take me up or out. Since I was giving up the fight *daily*, I thought it was more than likely going to be the latter.

On Wednesday, April 1, 1998, I left work headed to meet a date at one of my favorite local seafood restaurants for an early dinner. Let me tell you, *he* was the date from hell. Was God just out to get me? If so, after all I had done, part of me felt I deserved the loneliness, emptiness, and fear I was internally experiencing. That evening when the date ended, I had both the scariest and most awesome experience of my life. Following is the exact letter I e-mailed to some of my closest sister-friends who were praying me through when I didn't even know it.

The strange thing is I met this group of ladies online. I know that sounds weird, but it was on the sorority chat-line. Initially, the seven of us e-mailed and phoned each other for about a year. We dubbed ourselves "The Board" and, at some point, grew comfortable enough to start sending out nick-names for one another, based on different personality types.

One of them was given the name Quad, Inc. She is also from Louisiana. One Easter holiday when I drove home to visit my family, I called her cell phone and found out she was there visiting her family, too. So, I gassed up my car and drove the one and a half hour ride from Bunkie to Baton Rouge to meet her. This would be our first time seeing one another in person since we'd met online.

Meeting Quad and her family was so "natural." She and I instantly clicked. Whether it was that we are sorors, both GRITS (girls raised in the south), or simply that we have a genuine "love-hate" relationship over being college rivals we weren't sure, but after that initial visit the remaining Board members decided to meet. Our first trip was in September of 1998 over Labor Day Weekend, and we met at Walt Disney World in Orlando, Florida. This is the original e-mail testimony that was shared with them after my very first post-college, spiritual experience. Our Board Screen Names were used.

```
-----Original Message-----
From: OMNI
Sent: Thursday, April 02, 1998 10:50AM
To: CAT; QUAD; OPB; Q-TIP; DIVA; ESP
Subject: The Storm IS Over, Shaun's Testimony
```

First off, the date will not happen again. Not only does he have issues that I don't like, but just won't deal with. 1) He smokes (had three at the table AFTER I said I don't like the smoke because I have ASTHMA, and it makes it difficult for me to breathe). 2) He ordered a beer AND a Crown and Sprite/Seven Up... SOMETHING AT THE SAME TIME (not drinks one and orders another later). He asked for both of them then, and drank them while he smoked. 3) Is TOO finicky of an eater. Doesn't eat AYTHING (no seafood... few vegetables... no cheese…). It took HIM 30 minutes to decide on a dish for HIMSELF. He wanted it, then he didn't, then he wanted it again. 4) Too darn assertive. I hate for someone to answer my questions for me in THAT perspective (dating… when we're simply having dinner). Every time the waitress came back to ask if everything was okay he said, "Yes, it is." NO, it was not.

I explained to him that my pasta was DRY. There was not enough sauce on it. Also, I DIDN'T want wine last evening (get to that later), but he INSISTED that I get some. She brought me a glass of Merlot AFTER I maintained that I didn't want any Zinfandel and he gave up. He said, "I thought you like Zhin?" I said, "I do, but when I have wine I PREFER MERLOT." He said to the waitress, "Well, she wants the Zhin." EXCUSE ME!!! I said, "NO SHE DOESN'T. She PREFERS MERLOT." He then said it again, "I thought you like Zhin?" Yes, but I *PREFER* MERLOT! Then, I had to break it down.

I asked, "You drink Kool-Aid?" He answered, "Yes." I said, "Yeah, well I LIKE Kool-Aid, but I PREFER LEMONADE!!!! Understand the difference?" He just sat there and said, "Merlot." Ugh!!!!! I said approximately three times, "I was going to order Lemonade. I was going to order Lemonade. I was going to order Lemonade." He kept saying, "You don't have to." Like it was a kiddy drink or something?

Anyway, he KEPT calling me BABY!!! Ugh! I HATE that! We were having a dinner date. We were not dating. Then, he had the nerve to TOUCH me. Ugh! I think I'm going through WORLDLY withdrawal. Anyway, I wasn't very comfortable in his presence, and I'll have to let him know that if he asks me out a second time.

Guess what???!!! After the DATE from HADES, I was driving around. I realized it was Wednesday night and thought about something that I COULD be doing after such a LONG day. Well, Wednesday is my Bible study night. I drove to my church in Arlington, even though Bible study started at 8:00 p.m. and I didn't arrive until 8:45 p.m. Usually, if it will be after 8:15 when I get there, I just won't go. I know that was tacky, but something TOOK me there.

At any rate, when I arrived at the church I spoke with one of the ministers, but not the pastor. He answered every question I asked. Remember when we were having the debate about ministers and wine? Well, he explained (IN HIS OPINION) that ministers are not to drink, but some choose to do so with WINE.

He also said if you dance, then you need to be dancing to PRAISE THE LORD. (That negates dropping it like it's hot.) With music, he agrees with me. It's NOT THE BEAT, but THE WORDS that cause the ruckus. Dance, BUT praise the Lord. He answered every question I threw out there. I wanted to know just about everything.

Now, I also wanted to say that if I'm not as talkative for the next few days or so, ain't nothing wrong. God's just getting ready to USE me for something. The Board is (no offense, but...) IN THE WAY. There's something I'm supposed to be doing that I've been ignoring, and it's not working anymore. I don't know what it is, but I need to RE-FOCUS MY ATTENTION. I can't explain it, but I feel like God is getting ready to use me FOR REAL.

I called my pastor back in Louisiana last night, and he expounded on what the other minister meant when he said, "GOD IS CONVICTING YOU!!!" The other minister had already said, "I know what you're going through. I've been there. I know what you mean when you say you don't wanna BE TOUCHED no more. You don't wanna club no more. You don't wanna dance AS MUCH as you used to. You don't wanna drink no more."

He also said that if drinking wine has me that baffled, then I need to CAST that CARE UPON THE LORD. That's not to say there's something wrong with drinking wine, but if it's weighing that heavily on MY heart, then maybe it's not what I should be doing until God has had the final say for what He wants SHAUNDALE to do.

I also talked to him about some of my friends. I know we're close and all, but I eventually see us growing apart. They're going to still want to do all that stuff and I'm not. I was having problems figuring out how to tell them, and the minister introduced me to a new word: DESIRE. Now I know what desire means, but this DESIRE was different! He said to tell them I no longer have a DESIRE to do those things anymore. It was powerful and imperative! When he said that, I felt TRULY FREE.

Last night, I sat in bed and read my Bible. When I prayed, even THAT had changed. It was no longer the basic Lord's Prayer and then God bless... God help... God watch over... It was more so MY OWN PRAYER!!! Instead of focusing so much on praying for everybody else, I PRAYED FOR MYSELF!!! I prayed for strength as I attempt to walk the straight and narrow path, no longer DESIRING to stray. I prayed that ALL MY CARES (not just the wine one) be CAST UPON HIM. I did ask that He *PLEASE* ORDER MY STEPS IN HIS WORD.

I continued my prayer list and for the FIRST time in a LONG while, I felt like HE HEARD ME. I had an out-of-body experience. I saw a beautiful bright light before me, and it was as if I was floating on air. I was before myself, looking down on MYSELF, as I kneeled, cried, and prayed. It was warm and wonderful. It was peaceful and surreal.

So, WHEN I AROSE THIS MORNING, I DIDN'T HAVE ANY DOUBTS about my salvation. I KNEW THAT THE LORD HAD BROUGHT ME OUT, and I can say with a STRONG BELIEF that THE STORM IS OVER and MY SOUL HAS BEEN ANCHORED IN THE LORD.

Today, I am new! Today, I AM NOT JUST HIS, but HE IS MINE! Today, I am FREE, for I have been FED and my FLESH hungers no more... only my SOUL. I've got a new NAME, a new WALK, and a new TALK! So, bear with me as I start over while trying to live like THIS JOY I HAVE THE WORLD DIDN'T GIVE IT TO ME!

Yours in Christ,
Omni

Kleenex anyone?

-----Original Message-----
From: QUAD, INC.
Sent: Thursday, April 02, 1998 1:22PM
To: OMNI; Q-TIP; CAT; OPB; DIVA; ESP
Subject: Re: The Storm IS Over, Shaun's Testimony

Shaun,

I didn't want to address this to you on yesterday, because I could sense that you were wrestling between natural and supernatural. See what I mean by sitting back and letting God work? You are the apple of Christ's eye, and I give God all the glory. You have made a step that is truly ordered by Christ. I am getting ready to talk to you straight.

Everything happens for a reason. Everything we do is ordered by Christ. He has placed a certain conviction in your heart, along with a definite desire, to forever and always please Him. *Our convictions are based on what spiritual relationship we want to have with Christ.* If your heart is burning about certain subjects and you just can't seem to shake it, honey God is simply trying to get your attention.

From this day forward, surround yourself with people who want to do the same things as you. *It's hard for Christians to say they are changing and continue to hang out with the same crowd and go to the same places.* Temptation will try to override you, and peer pressure will try to take over. Girl, you are making me proud, but you know my feelings don't matter. It's not about me, but about Jesus Christ and Him crucified.

If you slip, don't hold your head down, and don't let the devil torment you by saying you're not saved. Speak the Word to him and he will shut up. Like, "Shut up, devil. I'm saved, by grace." The Word says if you confess your sins, He will be faithful and just to forgive you of your sins (see 1 John 1:9). Pray daily. Pray daily. Pray daily.

See, the devil can't stand what you did yesterday. Be prepared to have him come at you maybe through your family, friends, or job. When this happens, tell him he is a liar and call someone you know who will pray for you without thinking about your faults (someone who is sincere). You are welcome to call me at anytime of the day or night; my husband wouldn't mind. (No, I am not saying I am the only one sincere. Shut up devil!)

Shaundale, you may not realize it, but you have been born again!!! Everything is new. Your hands are new, etc. You've got me wanting to shout!

Shaun, you have been delivered! No more chains will hinder you. You've been set free! You've been set free! *God will always honor the hearts of individuals who want to do right and know the truth.* The ball is in your court. God's anointing is upon you.

QUAD

I felt so sure of my salvation after that experience, God could've called me home then. I was just that ready. I had fallen in love with Jesus *instantaneously* and suddenly all I wanted was to be with Him—to experience His touch forever. I decided, at that time, it was going to be Him and me from that point on. (Then, along came Derrick... another book in itself.)

I forwarded this exact testimony to my guy friend and our mutual friend, as well as his cousin (the gentleman I immediately decided not to continue seeing anymore as a result of my experience). At this point, I understood the passing away of old things and the coming of new (see 2 Corinthians 5:17). People began to distance themselves from me, and I began distancing myself from them too. Relationships on every level began to fail, so I surrounded myself with a group of the strongest Christian women I knew at the time. Now, five years later, I wondered if it was possible that I might receive an e-mail from one of the last people to contact me before God catapulted me into this new dimension of life.

Part of me wanted her to respond, but the other part wasn't sure how she would. Having sent my "What a Surprise" e-mail asking about life as it was as of right now, I braced myself for whatever. After wondering the night before what would happen if his wife intercepted my e-mail, I sat down to the computer the next morning. While waiting for my e-mail application to load, I held my breath.

When I received a reply amongst the new messages, I clicked on the bold lettered name under the Recipient List. As the message appeared in the preview pane, I exhaled and whispered a prayer. Once again, she had responded. The first sentence was "I see you are back again." As I continued to read, something would not allow me to become angered, nor offended. In my heart, I knew God was trying to either tell or show me something, so I read on.

As the wife posed several questions regarding the past and present, I was grateful to answer them. Over Thanksgiving weekend 2002, we covered everything that happened from 1998 up until then. *I'm serious.* She and I had even started talking on the telephone because our e-mails were getting too long. By the time God was finished with us, we were ministering to and encouraging each other. I told her how different my life was now, as compared to then.

For starters, God had called me out and I'd

rededicated my life to Him. During that time I had also cut off a lot of friendships. I was headed down the straight and narrow, and believed everyone was either for or against righteousness. Because our lifestyles were incompatible at that point, God led me in a different direction from most of my previous friends. So, thus began my journey; one I had been on for over four years at the time.

I then explained to her that Derrick and I had new "practicing" Christian friends and not just "professing" Christian friends. I told her we are also very active in our church by leading an in-home Bible study, volunteering in other ministries, and so on. I later mentioned to her how I was also sure that anyone who wasn't there yet spiritually probably didn't understand what all the hoopla of servant hood is about. I told her so much, I even mentioned the season of not dating I went through. Looking back, I realized God was preparing me for marriage. It was during that time when I noticed many of my single girlfriends slipping away. In hindsight, I was the one who fell off.

In the end, she and I discovered it was intended for us to meet and scheduled lunch. We continued to e-mail and speak with one another as our relationship quickly matured. As we shared more of our pasts with each other, I told her where I was spiritually prior to 1998.

For most of my adult life, I had been one of those Christians who wanted to throw their hands up in the club Thursday, Friday, and Saturday nights, and then shout praises on Sunday morning. I didn't even know what praise was. If I had, there was no way I would have been spending time with the devil all week and going to church on Sunday morning for a couple of hours, thinking I had done something. That was when God grabbed me by the collar and jacked me up, so to speak. After that, I got it and decided to truly worship Him day in and day out. I considered that my warning and have never regretted my decision.

As she listened to me, it became apparent I wasn't the enemy she'd imagined years prior. We were becoming great friends and even greater sisters. As our e-mails got longer and longer, and we grew closer and closer, there was an excitement that lasted for days. We were bonding so fast that when I learned my favorite female televangelist would be here in Dallas holding a revival at one of the local churches, I invited her. *Imagine that.*

Who knew what God was up to, initially? He had begun to turn things around *tremendously* and neither of us had a clue. I believed then, all things really do work for the good of those who love the Lord and are the called according to His purpose (see Romans 8:28). He had worked that one for the both of us, and now all things were becoming new.

THE PROMISED LAND

6 It was almost three weeks from the time my "new friend" and I first started talking. We'd shared so much in such a short time... from testimonies, to stories and laughter. Yep, all things certainly were becoming new. She and I continued to go back and forth both in e-mail and on the telephone. You'd think we had known each other most of our lives and had been separated for years. In fact, I began to ask her opinion on several matters of importance to me, and likewise she. There were several e-mails in particular when we, well I, just went on and on.

I had become accustomed to e-mailing almost everyone with specific and detailed letters regarding various supernatural experiences I'd had. The feedback was very positive and uplifting. Not only did it regard the testimonies, but the way I told the stories as well. I just knew I had a writing gift and various people were unknowingly confirming it daily. As far as a book was concerned, in the beginning I was slowly putting things together. I had begun to toy with styles, ideas, and content, but by now things were really beginning to come together and take form. See for yourself what happened.

```
-----Original Message-----
From: Shaundale Johnson
Sent: December 13, 2002 12:18AM
To: Undisclosed Recipient
Subject: Spiritual Gifts
```

I enjoy reading your e-mails -->

   Hey, for years I have felt like God was trying to get me to write a book. I'm a big procrastinator though. I wrote an e-mail to our Bible study members a while back telling them something God had recently taken me through, and I got some of the best responses. It was a LONG e-mail (gonna have to let you read it someday). Anyway, our growth group leader said my testimonies are like a gripping drama, not certain where they might be leading. I held on to that e-mail and shoved that comment in the back of my head.
   Lately, I've been asking God what is my purpose. I know He's telling me to write. It's something I've enjoyed every since I was a child. I would play school in the summertime. I was one of those people who wrote their name on the back and front of a whole sheet of paper, or doodled for days. At any rate, when I read that statement regarding my e-testimony, it triggered something that said, "Girl, just write." So, I've decided to stop procrastinating and just start writing what God's told me to. Do you think writing could be the *real* gift I've been asking God to reveal all this time, and I've just been sitting on it, saving it

for e-mails???

Shaundale

-----Original Message-----
From: Undisclosed Recipient
Sent: December 13, 2002 9:40AM
To: Shaundale Johnson
Subject: Re: Spiritual Gifts

   I am <u>SO</u> excited that I'm going to reply to this one first. I do think you have a gift. I've known you for almost 20 years (feels like it).
   I am a reader, a visual one at that. I love reading. Use the gift God gave you. Nurture it and it will flourish. God will take care of the rest. If you don't, you will probably miss your blessing. You will have a tremendous affect on someone's life in some kind of way. It's kinda like living and meeting strangers.
   Have you started a journal? You don't necessarily have to pick a topic to start a book. You can choose from several different things to write about. Start writing, and the next thing you know your book is finished. If you don't know where to begin with a topic, just start writing any thoughts you may have. A book can develop from that.
   Have you attempted writing anything other than e-mail? Maybe you can develop that one into a sample manuscript, put it on paper, send it out to a few publication companies or magazines, and see what you get. Yes, I would like to read that other e-mail also. Everyone has a calling, but everyone does not heed that calling. Don't be afraid. Trust in God, because He

provided that gift.

How is the conviction on your heart? I know mine is strong. When I even think about doing a lot of things I know are wrong, my heart tells me it is, and I know I need to either fix it, or not do it. I'm talking about little things you don't think about (i.e., taking a pen from work). Let that guide you with your writing. You will know when it is right or wrong. Don't be afraid to fail either. The devil will try to discourage you that way, but don't let him win. As long as the Lord is on your side, you will always come out on top. Remember, God never fails! PRAISE THE LORD!!!

-----Original Message-----
From: Shaundale Johnson
Sent: December 13, 2002 1:19PM
To: Undisclosed Recipient
Subject: Re: Spiritual Gifts

Oooohhhh, this is good. My conviction is strong. I used to get that feeling when I worked and thought about leaving with a pen or a pack of Post-It-Notes, too.

It's funny you asked about the journal. I have never been good at keeping one, but one of the pastors at church suggested it. He had no idea I was thinking about writing. I thought that was interesting and that God in some way might be trying to discipline my writing skills through journaling. Then, here you come.

I have several topics, but they all line up with testimonials. For some reason I know somebody will be blessed by it, but on the other hand the devil is telling me don't nobody wanna read about what I've been through. You know the devil is sly. Every time I hear that little voice, somebody comes back after simply reading an e-mail and says something along the lines of enjoying my writing. So, I think that's odd… like God is saying, "Girl, I done told you."

I'm gonna start journaling more seriously. It's been a couple of weeks since my last entry. There are even a few writers at our church with books out. Okay, I'm gonna really pray about this. I'm a technical person. I've always thought God was gonna bless me abundantly in the area of my degree. Lately, I don't even know if I want to keep working on computers. It's like I've lost interest. All I wanna do is write; yet, I won't write. Just might be fear. I'm gonna have to make the devil mad. I'm gonna write! I might have to start with writing my name over and over again just to get myself focused. You are so encouraging!

Shaundale

By this time, she and I had long given up on trying to figure out what God was up to. Things progressed to the point where I started to adhere to the call of writing more seriously, due to a combination of her comments as well as others. I had been *journaling*, but now I was considering *writing*. I hadn't quite gotten into a flow just yet, but I had begun to walk just a tad more closely with Jesus in an effort not to miss anything. There was no way I was going to write a book simply because I felt like it, or someone else suggested it. Especially, not a book of the magnitude I felt God was leading me to!

Within the next two weeks, things began to happen

that I *had* to be in the Spirit to receive. It seemed as though because I wanted more, God gave me more. I take that back. It wasn't quite that simple. Scripture revealed in James 4:3, *"When we ask, we do not receive, because we ask with wrong motives."* Well, trying deliberately to keep the channels clear, it was my desire to do whatever was pleasing unto God. I wanted to make sure whatever I asked for, I got. My motives *had* to be right. I wasn't planning on asking for snacks. I wanted substance! This was not the time to ask Him for bills to be paid or something material. I was headed for something *way* past that. Whatever it was, it would need a guaranteed answer. And, that was all I knew.

Having informed my newest girlfriend of who my favorite female televangelist was and of her upcoming revival, I decided it would be a great experience to share with girlfriends and invited her to attend the service with me. She wasn't able to make it, and it seemed no one else I invited could either. For some strange reason, the closer it got to the night I'd planned to attend the revival, I started to feel like maybe I was *really* supposed to go alone. I didn't know why; I just had this strong certainty beginning to stir inside of me that I wasn't supposed to be accompanied by *anyone*. So, I didn't ask another person to go with me in the days to come. *Boy! Was I on it?*

One day while watching Christian television, yes again, I saw my favorite female televangelist give a lady $2,000.00 to sow into her music ministry. I mumbled something like, "I wish it was me," and thought nothing of it. Usually, I tried never to wish for anything because, for some reason, I feel wishing is wrong. I felt I should just pray and be done. Either God would, or He wouldn't. To me, hoping was one thing but wishing was another.

The Friday I'd scheduled to attend the revival had finally arrived. The entire day I walked in the Spirit, as if walking on eggshells. It wasn't intentional, I was just careful of everything and hadn't a clue why. At this point, I'll just let you read the original testimony for yourself, because I couldn't explain it again if I tried.

```
-----Original Message-----
From: Shaundale Johnson
Sent: December 23, 2002 12:06AM
To: Undisclosed Recipients
Subject: Not going to believe this one!

Hello all,
```

   Just wanted to share an AWESOME experience I had this past Friday night. I made plans to attend a revival at a local church last week when I heard my favorite female televangelist was going to be in town. Her ministry has blessed me so much during this "valley" experience that I had to get there. The doors were scheduled to open at 6:30p.m., but I wanted to be there by 5:30. Well, that didn't happen. I left the house around 5:15p.m. and got there about 6:15. There were two bad traffic spots.
   Anyway, before I left the house I was urged in my spirit to print a copy of the vision I shared with you guys months ago. I didn't know why. I just remember saying, "Lord, for whatever reason I feel this urgency to put this letter in the prophetess' hand, You work it out." So I grabbed it and left.
   Well, on my way out I said, "Lord, I want to be seated on the floor." I didn't know why, I just felt this urgency to be on the bottom in the front pew. I said, "Lord, I want to be so close to the prophetess, I can feel her breath." Can

you imagine that? I don't know her like that. In fact, I know some of you way better and wouldn't think to make that kind of request.

Anyhow, when I arrived at the church, there was a line wrapped around two sides of the building. I had not planned for that. I stood in line, and one of the ladies next to me mentioned that she had been there the night before and was in the overflow room. Now, earlier I had prayed that God have a Word for me. I said, "I know the woman of God will have a Word for everybody in general, but Lord, I want my own rhema Word from You. Let her speak directly to me... to my situation."

I was in the Spirit ALL day and couldn't understand why. I had butterflies in my stomach and was just on a holy high, if you will. I couldn't even eat, so I gave into the fast I knew God was calling me to. At any rate, when that lady mentioned the overflow room I said, "Overflow room? Lord, I just want to be in the sanctuary!" At that moment, I just wanted to be in the same room with her. For some reason, I just HAD to get to the prophetess.

So, finally I got inside and was in the balcony. Now, I asked one of the ushers if there was room for one more on the floor. I went alone; don't know why. I just felt that I needed to go by myself. It was one of those things where I didn't know anybody there, and if I did they would be so far away it wouldn't even matter. I could freely praise and worship, and not have to be distracted by whispering or trying to hold back my praise. Does that make sense?

Well, in the balcony, I was moving and squirming. I mean, I was fidgeting around like a 2-year-old. In my head I kept saying, *I'm not supposed to be in the balcony. I'm supposed to be on the floor.* I repeated that continually to myself, "I'm supposed to be on the floor." Well, a man then went into the pulpit and said the people on the floor need to squeeze together, because they can seat some more folks down front. I sat at attention! I said, "Lord, if they're making room for me, You're gonna have to let me know." The last thing I wanted was to leave my seat in the balcony, and get to the floor to be turned around.

Within 5-10 minutes of that announcement, a fraternity brother of mine walked in with his wife and a group of people. (At least I thought it was a fraternity brother.) They entered downstairs and sat on the front pew. I said to myself, "That can't be him," and stared at the backs of those people's heads for at least ten minutes. Then, I threw my jacket over a chair and kicked my purse under my seat, as I stood and walked to the railing for a better view. I got the usher's attention and asked him to touch who I thought was my fraternity brother. Sure enough, it was him!

My frat noticed me, and then he and his wife came over. Now, I hadn't seen this man since maybe October. Matter-of-fact, I had only met him in July. It was now December. I said, "You're sitting on the front row! May I sit with you guys?" So, then he says he's under his pastor's favor and that he got in with him.

Well, I don't know his pastor and

didn't feel comfortable asking him. There was one seat on that whole pew and I knew it was mine, so I just asked his pastor's wife if they would mind if I sat with them. She said if the usher's didn't say anything, they wouldn't either. It was the reserved seating area, so my frat walked with me and asked the hostess if it was okay if I sat with them. She asked who he was and he told her, then he mentioned that he was with his pastor and turned to me. He said, "Go get your stuff." She then asked him who his pastor is, and he told her the man's name. She smiled and said, "Go ahead." Can you believe that??? Man, I leaped in my soul! I ran up those balcony stairs and grabbed my stuff so fast I don't think those people even knew I had come back!

Well, when I got down front to that ONE seat, on the WHOLE pew, of the FIRST row, I began to praise the Lord. I have reached a level so high, I cannot say nor do enough to show my gratitude on any given day. I mean, in His presence constantly is AWESOME, truly awesome. I was smiling because I was exactly where I wanted to be; exactly where I had seen myself when I first prayed to be on the front row.

Church began, and the Praise and Worship was high. When the prophetess walked out, I immediately went to a whole other level of praise. I have been watching her on TV during this whole "storm." I even bought her videos. Just to be in the presence of a woman of God with a ministry as anointed as hers changed my life, and she hadn't even spoken a word yet. I knew then that God answered prayers, most definitely!

Well, when she was given her microphone she came out prophesying and praying in Tongue. She asked various groups of people to stand, and began to tell them what thus saith the Lord pertaining to their ministries. When she called for all Evangelists and Prophets, I did not stand up because I was still struggling with what God was trying to tell me, specifically.

She then called again, "All Evangelists and Prophets stand up." I sprang to my feet like somebody had pulled a cord that was attached to my waist. She then began to speak these words as according to the leading of the Holy Spirit, "If you are in this place, I have called your ministry to deliverance; I have called your ministry to cast out devils; I have called your ministry to power and a great anointing."

The Spirit then led her to do the invitation FIRST. I mean, people flocked to that altar! Y'all what I experienced next was out of this world. We began to pray and continued our praise, because people were being saved right there at the beginning of the service. Not to be bound by the "traditional flow" of the program was truly great! We were really in revival, because the Spirit was having Its *whole* way!

Well, this one guy who I will never forget (in an orange t-shirt), got up, turned around, and tried to run. He was trying to step around people and get out! When the prophetess saw him she asked, "Where's he going?" That man turned around and y'all, I KID YOU, *NOT* — this is FIRST-HAND STUFF from me. I believe I'm a reliable source, don't you? — his face

Shaundale Hornes Johnson | 103

began to CHANGE. I mean, immediately I said, "A demon!" His mouth opened wide, and his teeth were exposed like a scene from a horror movie. You know, all sharp and pointy-looking. Then, he began to make sounds that resembled growls and his eyes got BIG. She immediately stopped and said, "Oh, I KNOW we're in revival NOW. A demon has walked up in here!"

A group of men were holding him. There were about five of them. People began to pray, and he began to struggle. They were trying to carry him to the altar, and all I could say over and over was (this should sound familiar), "I rebuke you in the name of Jesus! I rebuke you in the name of Jesus! I rebuke you in the name of Jesus!" She began to command the demon to come out of him. People were praying and stretching their hands toward him, and he fell out on the altar. I mean, stretched straight out.

The prophetess then said, "Okay devil, you want it like that?" Then, she began to call out every type of demon that may have been in that place. She said, "I command you to come out—you demon of adultery, you demon of drugs, you demon of this and of that. Now, this man was to the left of me; however, to the right of me a woman spit up some white stuff. I stood there with this look on my face with a scene from *The Exorcist* in my head, my left eyebrow raised, and a look that asked "Foam?" So, then the prophetess came to that side and said something like, "Lord, they're in here. People are spitting up demons. I KNOW we're in revival!" (Y'all, I know this sounds crazy! I'm sure of it, but I'm serious. I am SO serious. In fact, in a minute you'll know just how serious I am.)

So then I said, "Lord, I wanted to be on the floor, but I didn't expect all this to be going on." I just planned to sit on a front pew, receive a prophetic Word from God, give the prophetess a copy of my vision, and go on my merry way. Then God said to me, "Take out your envelope." I didn't know why He said it, but I did it anyway.

Before I left home, I put the copy of my vision in an envelope and addressed it to the woman of God. Well, during her sermon she said, "God has given some of you visions and dreams, and you need to write them down." I began to wave my envelope back and forth in the air. That was me! So, for some reason, I held onto it. I never put it back into my purse.

So, as the service continued, she then called for the offering envelopes. Well, while they were getting them ready, a lady walked across the aisle. The prophetess said, "Come here baby... you in the blue shirt. Do you mind if I pray over you? God has a Word for you." Well, a lady who doesn't look older than I am walked up to the altar. Immediately, the prophetess began to prophesy over her. She said, "God's doing something in you."

Then, she proceeded to prophecy. "God says, 'I've seen your faithfulness. I've seen you.'" "He said, 'My eyes have been on you and I've heard your cry, and I've called you out to let you know I heard you.'"

Instantaneously, it's like that woman was talking to me... like she was in my face, having a conversation with ME. There was nobody else in there; *she was just talking to me.* The prophetess then said,

"Bring me some money. God told me to sew $1,000.00 into your life because He said this is to let you know I hear you. He said, 'If I can do this, what else do you think I'm gonna do when you pray?" She then asked her husband to bring her $1,000.00. That's ONE THOUSAND DOLLARS.

When the prophetess got the money, she continued with, "God said I've given you an anointing to pray. That's why the devil tried to keep you out of praying. That's why he tries to hinder you every time you set aside time to pray. Because, I've gifted you to pray. Just like some people are gifted to preach, you're gifted to pray." He said, "I've honored your tongue and I hear your prayer. When you pray, I'm going to do it. When you tell me to fix it, I'm going to because I've given you this as your charge. This is your ministry. Eyes have not seen, ears have not heard, neither has it entered into the hearts of men the things that I have prepared for you. There's some stuff you've got coming to you in 2003. There are some doors I've got to open for you." He said, "While you're praying for everybody else, don't forget about yourself. Whatever you ask me to do for you I'm going to do it *for you,* because I've heard you. Don't stop praying!"

She looked at that woman and said, "Consider this as when the prophet Elisha asked the woman, "What can I do for you? This is a seed." I'm entering a new season in my life, and God told me to take you with me. I'm sowing a seed into that which God is birthing in you." She then told the lady, "Before you spend one dime of this money, spread it out on the table and take a picture of it." "When the photo comes back," she said, "tape it to a piece of paper and write these words on it: My life and my destiny are under the influence of the seed of the prophet."

Now, in my left ear I heard God say, "Write that down," like He was whispering over my shoulder (and NO it was not the people sitting next to me). So I asked, "Huh?" Then she began to repeat it, and I wrote it down exactly like she said it. After that, she put $1,000.00 in that woman's hand and my spirit leaped. I mean, I just got OUTRIGHT happy, because it was still like she had just said all of that to me… in my face.

Well, the next thing I heard in the distance was, "Come here lady in the red dress! Hurry." It seemed like she was calling me out of a dream, or waking me from a sleep of some kind. When I opened my eyes and looked up, she was pointing directly at me from the pulpit. I BROKE DOWN. I mean, I was bent over, crying, and trying to walk. You would've thought I needed a cane if you had seen me. I heard her say, "Help her up here." She then said, "Give me your books, Bible... all your 'lil stuff." It dawned on me I still had all my things in my hands.

Now, normally you would think to put everything down. I kept mine, so I gave all of it to her. Then, I heard her say that when she put that $1,000.00 in the other lady's hand, this lady (me) started praising God so hard for her, she praised her way into the other lady's miracle. And, God told her to give me $1,000.00 and declare the prophet seed over my life, too. I was too through! In fact, I'm *still* through. She then said, "You are under the prophet's seed. Spread the money out on a table and then take a picture of it. Tell the devil he is a liar and you don't need *nuthin'* he's got. Then, point to the picture as a reminder." She then placed her hand on my stomach and began to pray. When she touched me, y'all I fell out.

I was so glad I had heeded the voice of God when He told me to wear something long. I didn't understand it but said, "*Okay*." This red dress comes down to my ankles, and I put my black knee boots on with it. I was on the floor, and my feet were up on the steps to the altar. When I say I fell out, I mean, I *literally* FELL OUT. All I heard on the way down was her saying something to the effect of doing exactly what she had told the other young lady to do, but I didn't hear what. Then she said, "When that baby gets up, this $1,000.00 is hers!" I'm shaking my head now. (Gonna have to take a praise break and come back to y'all.)

Okay, I'm back. I realized when I got up, although I did not hear what I was instructed to write when she told me to, God had already informed me of it earlier. So, I got it when she was telling the other young lady. *God is so good. His Word is SO true.* I remember a feeling of total peace; it was like I was looking up into the heavens! I said, "Lord, I'll never doubt You again."

I hadn't been having the best week. It's the Christmas season and we're living on answered prayers, because we can't even afford to pay for the air we breathe right now, and thank God He's not charging us for it. At any rate, I'd said earlier

108 | *Once Broken, Now Blessed*

during the week, "God, we have a big beautiful tree. It's decorated wonderfully and we have one big box under it for Emahn." Then I said, "It's not even about that, Lord. I'm just thankful she has this tree, but it would be so nice to put some more stuff under there, even if not just for kids." Then, I began to thank Him for all of the things I already have, for instance, this house, my husband, and my child (just those three things mainly). I didn't feel like I had made any requests; I just had thoughts of a beautiful tree filled with lots of gifts like our first Christmas in this house.

Well, needless to say, I had started thinking about what it looks like from here going into 2003. So, while I was on my back — and now I literally know what people mean when they say that when you're on your back, the only place to look is up — I felt the peace of God. In fact, I knew the peace of God and brought some of it back with me. Isn't that amazing?

When I got the money, one of the prophetess' people handed me back my stuff. I thumbed through it and handed her an envelope. She looked at me strangely, but when she read who it was addressed to she took it, put it in her Bible case, and zipped it up. I trust God fulfilled that as well, and she got my vision for whatever purpose(s) He designed. Notice I said "designed."

I now *truly* know God has a purpose and a plan for my life, as according to Jeremiah 29:11. There's just no way that entire evening of events could have been more perfectly orchestrated if there had been a program! Out of the thousands of people in that church, I only knew the two I'd sat next to under their pastor's reservation; so I thought.

During the offering, one of my girlfriends came through the crowd towards me. She just hugged me and whispered, "God is so good," in my ear continually. I was equally glad to see her, because the whole thing felt like a dream. Seeing her was my reality. *Man!* God answered every prayer I prayed, from leaving the house to getting to the church, *and then some*. How awesome!

That's why I couldn't contain myself in church this morning. My frat brother, the minister who got me on that first row (in the natural), called me yesterday morning and said he'd gotten his answer. He said that he prays to know why God sends people into him and his wife's life. He also said he knew, on his way home from church, it was meant for me to meet him in order to get me into that seat on Friday night. *Unbelievable!* (I'm trying my best to hurry up y'all.)

This morning I was still full. In fact, at first I was wondering Friday how long this "high" was going to last. Then one of my other girlfriends, who had heard about it from the girlfriend in attendance, called me last night. When I mentioned it to her she said, "Girl, you don't ever have to come down off that high." For the first time it hit me that I don't. I've been elevated behind the veil into the holiest of holies, and I have been given the right to remain. "I've seen the mountaintop," if you will. So this morning I just could not sit still! I had to excuse myself when the choir sang that *Now Behold the Lamb* song.

While I was out there in the back, God spoke to my spirit. He said, "I have something for you to do. I have prepared you for such a time as this." I stood still. Then, when I finally came back in, the man sitting behind me gave something to me. I don't know who he was, but he stood as a visitor. He handed me a pocket card (one of those cute little plastic picture cards with scriptures on it) that says: *Whoever follows Me will never walk in darkness, but will have the light of life* (John 8:12). I smiled.

When I sat down, the same minister I had been sharing my visions with was up preaching. He was making mention of Mary and people knowing her name for thousands of years to come over the nations. Then, his sermon title went up on the screen which was "How God Does Great through Everyday People." I mean, it just kept coming.

When he acknowledged that how deep you let God take you in the valley is how high He will take you on the mountain, he reminded me of something. When I was in line Friday night, one of the ladies standing in front of me was talking to some other women who were in line with us. One of the women said her pastor told them that however bad the storm, that much better the blessing. I thought about Derrick and me. Then, another woman said her bishop told them that however deep your hurt is however high the reward. I thought about me.

Not being selfish, but nobody but God knows the tears I've cried. I felt like that was my Word right there standing in line. So, for the preacher to just come out and say that was like a breath of fresh air to me, because on the mountaintop I can breathe. There are just too many things working against me in the valley.

The prophetess said to those who stood as Prophets, Prophetesses, and Evangelists that in 30 days doors which have been closed and have never even thought to be opened will begin to open up, and in 12 months there would be a switch of faith with no fear at all of the enemy. We would be at a new level of trust in God, and that some people are going into the fourth level. Anybody can be in the outer court, but the fourth level is where you're steadfast in the things of God... when you speak it and it's done. Okay, I'm done. See, I try not to write too often, but when I do, I do huh?

I've been praying about the money. I know she didn't give me $1000.00 to go shopping, and my spirit is telling me not to pay ONE bill with it. I was preparing our tithes and was immediately hindered because I remembered I have to take the photo, write on it, and put it up. So, after I get the picture put up, I will tithe and put away rest of the money away. I don't think you guys know this either, but I've started writing my book "Once Broken, Now Blessed: A Testimony of Trials and Triumphs." It's based on the 23rd Psalm. Pray about that, too. Maybe the money is supposed to be going towards its completion.

I LOVE YOU GUYS! As always, I have not shared this with lots of people, but I always think of you guys first!

That was it, the height of my brokenness. When I got into my car after the service that evening, the very first thing I did was pray. I asked the Lord specifically for a role model. Not exactly knowing the extent of what He was preparing me to do, I did know I needed a good and solid example to follow. It's not that Jesus wasn't enough; I just wanted someone I could relate to naturally. I could never compare myself to the One, but if a regular Jane Doe said she'd come from the back roads of the bayou and God raised her up for His glory, then I could relate to that.

Having gone through various *super*-natural experiences over the past eight months, every time I saw my favorite female televangelist on the TV prior to that incident I had begun to say, "Lord, that's what I want." Now, I didn't want her ministry or her anointing, because only the Lord knew what she had gone through to get them. What I did want however, was to be used to the equivalency of her… just the effectiveness, even if all I ever got to do was write. That's what I wanted prior to seeing her, so when I saw her at the actual revival that's what I said again, "Lord, what I want is a teaching ministry as effective as hers, through writing. I just don't want to go through what she went through to get it." Then God spoke to my spirit. He said, "That's the problem. People don't want to go through."

When I thought about that, I wondered how many wives would support a husband who hadn't had a real job in 19 months. Contract work was fine, but I was a consultant long ago. When I didn't work, I didn't get paid—and neither did he. Then, I thought about the number of women I knew in my situation who had left their husbands within a few months of being laid off. Here it was going on years. I told Derrick once, "Either

I'm dearly devoted or dearly dumb." God was proving my devotion *to Him* outweighed all else.

I soon remembered something one of my girlfriends once commented on: her pastor's wilderness experience message one Sunday. She looked at me and said, "I'm not ready to go through the wilderness. Yes, I know there's a blessing on the other side of the storm. I also know when God takes you through, He brings you out. But, I don't want to go through *nuthin'*." That was confirmation to what God had spoken right there. I realized then most of us just want to magically end up in Canaan. It was as if we snapped our fingers and said, "Abracadabra, to the Promised Land!"

Now Blessed: The Triumphs

He restoreth my soul: he leadeth me in the paths of righteousness for His name's sake. Yea, though I walk through the valley of the shadow of death, I will fear no evil: for thou art with me; thy rod and thy staff they comfort me. (Psalm 23:3-4, KJV)

"Blessed is the man who perseveres under trial, because when he has stood the test, he will receive the crown of life that God has promised to those who love him." James 1:12

"Then the King will say to those on his right, 'Come, you who are blessed by my Father; take your inheritance, the kingdom prepared for you since the creation of the world." Matthew 25:34

"For his anger lasts only a moment, but his favor lasts a lifetime." Psalm 30:5

"The Lord redeems his servants; no one will be condemned who takes refuge in him." Psalm 34:22

"Blessed are those who hunger and thirst for righteousness, for they will be filled." Matthew 5:6

"The end of a matter is better than its beginning, and patience is better than pride." Ecclesiastes 7:8

"Blessed are the pure in heart, for they will see God." Matthew 5:8

"But many who are first will be last, and many who are last will be first." Matthew 19:30

"Blessed are those who are persecuted because of righteousness, for theirs is the kingdom of heaven." Matthew 5:10

LET IT HAPPEN

7 Ever since Friday evening (at the revival) when the Lord blessed me with a rhema word, I knew I was definitely headed to the Promised Land and felt new. That prophetic word from God was the something extra I'd held on to Him for in my closet when I cried out about the lawsuits, the headaches, and the heartache. The day He anointed me and I said, "Now, bless me too!"

As time progressed, I found myself calming down because of that prophecy. I started to think about foster parenting again, but didn't share it with Derrick because I had failed to convince him before Emahn came along. Also, I found myself changing more and more in my thought process. In fact, I thought about introducing myself as Josephine. You know, as in the female rendition of Joseph, whose life went from one level of brokenness to another. Really, my whole mindset had changed regarding my family's situation after just one night.

Feeling like Jesus Himself would open up the heavens and come down here if need be, it had finally dawned on me where we were in relation to the man in charge of the rations. Yes, we were still in the famine, but once I realized the man in charge of the supplies is my brother, of whom I am joint heir of *His* inheritance, the burden of trying to figure out what we would do to survive was lifted.

Like Joseph's brothers, it was scary for me remembering all of the things I had done in the past that were in outright disobedience to my Father, concerning my brother; however, because Jesus still loved me, He was willing to make arrangements for my household and me. He was especially willing to provide for our well-being during the crisis, which was all that mattered. Our situation wasn't as bad anymore, because I personally knew the man who could speak peace be still and quiet the storm. All I had to do was wait. When He was ready, He would call. When He was, He did.

The morning of December 27, 2002 I awoke to a whisper which said, "Shaundale, voice of power. Shaundale, voice of power." So, in that "I'm just waking up" voice I answered, "Huh?" Derrick then rolled over and asked, "How did you know I was calling you; I didn't say anything." "You were calling me?" I asked. He said, "Well, I was in my head." Then, he explained that he had just awakened and was about to say my name when I answered. He wanted to know how I knew to answer him when he hadn't even spoken yet.

I lay in bed for a minute and said, "You didn't call me." Derrick then said, "Not out loud, I didn't." So I just laid there a minute longer and said, "I didn't answer you," in one of those "something weird is going on" voices. "I answered," I replied, "to Shaundale, voice of power." It was as if someone had said Oprah Winfrey, talk show host. It was a name followed by a title. That's when it dawned on me it was God; *He* had called me. Totally awake by this time, I was convinced He was telling me my new name: Shaundale, voice of power. Derrick just confirmed that someone had audibly spoken. What a wonderful and blessed experience! It was next followed by a vision. Tune in.

Several other people and I are in my middle school cafeteria. Some of them I recognize, while others I have never seen before; although, there are some who appear to be shadows in the background. There is something going on, so I sit down. Emahn, who appears to be around four or five years old, goes around and sits on the other side across from me. To my right is an old man. He appears to be a regular guy in a suit, but I know he is the devil.

The man turns to look at me, and the other people who are seated between us get up. He then tells me I am the only person present who knows what to do. I say, "Nah-uhmn." (I'm country even in my dreams). Then he says, "Watch," and gets up. Unsure of what he is about to do, I go around to the other side of the table to pick Emahn up. He then starts charging at people and running towards them, jumping around and making "boo" sounds as they run away. He starts running towards me in the same manner, and I hold up my right hand, palm out, in an authoritative manner. He says, "See?"

The man then runs toward some more folks and they take off. He later tries to come at me again. He backs farther away and runs harder, like he is picking up speed. At that time, I lift my hand and open my mouth to speak. I don't have to though, because he immediately stops. He then says, "See, you're the only one here who knows what to do." Everyone else is still in an uproar. I'm holding Emahn and she appears to be okay. She isn't crying or showing signs of fear at all.

Later, God revealed to me the time was coming when

I was going to have to carry some people by myself. It wasn't about Emahn. It never was. She represented the children, just as He was about to reveal Bunkie represented the Church. As I thought about the first vision some more, I continued to focus on the child standing in the doorway. Then, I asked myself if I could carry him. The more I thought about it, the more I believed I could.

It didn't sit so well with me though remembering that both times I was preparing to fight the enemy, Emahn was in my arms. Could he have been after my child? The thief *does* come only to steal, kill, and destroy according to John 10:10, but *surely* even the devil knows he would have to take me *totally* out to get my child, and God had already proved He's not having that with the car wreck.

Thinking more heavily about the devil coming after my child, I still didn't know if God was referring to spiritual or natural children. There was a huge difference between someone who could not grow due to a *natural* handicap, and somebody who chose not to grow due to *spiritual* hard-headedness. One was dumb in the sense that he couldn't do (whether he knew or not); the other was stupid in the sense that he wouldn't do (what he knew to do). Knowing how I am about people who don't want to do better, I wanted to know just who I was going to be responsible for carrying. *Dumb*, I'd muster up every ounce of strength I could find to carry, but stupid? *Stupid*, I'd try to flat-out leave if I knew I could get away with it.

Later that day, I turned on Christian television. A very prominent and influential televangelist in the Atlanta area was on who asked the question, "You've heard from God, now what?" *Amazing!* As always, God was right on time. I was wondering the *same* thing. *Now what?*

I later decided to phone a minister-friend of mine from home. I was excited to tell him about my latest supernatural experience with the prophecy. I began to talk and share that testimony, as well as other experiences, when mid-sentence he spoke the words, "Well, you know," and immediately I knew what was coming, although I wasn't ready for it. "You have an open invitation to the pulpit whenever you're at home," he continued. I was speechless. Never in a million years did I anticipate that. That's nothing personal against him; I just never expected that from a church in my entire hometown.

My mind instantly drifted back to another vision I had immediately following the sound of God's voice telling me to save the children. In that particular dream I was standing at the podium in my home church, speaking to the youth and children. There were two groups of them seated on both of the two front pews, wearing the same choir robes we'd worn as children. The interesting thing was that those robes hadn't been used in years. Back then we would have someone from the community come and speak to us once a month, but that had stopped long ago.

After that vision, I said, "Lord, I won't go without an invitation." My interpretation of being at the podium meant I wasn't welcomed in the pulpit, but in my spirit God told me I'd already received a request from Him. He was referring to what He had just said concerning the children. When I later shared that revelation with my former "How to Listen to God" CCBS Instructor, he said the *exact* same thing, "You've already got one."

The next day I received a phone call from my sister. The conversation was about the upcoming Youth Church anniversary program back home. Derrick and I were scheduled to head home Friday and I thought, *it's just like God to do something like that.* I felt like I was going as a spectator, only to end up a participator.

As my nerves grew shaky and I tried to figure out what God was up to next, the butterflies in my stomach (which I now refer to as my Holy Ghost or conviction) returned. I felt a constant need to fast. It was as though each of my earlier notes regarding children were brought to my remembrance. With something boiling over in my belly, I made up my mind to give into the fast until God said to eat.

Oddly enough, I was cooking dinner when the phone call with my sister ended and the thoughts began. Once I finished cooking, I prepared plates. Although I had no appetite or desire to eat at all, I fixed me a plate of food to dine with the family as always. *Go figure.* I sat down, blessed my meal, picked up the fork, and dropped it right back onto the plate. It was as if God said, "I told you not to eat." I couldn't explain it, but this feeling came over me. This strong conviction was boiling over in my stomach, and I remember telling Derrick I couldn't eat. I then got up, headed into the master bedroom, and grabbed my Bible, notebook and journal. I was preparing to do my Father's business; I just didn't know what "His business" was.

I went into my office and locked the door. Stretched straight out on the floor, while lying prostrate, I began to praise the Lord and prayed immediately. I knew He was there, because His Spirit was all around me. Standing, I stretched my arms toward heaven and said once more, "Lord, I'm available to You."

As I began to write, the Spirit of the Lord poured out on the sheets of paper before me. When I was finished it was 11:20 p.m. and an entire message had come forth. I exhaled upon completion, and God dropped into my spirit His approval for me to eat. I felt like my due date for whatever He was preparing me to deliver, on a larger scale, was growing near.

While still in my office, as I flipped through pages and pages of old journal notes, I came to one sheet in particular that regarded a local minister mentioning that

God's promises are for God's people in a sentence. I knew that should have been the focus, because I wrote that down months ago in reading 2 Chronicles 7:12-16. In that passage, God spoke to me as He did Solomon. He said, *"I have heard your prayer, and have chosen this place for Myself as a house of sacrifice. When I shut up heaven and there is no rain, or command the locusts to devour the land, or send pestilence among My people, if my people, who are called by my name will humble themselves and pray and seek my face, and turn from their wicked ways, then will I hear from heaven, and will forgive their sin and heal their land."* First, you had to be His people; I was. Secondly, you had to be called by His name; I was. Third, you had to humble yourself, pray, seek His face, and then turn from wickedness; I had. I knew the promise of God hearing and forgiving us, as well as healing our land, was mine. For me, our land included my hometown. I was just awaiting visible evidence of God restoring it to manifest.

The next day was so productive that I was able to organize my file cabinet. In doing so, I came across a printed e-mail entitled "The Storm is Over, Shaun's Testimony." I had written that letter to The Board back in 1998. It was the testimony of my rebirth experience. God definitely led me to that paper, because I had been looking for it about a year. I knew I had it; I just didn't know where it was. I felt especially good knowing He was getting ready to confirm its contents and use me for something tremendous. That testimony was going to be vital for someone else.

Throughout the night, God continued to talk to me. I could not get any sleep and was tossing and turning. Normally when I had trouble falling asleep, I just laid down until I decided to get up to read and/or pray. However, on this particular night, I rolled from one side to the other. I think I even put the pillow over my head.

By this time, God had consistently been keeping me up for months, and the lack of sleep was finally starting to get to me. I sat up, grabbed the pen and journal off the nightstand, and began to write "sink or swim," only because I kept hearing those two words repeatedly. So, I wrote it in the form of a question that I was asking God, "Sink or swim? What do you mean sink or swim?" Then, silence filled the room as my spirit overflowed with the words of the Lord, and my pen moved to every thought and conviction of my heart, *some are waiting to catch the next ship and there isn't one.*

As I placed my things on the nightstand again, I turned out the light and snuggled in for a good night's sleep. Five minutes after closing my eyes, I sprang up again. Reaching for my things, I was captured by the thought, *always a runner-up.* So, sitting up, I asked God why I was always a runner-up and never a queen." Now, first of all, it was somewhere around one o'clock on this particular morning. Why in the world was I lying in bed having beauty pageant flashbacks? Then, with pen and paper in my hand expecting a response, I heard in my spirit, "Because if I had let you win, you'd be stuck on doing something that *I* never called you to do."

I then recalled the times I had run for the crown and title of Miss Bunkie High School and Miss Black History back home. With that, I laid back down. Within minutes it clicked like a light switch! I flipped the lamp power to on again and sat up. I imagined if God had let me win a pageant or two, I would have more than likely attempted to win more of them. I would have probably never sought Him for direction—let alone destiny—because I would have chosen a different path altogether. *Talk about being off track.* With that, I laid down again. In another five minutes or so I sat up, flipped the lamp on, and reached for my things all over. Then I asked, "Now, Lord, how am I supposed to get any sleep?" *Isn't that crazy?*

To be honest, I hadn't quite grasped a high level of compassion for folks who were carnal, or immature Christians. Remember, I classified everyone as spiritually dumb, spiritually stupid, or sanctified. Either you couldn't do right because you were unsaved (spiritually dumb), you didn't want to do right because you were immature (spiritually stupid), or you were spiritual and sold out to Christ. In my case, I was stupid. I knew to do right; I blatantly opted not to. That's the only way to call it; tell truth and shame the devil *again*.

Spiritual children, of any natural age, who do not want to do as they were instructed by God are pretty much saying, "I don't want the responsibility of following through with what I've been given to do." So, I was immature. I didn't want to grow in Christ and take on the full responsibility of being a mature Christian. However, the problem I had now was if I couldn't even tolerate my own season of "laziness" how was I expected to put up with someone else's? I soon got it though, because Daddy said so.

I continued to listen through the silence of the room and discerned what God was telling me. The truth was that some of us have been stuck on what we want to do for so long, we don't realize that what He wants to do is help us push the pedal and give us favor. *Another stunner!*

Growing up, almost everything seemed to come naturally to me... until my sophomore year in college, that is. Yep, up until then, everything my hands touched prospered. I knew exactly when I had gone too far before and the hand of God snapped back into the heavens the first time. I pin-pointed it to just before the summer I moved to California, for an internship in May of 1993, and turned twenty-one the following June. *Man! Did my life take off?*

I had just joined a Greek Letter Organization (GLO)

that previous April and had become a bit more social. When I moved to California, one month later, my eyes were opened to a whole new world *literally*. Attending Grambling State University showed me there was life outside of Bunkie, but living in California showed me there was life *period*. One I was readily excited to try out and, thanks to my newfound courage and confidence as a member of a GLO, I did.

Having the boldness of a lion, I knew exactly what God was talking about in telling me some of us have been stuck on what we want to do for so long, we don't realize He wants to give us favor. I had been stuck on stupid from 1993 to 1998, boldly sinning against God. In fact, I was on cruise control! While I certainly can't blame pledging for my years in Egypt (bondage of sin), in all honesty I believe that's when the enemy got his greatest foothold over me.

Thinking back, I've asked myself what was my purpose for joining the sorority? Well, I wanted the same things most other young women want: to be desired, to be accepted, and to be appreciated. However, this was the killer: Jesus had *already* called me beloved. He had *already* acknowledged me. He had *already* accepted me; He *already* treasured me as His own. Because *I failed* to recognize my own self-worth in Him already, the enemy had a field day with me when I pledged. Nevertheless, the prodigal daughter came to her senses and returned home with far more baggage than she left with, and way too much dirt to wash away in one cycle.

After that earlier conversation with the Lord, I put down my things and thought, *I'll get off the boat and go get 'em.* At that point I had *really* gotten it. It wasn't about me, and it had never been. It was about *Him*. Realizing that now, I was ready to carry whoever He sent me for… spiritually dumb *or* spiritually stupid. I surprised even myself, by this time. Then, there it was:

compassion, understanding, and patience. Would you believe then He let me fall asleep?

God took me through all of that for a lesson in understanding other people's hurts and needs. I had to learn to deal in the natural, before I started dishing in the Spirit. I learned long ago you can't take anyone anywhere until you first acknowledge where they are now. Muh, my grandmother, helped with this lesson. Because she wouldn't go *anywhere* (except to the shopping center), if we did get her to ride somewhere else with one of us she had to know why, how long we'd stay, and so forth. Because she was most comfortable at home, and since we all knew this, we'd have to constantly acknowledge, "Yes, Muh, I know you'd rather stay here, but just come along for the ride." Then, as we're headed to the car someone would say, "A ride to so-and-so will do us some good, just to get out of the house."

Remembering that scenario, it dawned on me that it would do no good to tell a hungry man about Jesus, because he's not listening to me in the Spirit. He's listening to the growls of his stomach in the natural. First, I had to meet his natural need by feeding his belly (telling him it's okay to want to stay home), and then he'd allow me to meet his spiritual need by feeding his heart (telling him a ride would do some good and helping him to the car). If I tried to do the latter first, he would automatically shut down and put up a defense as to why he didn't need my help, or at least my grandmother would.

For the longest time, I didn't comprehend how a person could know better and not do it. Truthfully, I had forgotten. On that night, God helped me to remember my own enslavement-to-sin experience, when I was stuck on stupid, and let me know I needed to meet people where they were. I needed to take them by the hand, just as He had done for me. I didn't have to be cynical or condescending, because it wasn't about *stroking* them. It was about *serving* them—through Him.

God knew I would be in no position to serve anyone if I lacked compassion, understanding, and patience. I learned then that ministry is in the heart, not the head. In the end, His only concern was whether I'd connected with the person's heart or spirit. If I never did, then more than likely the only thing I had done was clash with their head. The same minister who continued to help me with my visions taught me long ago that hurt people, *hurt people*, and I added, *even if it's themselves*.

I realized then individuals are going to do what they want to, whether it pleases God or not. If it didn't, it wasn't up to *me* to go Bible on them first. It was up to me to go back to basics *with* them. One, I was to acknowledge their struggle, or recognize the sin. Two, understand their grief, or get to the root of the problem. And three, encourage them in the Word, or offer support—as in minister. I was also to do it *in love*, because an alcoholic didn't want or need to hear, "…be not drunk with wine," (see Ephesians 5:18, KJV) before they heard, "I see what you're going through (recognizing drunkenness/alcoholism is the sin), and I understand what you're dealing with (recognizing the root, for instance depression)."

Prior to this revelation, I always felt in my heart I'd done what God wanted me to, but in honesty I had not. He wanted me to be a witness, but I let my head get in the way of my heart. I hadn't ministered at all. I had judged and I had condemned, but I had not convicted. Only the Holy Spirit can do that, and He exited as soon as my head entered. It's because with my head came vanity, pride, and conceit—neither of which are of God.

It was only a day later when the dreams started again. It was as if every time God spoke to me He began to show me things. Soon, I developed a level of expectancy I didn't have before. It didn't even have to be a prayer request. I could make a comment about something and hear a verbal response, receive a visual reply, or feel a spiritual answer. It wasn't something I could turn on or off. I wasn't sure I even wanted to because, once again, I had tapped into something. God was definitely working on me, so I just let it happen.

THIS OPENED DOOR

8 Nights after connecting with God in the Spirit and learning the lesson on compassion, I had a bad dream regarding my family. I didn't know whether the devil had changed lanes again or if God was responsible, so I started praying. Although I don't particularly know why; it just happened that way. The visions continued to come, even though by this time most of them had become nightmares. Now, it was personal, but I was consoled in the Spirit when God revealed what this latest one meant. The significance of this particular dream was clear and openly received.

God was showing me that our relatives are our earthly family, and just as we are in this world but not of it, we are *in* but not *of* our natural families as well. For the first time I understood, in a sense, we are all equal but separate. Anyone who is not covered by the blood of the Lamb is not considered family in the Spirit realm... *equal in mom and dad, but separate from God.*

It was an eye-opener for me to think how we, as people, are quick to claim one another and welcome each other into our lives, but dogs have sense enough to sniff first. I noted then, as Christians, the closer we get to one another the more we should smell some form of the crucifixion. Either we would detect each other's death as we listened for a testimony, sense one another's burial while we watched the passing away of old habits, or discern each others' resurrection as we tasted and saw the manifestation of the goodness of God in one another's actions. Somewhere, somehow our crosses should *always* come forth. If not, we have neither seen Him or know Him (see 1 John 3:6).

With all of the things happening in my life at that time, my prayer list grew longer and longer. I found myself praying for people's salvation (people who'd told me they were already saved). I felt the need to pray for their salvation based on the lifestyles I witnessed them live. I knew what they were saying, but what I was seeing spoke more loudly than what I was hearing. Then, one day God spoke to my spirit and told me I needed to stop praying "save" and start praying "draw." It was because I couldn't honestly know if anyone was ever truly saved or not without looking within their soul, only He could. I just wanted Him to draw the sinner unto salvation and the saint unto sanctification, so I began to pray for God to draw everyone I knew, *including me*. That was exactly what I wanted with God spiritually, and that is precisely what I got.

One morning, while lying in bed asleep on my back, I saw a face that was beautifully bronzed with white hair that looked like cotton. The face had a nicely groomed mustache and beard. As this person leaned over me and came closer, I began to smile. I opened my eyes as I felt his lips touch my forehead. I immediately recognized the face raising up as that of Jesus. As He drifted farther away, I leaned forward and began to look around with my smile still in tact. It was the crack of dawn, with little sunlight shining into the bedroom. I looked over at

Derrick and he was still asleep. I laid back down in awe. Amazed that Jesus had taken time out of His morning to greet me with a kiss, I was convinced that I was definitely on the path of righteousness, which would eventually lead to my destiny.

That afternoon, interestingly enough, I caught a glimpse of another Christian television show. The program highlighted a couple testifying about how they had both seen images of Jesus, at different times during their lives. The wife testified of her experience first. She told of a time when she had contemplated ending their marriage. She then shared how she was crying and pouring her heart out to one of her girlfriends while sitting at the kitchen table. As she was talking, Jesus appeared unto her over her friend's shoulder with a message that she had to forgive her husband for something he had done.

Later on, in the same segment, the husband's interview came on. He was testifying that after his wife's encounter with Jesus, her attitude had changed. He couldn't particularly put his finger on it, but there was something different about her.

Although life continued on and he could tell she had truly forgiven him, he had not yet been able to forgive himself. Well, one day he was so grieved by the memories of his past actions that he began to pray. He specifically told Jesus if He was really working things out to show him. As he looked out of the window, he saw an image of Christ in the sky with a tear falling from His eye. I attributed his vision to the grief we cause Jesus when we don't trust Him totally and completely to do what He has promised us He would... to set us free indeed (see John 8:36)!

I was also reminded of a sermon I'd heard in the past. The minister spoke on the rapture and mentioned that we will not see Jesus until He comes again. He continued by saying, "If anyone says Jesus visited him or her, or they saw Jesus, then tell them they're crazy because the Bible says we will not see Jesus until He comes again." I laughed, because although I believe that I take it literally. *We* will not see Jesus. The word "we" is plural and means collectively [as a group]. We, as a group and body of believers, will not see Jesus until He returns. However, that doesn't negate the fact that I, as well as others, have had *individual* experiences of seeing Him for ourselves.

Nevertheless, trusting and believing God for His promises, I began to pray for the assurance that I was not losing my mind. Did you really think all of this was happening and I was just going along with the flow? *No indeed!* I thought I was crazy for months, *for real*—not the "Shaundale is so crazy" kind of crazy, but the "Shaundale is losing her mind" kind of crazy. And, I certainly did not need anyone trying to validate it without hearing my story.

Another morning, in particular, I opened my Bible and let the Spirit of God lead me. I bowed my head and said, "Lord, I need assurance. Please, let me know I'm still on the path." My Bible fell open to Deuteronomy 28 (KJV). So I read, *"And it shall come to pass, if thou shalt hearken diligently unto the voice of the LORD thy God, to observe [and] to do all his commandments which I command thee this day, that the LORD thy God will set thee on high above all nations of the earth: And all these blessings shall come on thee, and overtake thee, if thou shalt hearken unto the voice of the LORD thy God.*

The text then went on to specify what exact blessings would come upon and overtake us if we stay in the will of God. When I finished reading the passage, I could not believe how easy that was. *Talk about an on-time God!* To be honest, I could not have even stumbled upon that on my own anyhow. Realizing now that even if I had "just happened" upon it, the promise would not have been for me. It was for Israel, but because I *specifically* asked for a Word, on that day it was my *specific*, or rhema Word.

I had read through the Bible over the years, but that was just it. I'd read it as if it was a typical book. I wasn't looking for anything, so I found nothing. I had even read several of the books of the Bible repeatedly, but couldn't particularly remember anything I hadn't already learned as a child. Now, because I was actually studying, I could remember where things were and what a particular passage was really about.

I would start to read and, on those occasions when I forgot to pray first, my attempt to study became like reading a literary work all over again, which I never wanted to experience another time. After reading like this for a little while I would close the Bible, ask forgiveness over rushing in without proper preparation (bless my food), ask for revelation and understanding (strength and nourishment), and ask that God would speak to me specifically in whatever text I was preparing to study on that particular day (sustain).

On rare occasions, when I felt myself getting low or feeling drained, I would blurt out, "Lord, take me where You want me to go today." I did this because He knew what I needed, and to me there was no sense in flipping through pages and pages looking for something to read when He could just take me there—and the sooner, the better.

When I finished reading Deuteronomy 28, I raised my head and asked, "Lord, what specifically are You saying?" To my spirit He spoke the words, "I'm taking you to a new place." I breathed easier the remainder of the day. Even after that incident when I felt myself becoming emotionally exhausted while trying to wait it out in the valley, I said, "Oh no, the devil *is* a liar. My life and my destiny are under the influence of the seed of the prophet, and my God is taking me to a *new* place." I had much attitude about it, too.

Part of me was excited beyond measure to think God would use *me* in this way. On the other hand, part of me was disappointed I hadn't walked the path He'd obviously planned for me all along. As my mind drifted back to when I was a child who always had a book, was always writing or dreaming about it, I was saddened to know that somewhere along the line I grew farther and farther apart from God and in essence delayed my own destiny.

Having prayed over what to do with the seed money I'd received on the night of the revival, I thought about suits. Initially, I didn't want to spend the money on anything, but quickly began to feel convicted when I considered the parable of the man who hid his money in Matthew 25:25-28. As I continued to pray more over what to do with portions or all of the money, I decided to purchase myself a couple of fashionable ensembles.

One reason I decided to buy the suits is because I hadn't purchased anything in a while; and secondly, it dawned on me I needed to make sure I had something decent to wear since I knew God was preparing me for ministry. Keep in mind I had been a stay-at-home-mom for almost four years, so most of my dry clean only items were replaced with cotton and machine washables after a few too many spit-ups and one too many sticky hands. Therefore, Derrick accompanied me to the mall as we went looking for suits.

For me, shopping at the mall was a chore. I had gotten used to catalog shopping or simply buying online, but because I wanted to get out and was determined to stay within a set budget, I headed for one of the local malls. We walked and looked. I frowned and turned up my nose. It was awful. When I was ready to head home empty-handed, Derrick headed towards another store. I guess he figured I hadn't gotten him out to the mall for nothing, and we were going home with exactly what we came for.

By that time, Derrick and I both knew what my problem was. I wasn't finding the quality I wanted. The styles were okay but, to me, the fabrics were awful. So, coming out of the last dressing room, I prayed. I remember saying, "Lord, You are going to have to help me out here. You and I both know what I want and what I'm looking for. We both know I have expensive taste, but today I'm on a bu...bu...budget."

Still struggling with a clothing budget, something I never had before the lay-off or before marriage, I had already stopped buying clothes for myself because I wasn't able to get what I wanted. Used to buying any- and everything on a whim, I had gone from shopping once a week to once a year. *Talk about hard.* It was also during this time when I was reminded of one of the worst incidents of my life. *The story goes:*

When I relocated from Arlington to Dallas, I was in such a hurry to move that I left a piece of my luggage inside a closet at the old townhouse. I moved on a Friday, so when I noticed the suitcase wasn't with me in the new townhouse, that evening I called my old property manager but the office was already closed. I blew that phone line and voice mailbox up all weekend, because most of my best clothes were in that one piece of luggage. I probably would have traded all of the other suitcases for that *one*.

On Monday, when someone *finally* answered the telephone, I spoke with person after person in Management. I was glad to be able to speak with someone who actually looked for the suitcase and found it. I rushed over to the property manager's office after work wearing jeans and a t-shirt (the best I could find of the remaining items) and picked up the luggage. I was very grateful, that is until I opened it later that evening and found my best *and* favorite clothing items gone.

At that point, I was so furious I called my old property manager back *and* a few lawyers (all of whom advised me to write a letter explaining my situation and requesting the items be returned). The property manager then gave me some selfish mumbo-jumbo. I was told that since I'd relinquished my keys, I had also given up ownership of any personal items left as well. Finally snapping back into reality, I wished I had already met my Jabez-praying girlfriend, at that time.

After shopping all day and having gone through racks and racks of clothing, I saw an outfit I liked. However, the price tag wasn't as flattering as it once would have been. I really wanted that suit, but knew I could not spend that amount on one outfit alone, not on that day anyway. *Talk about getting an attitude.* It took everything in me to hold my composure, keep my neck from rolling, and stop my lips from smacking. I fought back the words "There was a time when I could've bought it just because I wanted it." Then I prayed with both a humble and heavy heart, "Lord, if I have to sacrifice what I want for what I can afford *this time*, then I will. I know the time is coming again when having to sacrifice like this won't be even an issue, amen." Then, I heard, "Look over here!"

Derrick had found an entire section of suits, by the same designer, on sale for 80 percent off of the original price—including the first one. I liked most of what I saw and grabbed all that he handed me, as I headed into the dressing room. When I came out modeling the first suit, which I knew I wanted, I started doing my "glory hallelujah" dance. Despite the sale, I kept my word and left the store with only the two suits I'd come for. These weren't just suits, though. These were two three-piece suits with the long suit-jackets. They were tough! I barely paid $100.00 for suits that were well over $500.00. *Talk about answered prayers and desires of the heart!*

Having purchased the suits *with* shoes, and still under budget, Derrick and I headed home. Although I was thrilled with the items, I wanted to be sure I had done what was pleasing unto God with the money. I still wasn't so sure I was supposed to buy the suits, but knew it wouldn't hurt since I needed them. Well, I was so happy and excited about the outfits when we made it home and I took them out of the bag that I went online to find the designer.

Automatically assuming there was a registered domain name for her, I was highly disappointed when the search page errored out. So, then I typed the name "Amanda Smith" in the Address Bar in order to search again. I had never heard of this designer before *ever*. Well, as soon as I typed the name Amanda Smith and hit the Enter key, you will never—in a million years—guess what popped up.

The very first thing to appear on-screen was *Amanda Berry Smith: An Autobiography of the Story of the Lord's Dealings with Mrs. Amanda Smith the Colored Evangelist; Containing an Account of Her Life Work of Faith and Her Travels in America, England, Ireland, Scotland, India, and Africa, as an Independent Missionary 1837-1915.* My bottom lip dropped as my mouth opened, and I began to rub both my eyes as if I had just awakened.

I stopped and began reading the preface of her book, which read: For a number of years many of my friends have said to me, "You ought to write out an account of your life, and let it be known how God has led you out into His work." I stopped right there. I knew this couldn't be. It just couldn't be. Not that I wasn't satisfied with the information I received, but I was looking for something on Amanda Smith the fashion designer. So, what did I do? *Glad you asked.* I'm only human, so I modified my search criteria and re-typed "Amanda Smith, fashion designer." My revised search then took me to another page which listed several people who shared the first name Amanda or the last name Smith, but no Amanda Smith. So, I modified the search criteria again, several times, and re-typed "Amanda Smith" followed by every possible thing I could think of relating to fashion.

Having not found anything at all on Amanda Smith the clothing designer, I re-typed "Amanda Smith" and hit "Enter" once more. Several other Christian links came up, but nothing ever took me to the fashion designer's website. I searched one last time that night and was taken to a link which listed four different sites where Evangelist Amanda Smith's autobiographies were available. God definitely had something in store for me this time. First, He definitely wanted me to buy suits; and secondly, He definitely wanted me to get the ones I got! *Oh, blessed assurance!*

At that instance, I grabbed my journal and prepared for a long night of "chit-chat" with God. I would not have missed that opportunity for anything short of somebody falling dead in my house. This was getting deep. I knew from that moment on I wouldn't buy any other suit by any other designer, for as long as possible. If I had to go to the mall just for Amanda Smith suits, then you might as well start calling me her poster child.

Before my prayer and meditation time with God, I decided to get up and go back to the first site where I re-read her book title once more *thoroughly*. I choked on the words "An Autobiography of the Story of the Lord's Dealings." I knew I had to purchase the book, because it was both by and about Evangelist Smith, so I clicked on the link. There was a site where I could download the entire book and read it online, or several sites where I could order it. I wanted the actual book in my possession, and I found two independent bookstores that each had one copy for hundreds of dollars. If it came to me purchasing a book at one of those online stores, I was prepared to do so. The remainder of my seed money would have been used to purchase it. I could not have thought of a better reason for spending it, other than on Miss Amanda Berry Smith in one way or another.

Looking back, I didn't even realize God was working that clothing situation for my good. As hurt as I was, had I not left the clothes in my old townhouse and the employees hadn't stolen them in the first place, I would not have even needed new clothing items when I did. I would've missed finding Miss Amanda Smith altogether.

There I was holding onto the bitterness about those clothes years later because my closet has never been the same since, and God was trying to get me to release it so I could grab onto something much better. He knew, before even laying the foundations of the earth, that in 1998 I would have to be stripped of some of my most prized possessions, my clothes, in order for Him to be glorified in starting to replenish them in 2003. Not to mention the added blessing of this new journey He'd started me on with Miss Smith. Had He not allowed any of those circumstances to play out *then*, even knowing the extent of my resentment that was to come, *now* I would not be seeking His will at all and would have missed this opened door.

HEAVEN AND EARTH

9 After searching online all night for Miss Smith's book at a more reasonable price, I found four copies at Barnes & Noble. The next day I visited the local store and ordered mine, as I eagerly continued through this opened door. I was told it would take eight days for the book to arrive, so for a week I prayed, studied, and researched Miss Amanda Berry Smith as best I could.

During the days to come, I asked myself a couple of questions. One was, "What could God be trying to tell me through this woman or her book?" Then two, "What kind of connection could we have, if any?" Then, Derrick said something that made all the sense in the world to me. He said, "She could be your role model." It clicked just then.

God reminded me I had specifically prayed for a role model *consistently* since the night of the prophecy at the revival. I decided that same night, on my way home from church, whatever path God was having me to take I wanted someone there who would help me to reach the end successfully; someone who wasn't headed there, but had already been there… for a long while.

The odd thing was Derrick didn't know that particular request. It wasn't something we prayed about during *our* prayer time. I prayed about it during *my* prayer time. So, how could he have known that, and why would he mention it now? I've said it before and I'll say it again, "Because God speaks through other people. We've just got to position ourselves to hear Him." *Praise the Lord! I was right where I should be!*

Amanda Berry Smith could very well have been meant to be my role model. *Why not?* She received her call, had an international ministry which lasted twenty years, *and* she wrote about what I'm trying to write about at this very moment… an autobiography dealing with my story of how the Lord has dealt with me. Although, even after all I continued to learn about her, the question still remained in my head "Who is this woman?" In thirty years I had never heard of her, but I welcomed the opportunity to learn all I could now and follow in her footsteps, as Jesus leads.

I awoke the next morning with such joy. I had been online the night before until 2:30a.m., just reading and marveling over the life of Miss Amanda Jane Berry Smith. She was born in 1837 and lived to be 78 years old until her death in 1915. Once again, who was this woman who'd died 90+ years ago, and why did she show up on my doorstep, so to speak, yesterday?

When I finally fell asleep and awoke later that morning, I could feel the Spirit of the Lord all over me. My heart was full. I got up and opened my organizer and right there on the page for January 26, 2003 were the words "Expect a miracle this week." I thought back to the night in December concerning the prophecy and heard *with precision*, "In approximately 30 days, doors will open you have never even thought about. Be still. People's lives are at stake."

I'd written that statement on the night of the revival when the prophetess spoke to the attending Prophets, Prophetesses, and Evangelists. When I made it home, I flipped ahead thirty days from that date. Since she said *in approximately 30 days*, I did a "give or take a day or two" and picked a day during that week of the 30th day. Once I had it, I simply wrote "Expect a miracle this week." For me, that meant exactly what I intended it to: expect a miracle everyday that week. It would fall on one of those days, and sure enough it did.

There I was expecting a job or career shift, and God was taking me in another direction… a spiritual one. He certainly had my attention. He let me know that while I was looking for things in the natural, He had already worked them out in the *super*-natural. So, guess what I did? I stopped looking for things that were normal!

While still awaiting the arrival of my book from Barnes and Noble, I continued my walk with the Lord just a little closer than usual. I was searching, listening, asking, and praying. Still researching Amanda Smith online, I continued to wonder what the connection was. Could God miraculously be reconnecting me to my past? That *would* be something spectacular. So, I did what now comes naturally; I asked Him. I prayed and asked God that if anybody who was somebody *for Him* was linked to me, then could this woman be the one? His response to me was, "She is. The blood of Jesus covers you as it did her." That was the end of that.

In studying Miss Smith's biographies, I discovered her final ministry was carried out at an orphanage in Harvey, Illinois. Her passion was children, and I knew surely God was working on something. This sense of conviction had little to do with Him mentally taking me back to if you want to save them, save their children. Neither did it have to do with Emahn or my love for children. What it had to do with was the return of the burning desire I had for adopting/foster-parenting. I knew convincing Derrick, prior to this point, had been a struggle. However, after this, I knew it would be a piece of cake. (And, it was!)

All my life I have been around children, so I surprised myself when I prayed and asked God to somehow use and equip me to continue this woman's legacy and her works. We had so much in common; I simply couldn't understand the possibility of *not* being connected to her in some way.

Throughout the remainder of that day, I felt somewhat empowered. Call me crazy, but it was as if living the end of "Malcolm X" the movie. I am Amanda Smith. I *am* Amanda Smith. *I* am Amanda Smith! It was then that I prayed, "God, please let me be this woman's Joshua. Prepare me to lead others into Canaan."

Later, there was a song in my head. I had learned it awhile ago from one of Derrick's aunts. It's called "Whisper a Prayer." It's a very old tune; so old that when I did an online search for the artist, the results said composer unknown. For some reason, while humming that tune, I felt a kindred spirit with Miss Smith that was unexplainable. It was almost as if there was a burden on me to carry some imaginary torch. I felt somewhat overwhelmed at the thought of having to fill *her* shoes. It was then I remembered Proverbs 3:5-6 which says, *"Trust in the LORD with all thine heart; and lean not unto thine own understanding. In all thy ways acknowledge him, and he shall direct thy path."* I was definitely a witness that He was directing my path, so I decided to keep right on trusting and acknowledging Him.

For some strange reason, I developed the urge to go to Chicago. I didn't know why, nor did I understand it. I just knew I felt I had to go. Derrick started making arrangements to get my airplane ticket online. I then called two college friends in the area to notify them of my expected arrival.

Weeks later, as I prepared for my upcoming trip, I "just-so-happened" to catch another profound woman of God on television who said, "Arise Joshua. You have to get up and do something." I knew I had to write. She continued with, "Don't look at your situation, look at your revelation." I thought about my photo of the one thousand dollars. She then went on to say, "God is beginning to show you things that have been hidden." *Wasn't that the truth?*

The very next day I received "the call" from our local Barnes & Noble. My book had arrived, so I went to pick it up. While out getting it, I decided to run more errands on the other side of the city. Then, I remembered I had not eaten since breakfast. It was almost 3:00p.m. and I was *hungry*.

While driving, I slowly merged into the left turning lane to get onto I-35 South in Dallas. At the stoplight, while waiting to get on the entrance ramp to the Interstate, I saw a homeless man. He was talking to another man who was in the car at the beginning of the line. As he left that car and moved on to the second, he staggered. I thought to myself, *He just looks intoxicated*; however, something in me would not let me pass him by.

As I moved up in line and inched towards the light, the man staggered towards me. I promise you, I intended to drive right past him, but something in my gut told me not to. I said, "Lord, I haven't eaten since this morning." God spoke to my spirit, and I felt convicted because I knew I would eat when I made it home. So, I partially rolled down the window and handed the man my last few dollars. I figured even though he looked like he was going across the street to the liquor store, some good would come out of it somehow.

When I made it home I ate, but days later while still

walking and talking with the Lord on my Amanda Smith "high," I thought, *salvation is free*. Then, I wondered why in the world everyone won't just get in line for it. That's when I heard this voice say, "It may have been free to you, but it cost *Me* My son." Well, that triggered a thought. I was reminded that giving my last $2.00 to some homeless man seemed free to him, but it cost me my lunch—a $1.89 super-sized McDonald's french fry to be exact. I then began to think just how minute that meal was compared to the life of Christ, but the lesson I learned was grand: "Don't Waste."

Just like I was concerned about that possibly intoxicated homeless man misusing my last $2.00 on liquor (when I could have been comforted by it myself for food), God was saying don't waste the blood of my only Son, Jesus, on sin. Sure, the crucifixion was free to us, but it cost God *His* only begotten Son!

I'd even told God when I saw the homeless man, "Lord, he just looks like he's going to drink my money up. He's stumbling now!" But, God told me to give it to him and not to worry about what he did with it, because that was *His* business to tend to. So, I gave the man *God's* money, prayed, and drove home.

Here it was days later and I was still being reminded, "Just as you were concerned about your $2.00 being put to good use, don't you think I'm concerned about my Son's blood being put to good use, as well?" *Man! What a lesson to come out of $2.00? Talk about a perfect example of grace and mercy.* I determined then this lesson must have been preparing me to share the gospel and let God do the rest, because whatever happened after the seed is planted is His business to tend to.

I made a major connection with the Father on that day. That was some serious stuff. So serious that when my sister phoned and told me she had just finished talking with her father, I was speechless. When she told me she had been calling him for years, I was too through because I was convicted again. Here I was still holding grudges against my own father after all these years. I was 29-years-old, at the time, and had never phoned him *ever*. I admit after hearing my pastor's 2001 Father's Day message entitled "Celebrating the Empty Chair" I wanted to contact him. I just never did. I even planned to write him a letter once; however, I simply never got around to doing it. So, after listening to my little sister talk on and on about how she and her father were talking now, even over the distance, I called mine for the first time.

When he answered the telephone, I spoke and told him who I was. I could actually hear excitement in his voice. It was then I felt I could freely talk. Although there were several questions I wanted to ask him then, I decided to save them for another time. I wanted this experience to be a pleasant one, so I decided to keep the concerns I had to myself. However, I did mention that I do have "issues," and he told me to call at anytime to discuss them with him.

Even though I have never taken him up on that offer, that particular conversation lasted twenty minutes, and I was surprised when it ended with an "I love you" from my father. For the first time in my life, to my recollection, he'd told me he loved me and I couldn't see his face to search his eyes when he said it. *What an emotional day.* Yes, I cried, but I was also able to tear down walls that had been up for most of my life.

I found out who my biological father was around the age of eight. For at least the past twenty-three years of my life I had been an angry and heart-broken little girl, as opposed to daddy's little girl. On that day, I even began to see how I had put up a wall between God and me in relation to *Him* being *my* concerned Father. I'd never trusted God totally and completely to come through for me, which meant I'd never ask Him for anything and *really* believe I was going to get it. In the back of my mind there was always doubt. Because something always came up in the natural, I assumed the same would take precedence over me in the Spirit, as well. I didn't learn that because I doubted, and not because God isn't concerned, is why I wasn't getting my prayers answered until I actually started to mature as a Christian. Matthew 21:22 says, *"If you believe, you will receive whatever you ask for in prayer."* Truthfully, I didn't believe, so I didn't receive either.

God was entering into rooms on the inside of me I had locked, and it didn't feel good at all. I didn't like it because I wasn't even sure I wanted it. It was so much easier for me to hold on to the hate than to embrace the love. I knew I needed deliverance, and I thought I wanted it, but this didn't feel good in any way. *All of this because of a homeless man and $2.00*, I thought. *Why couldn't I just have the fries?*

Later that night, I soaked in a hot tub of water. As I read the autobiography of Amanda Berry Smith and finished chapter four, I skipped ahead. (It's a habit, something I've always done.) When I read the last paragraph of the entire book, tears began to stream down my cheeks. This woman prayed for her own Joshua as late as 1893 when the book was first published. Her exact words referenced that some of the younger women would pick up where she left off. *Could I be one of them?*

My heart rejoiced, as I called Derrick in and asked him to read the words of Miss Smith. He sighed as I repeated to him my private prayer in which I had prayed to be her Joshua. I had also asked God to somehow allow me to pick up where she'd left off in order to continue her legacy. Now, in her very own book and in her very own words, I was reading where she herself prayed that the Spirit of the Lord would come upon some of the younger women who had talent, and who had better opportunities than she did, in order to do a better work for God. She also requested that we, the younger women, would take up the standard and bear it on with the remembrance that "...Without holiness no man shall see the Lord." (Hebrews 12:14) After that, I wondered if I could actually be amongst the "some" she prayed for. So I *really* prayed then, because I knew God was definitely ordering my steps.

As I continued with my reading, I finally stopped after reaching the part where Miss Smith talked about receiving misinformation from her pastor. My mind immediately went back to a book I'd read several years prior entitled "A Divine Revelation of Hell" by Mary K. Baxter.

In this particular book, God used Baxter in a most remarkable way. For 30 consecutive nights she accompanied Jesus to hell, as He showed her what things to write about on earth. She described an incident in one of her experiences where a minister was being tortured, around the clock, by demons. While he lay in a casket crying out, the demons were taking shifts piercing his heart with a pitchfork. It was his eternal damnation for irresponsibly teaching the sheep in God's flock while under his care. God immediately reminded me of the book of Daniel, where I'd read about the irresponsible shepherds, and this all seemed surreal.

As God continued to show me more and more, it dawned on me that all of this really had very little to do with Bunkie. Just like Emahn symbolized the children I would carry, Bunkie simply symbolized the world; however, a little closer to home was *the Church*. Because I have heart ties back home, God simply chose to tug at them in order to get my attention.

For the longest time, I could not figure out why I was so burdened over some of the people back home. They weren't any worse off than people in New York,

California, Chicago, Florida, or even Texas, as far as I was concerned. Sin is sin, but home is where my heart is, and God was trying to get me to see the bigger picture. Just as He did not want anyone to die and go to hell, neither did I—*especially not my own people.* Besides, Bunkie wasn't just about *my* family; Bunkie *is* my family.

God was showing me that if I'm just as passionate about the rest of the world as I am over the city of Bunkie, then I'd be able to move to a bigger realm—the children of His kingdom. In a sense, the same zeal I have for home, I would use to light the world. And, I thought that was amazing. God cares so much about little ol' me, *and you*, that He went as far out as He did. He drew me closer to Him, so I would hear Him when He called.

The very next morning I awoke in horror to a bad dream. Either God was trying to tell me something else, or the devil was working a good one on me. In this particular dream, the details are as follows. Tune in.

Quad and I are in Bunkie at my grandmother's house. Because the house is so small, she and I are sharing my mother's bed and Emahn is between us. We appear to be adults and Emahn appears to be six months old or so. Quad looks at me and asks if I really want to please God. I know in my heart she's asking if I really want to serve Him, so I answer excitedly, "Yes!" It was almost like one of those "Tony the Tiger" yeses. She then asks me how old Emahn is, and although she appears to be six months I say, "It's been about a year." She says, "Uh huh, I thought it has been about a year." (Like it was just in time for something.)

She then grabs my arms from behind and crosses them over my chest while I sit in the "V" of her legs. My arms hurt somewhat, but I think about the crushing of grapes for wine, or one of those "God never uses a man without crushing him greatly" experiences. So, although it hurts, I accept the pain and look forward to it as a pruning process. Then out of the blue she says, "Open your mouth and praise the Lord." Without hesitation, I open my mouth to glorify God and a growl comes out. I start to squirm and shake vigorously, as if trying to get free, and hear Quad praying for me in Tongue. I can't get loose, but I hear her scream and then moan.

I think with the little part of me I can still feel of how I must be hurting her, but it seems I just want her to stop praying. I open my mouth to praise God again, but a growl comes out once more. I refuse to believe this is part of who I am and want to cry out to the Lord, but I bite Quad instead as I put my mouth over her lips. My arms are still crossed over my chest, and my hands are still pulled behind my back. I cannot get free and I just want her to stop praying, so I bite her lips. She has her head rested upon my right shoulder and won't let me go for anything. I bite down on her lips, because I am being possessed by a demon. Then I hear her scream and squeal, but she never stops praying for me.

I begin to think to myself of the pain I'm causing her with the little bit of me that is fighting back. I want to let go of her lips, but the evil spirit won't let me. Then, when I finally let go, I feel like I will give up or out, but never in. Afterwards I whisper with the little bit of sanity still in me, "I love you, girl." I want her to know that if I don't make it through, or if I hurt her, I'm sorry and I love her—especially for trying to help me, for not giving up on me, and for being there to pray me through.

I awoke, but didn't exactly know what had taken place in the end. I did remember kind of sinking, or just giving up the fight and passing out. I recalled glancing at Quad and she appeared to be someone else. She actually appeared to be dead. She was pale and fair-complexioned, almost white-looking. Not White, as in Caucasian, but white as if she had been dipped in flour from head-to-toe with her dress still on. She looked like a zombie of some sort, with a torn dress and unkempt hair. Pacing at the foot of the bed was also a huge demon with a pitchfork. It was as if it was waiting to see if something would happen.

Thinking back, I wondered if it could have been that I was giving birth to something—something spiritually dead people, who are closest to me, would try to assist me in bringing forth. Bunkie did represent the Church now, so who were these people God was trying to warn me about? Zombie or no zombie, Quad was praying in the dream. "To whom was she praying, and where did this demon come from?" were the questions I asked myself, though. "What could it have been awaiting the arrival of?" was another. Perhaps, the book? Or, maybe even a ministry, or my child? Whichever it was, we all know it meant me no good. It was on assignment to steal, kill, or destroy. *That we know!*

It was around 3:50a.m. when I woke Derrick and asked him to hold me. Then, I asked him to pray with me. After that, I asked him to put the CD's on and to check on Emahn. Now, at any other time, the CD player would have had Donnie McClurkin, Richard Smallwood, Fred Hammond, etc. already in place. On this night it was empty, because all of the CD's were in the car.

Derrick actually had to load the tray when all I wanted him to do was push Power and Play. I decided then I'd play our CD's every night to help me sleep better. I also felt that even if no one was awake to say "Jesus" and cause demons to tremble, Yolanda Adams, Kirk Franklin, Karen Clarke Sheard, *or somebody* was going to have us covered. And, let me tell you this, there's no sleep like drifting off to the assurance that this battle is not yours.

When Derrick came back to bed I wanted to call to

Beaumont then, but decided against it. I sat and stared at the clock, wanting to call Quad at four in the morning. I knew she and her husband would be up as early as five o'clock, so I waited. I was up the remainder of the morning and when that clock displayed 5:01a.m. I was dialing Quad's number. I remembered how I was too afraid to even get up and go to the bathroom alone, but after the music sank into my spirit I was calm.

Quad's husband answered the telephone and gave it to her. When I told her the details of the dream, the first thing out of her mouth was, "Oh, uhn-uhn! We rebuke that *right* now." She's a minister, but still I was on the telephone wondering, *Can you really rebuke a dream?* She started affirming the Word of God and speaking those things in our lives that are of the Spirit, so I followed her lead. She went on to tell me that I need to be careful of the people I associate with, and to also be aware of some of the people who pray for or even hug me. Afterwards, she prayed and we hung up.

I sure felt better, but what Quad said didn't start to really sink in until later when I began thinking about hugging a little more. I told Derrick what she had shared with me, and he said it made sense to him. He saw it as a transfer of energy. Whenever I reached out and hugged someone in the spirit of God, something good and positive left me. Likewise, something left the other person as well. The question was "What?" Not only had strength left me, but some form of weakness possibly entered in.

After that I started to think about my "off" days, as well. I wondered about the times when my own attitude needed checking and I passed my spirit of depression, unforgiveness, or resentment on to some unsuspecting others. Derrick and Quad had me thinking *way* too hard, but the last thing I needed or wanted was to be the recipient or giver of ungodly spirits.

I didn't know what God was trying to tell me, if anything; however, I was getting tired of having demonic dreams. I started wondering if God was trying to tell me to watch my friends, watch my back, watch my family, or if the devil was just messing with me about the people closest to me. He could've been changing lanes again, so I decided I'd just read my Bible and journal. I trusted God to take me to the scriptures He wanted me to get to on that day.

I started flipping through my Bible while noting some scriptures in Ephesians I'd previously read and highlighted. Those not being it (I can usually tell in my spirit when I'm in the right place or not), I continued to read on as I turned more pages. Then, there it was, the armor of God. That's where He wanted me. I knew that was it! In fact, our pastor had spoken briefly about wrestling against principalities and powers the previous Sunday in church. I read on in chapter one, through to the 20th verse, and knew God was telling me something in regards to being prepared. It read, *"Pray also for me, that whenever I open my mouth, words may be given me so that I will fearlessly make known the mystery of the gospel, for which I am an ambassador in chains. Pray that I may declare it fearlessly, as I should"* (see Ephesians 6:19-20).

The devil was trying to silence me! In the dream all I wanted to do was praise the Lord, but couldn't because there was a growl in my mouth. After reading these scriptures, I decided then I would praise God freely, because He would give me the words even when I didn't feel like it. I'd be doggone (my country side) if I was trying to exalt the Lord and allowed the devil to steal my praise.

That morning, when the sun came up, I prayed Ephesians 6:10-20. I said, *"Oh, God, help me to be strong in the Lord and in His mighty power. Help me to put on the full armor of You, so that I can take my stand against the devil's schemes. Remind me daily that my struggle is not against flesh and blood, but against the rulers, against the authorities, against the powers of this dark world, and against the spiritual forces of evil in the heavenly realms. Help me to daily put on the full armor of You, so that when evil comes I will be able to stand my ground, and after I have done everything, to* stand. *Please help me to stand firm with the belt of truth buckled around my waist, the breastplate of righteousness in place, and with my feet fitted with the readiness that comes from the Gospel of peace.*

Also, Lord, in addition to all this, help me to take up the shield of faith with which I can extinguish all the flaming arrows of the evil one. To take the helmet of salvation and the sword of the Spirit, which is the Word of God, and to always pray in the Spirit, on all occasions, with all kinds of prayers and requests. Please help me to keep this in mind, to be alert, and to always keep on praying for all the saints, as well as myself. That whenever I open my mouth words may be given to me, so that I will fearlessly make known the mystery of the Gospel for which I am an ambassador in chains for Christ. I pray that I may declare it fearlessly, as I should, in Jesus' name, amen."

After that, whenever I felt fear trying to creep up on me I would do a number of things, but I remembered that prayer. It was also on that same day when I thought about and prayed for all the women in the world who can't roll over and ask their husbands to pray for them. It was one thing to roll over and have nobody there, but it was something altogether different to roll over and have someone who shouldn't be there. Holding was nice, but praying was much nicer. It was then that God dropped the words "hold tighter, pray harder," into my spirit. It was in reference to Him. I was determined to see the manifestation of whatever He was working on in the Spirit come to pass in the natural. So, I held tighter and prayed harder.

I realized then we *need* the whole armor of God. Otherwise, we would be half-cocked as in knowing the Word of God, but living by way of the world. At that point, my mind drifted to Judas. "What about Judas?" I asked God. Well, Judas was as half-cocked as anybody. He knew the Word. He walked and talked *with* the Word. Heck, daily he was in the presence *of* the Word, but he still had an open door to sin that the devil gained access to him through. Now, I know it was Judas' destiny to betray Christ. But, is it ours?

In Galatians 2:20-21 the text reads, *"I am crucified with Christ: nevertheless I live; yet not I, but Christ liveth in me: and the life which I now live in the flesh I live by the faith of the Son of God, who loved me, and gave himself for me. I do not frustrate the grace of God: for if righteousness [comes] by the law, then Christ is dead in vain."* That verse, simply stated, means we [the old us] died in Christ, but still we [the new us] live. It's not really us who lives though, but Christ who lives *through* the new us. Therefore, we do not mock God's grace because if righteousness could come by simply following the law, then Jesus died in vain and righteousness can't truly come through Him. Haven't we all made that statement at one time or another? *Sure we have.*

Whether we realize it or not, whenever we continue to sin we all but say with our actions that righteousness couldn't honestly come through Jesus. Then, we crucify Him all over again just to be sure it does. Every time we sin, we put Him back on the cross to go through the crucifixion all over again. Just like I was looking out for my $2.00 with the alcoholic, homeless man, God was still looking out for Jesus.

The day after waking from that horrifying dream, I continued to read Amanda Smith's autobiography and learned about her experience of seeing Jesus. My mind raced back to the morning I awoke to the kiss on my forehead. The same Jesus she saw and described is the same Jesus I saw, with the exception of the beard and robe. I saw a white, curly beard that was short. She saw a white, curly beard that was long.

Miss Smith described Him as the lovely, beautiful Jesus. She said He seemed to stand about six feet high in a loose, flowing, purple robe. According to her, "His hair and beard were white as wool, and His beautiful beard covered His breast to His waist. His face was indescribably lovely," she wrote, and I agreed.

The thought that both Miss Smith and I experienced the joy of seeing Jesus, only with different lengthened beards, reminded me of a question I once heard asked on a local Christian radio talk show. One of the callers wanted to know why people keep saying God is doing a new thing when the Bible says He is the same yesterday, today, and forever. As I thought about that question, I began to pray for clarity myself. The caller did pose a good question.

Well, in time, God revealed to me that yes He is the same yesterday, today, and forever (Hebrews 13:8); however, He does new things. His teachings are consistent, but His actions change. In Isaiah verses 43:18-19 the Lord said, *"Forget the former things; do not dwell on the past. See, I am doing a new thing! Now it springs up; do you not perceive it? I am making a way in the desert and streams in the wasteland."*

God already knew most of us would try to make our ways His, and just because we get caught up in monotony doesn't mean He has to. He is God always, but He can do things differently or altogether new for those who can *perceive* it, and therefore will *receive* it. He has said in Isaiah 55:8-9, *"For my thoughts are not your thoughts, neither are your ways my ways. As the heavens are higher than the earth, so are my ways higher than your ways and my thoughts [higher] than your thoughts."* (Inserts added.)

Just because God *is* the same, doesn't mean He would not *do* things differently. *We do it all the time.* God could make streams spring up in the desert and wastelands if He wanted to. He did, after all, create both heaven and earth.

DESTINY IS FULFILLED

10 Having put into perspective just who the Lord is, and the severity of what He was preparing me to do, I decided in my *definitely finite* wisdom to run. Yes, I said it... *I ran!* As if there was someplace I could hide between heaven and earth. Reflecting upon one of my most frequently used phrases when someone asks me to exercise, which is, "I'm not running unless somebody is after me," I hadn't lied. I guess God was coming in for the kill.

Since I had spontaneously joined the music ministry at church, I was trying my best to fit in. I jumped around so much from week-to-week that I was in the choir, out of the choir, on the praise and worship team, off the praise and worship team. I got on my own nerves until one evening in rehearsal one of the leaders mentioned we are *called* to the music ministry. I looked away, knowing I hadn't been *called* to do anything that even remotely resembled singing. What I did know was that I had been called to preach, teach, and/or evangelize. I just didn't want to. All I wanted to do was write. I didn't want to tell anyone anything verbally, so I tried to get as close as I could vocally and started singing.

The ministry leader then went on to say anyone involved in any area of church ministry is to be called to the particular organization they're working in. It finally registered in my mind why I was flip-flopping from week to week. I had tried to make myself fit into the music ministry, because I grew up singing in the choir. I felt if I was going to be active in any area of the church it would be that one. Singing was all I knew. It was what I had always done, partially because it was my only option growing up. I didn't know anything about being called to the choir. I just knew about singing.

I left rehearsal that night, having bounced back and forth for almost a year now, with my mind made up. I was not going back. Not because I didn't want to, but because God didn't want me to. There I was throwing off my own agenda, and everyone else's in the music ministry, because I was trying to fit in somewhere God never ordained for me to be. I was so mad. Up until that point I didn't recall ever being taught that I had to be called to *a* ministry in the church; only that some people are called to be in *the* ministry of preaching the Gospel.

As I continued to grow and learn, God took me specifically to Deuteronomy 1:6-7 (KJV) which says, *"Ye have dwelt long enough in this mount. Turn you, and take your journey, and go..."* I had finally gotten it. God was saying it was now time to break camp and move full speed ahead. I heard that loud and clear.

Knowing the promises of God were just over the horizon, I started to struggle with impatience. I wasn't lacking in faith at this point, because I knew the Promised Land wasn't far away. I just didn't know when I was going to get there. So, I listened on and continued to write as the Spirit led.

God showed me that He had given the land in the remainder of Deuteronomy 1:7 (KJV); however, in

Deuteronomy 1:8 (KJV) He started with, *"Behold, I have set the land before you…"* In other words, He told me, "Look, I have shown you the land." My question was what do I do now that I have seen it? What do I do now that I've heard from You… now that I've seen Your face? What do I do now that I've touched You? His answer? "Wait." So, I waited in the presence of the Lord. Ever since that day in the closet when the anointing took hold of me, and I took hold of the blessing, that was where I tried to stay.

It was in God's presence where things came to life. Suddenly, things made sense in the Spirit I had been trying to figure out all my life in the flesh. I will tell you this: God showed me things in five minutes in the Spirit that would have taken me nearly 50 years to figure out in the natural. I wanted to know everything about His plans for me from the beginning to the end. Then again, I realized I didn't even want to know the end. I just wanted to be brought up to speed regarding what was going on now and coming right over the horizon.

Some days I awoke in the early morning and, before demons would get busy around me, I would begin to pray and praise. God was telling me about Himself. He was even telling me about myself. I needed to be in His presence. I trusted Him completely, because I realized prayer is a two-way conversation. If He was courteous enough to listen to me ask, then I would be respectful and listen as He answered. In God's presence things happened that were unexplainable. Believe me, I've tried. Spending time alone with Him began to fix things. I started to heal in areas I never even knew I hurt.

As I sat down to dinner one evening, I began to cry. Whenever the Holy Spirit grabbed my heart I never knew what to expect. Having begun to go through a series of supernatural heart transplants, I went from blessing to blessing. I remembered on that day, in particular, Emahn was still a baby in her highchair. Derrick just sat there and looked at me. After he asked me several times what was wrong, I finally told him. At first I didn't answer because I didn't know. Then, it registered in my mind what the problem was.

I'd received a phone call that day from my maternal grandmother telling me she had decided not to visit for the holidays. I felt so much like a baby, because I could not stop crying. I looked up at Derrick and said, "They've never said they're proud of me." Then, I exhaled. The tears dried up and it was over; that was it. After all that time, I guessed I just had to get that out.

No one, who *really* mattered, had ever told me they were proud of me. Not for my high school graduation with honors and scholarships; not even for my college graduation with job offers; even still, not with the success of my career and accomplishments, or the success of my marriage and family—*nothing*. I realized then all I had ever been working towards in my life was the satisfaction of pleasing others. In my mind it had never come, because my ears had yet to hear any praise.

Well, in His presence I learned that God is not only pleased with me, but delights in me as well. I had waited twenty plus years to receive verbal validation and approval, but God alone declared me free in one day. Free from other's expectations, as well as self-gratification. I was determined then to only please Him because, even when I fell short, He still picked me up and held me close. He still loved me and stretched out His arms to say, "Behold, I have set the land before you. Now, get up, dust yourself off, and wait for Me to give it to you. If you'd just wait for Me to lead you, you wouldn't fall as much, and especially not as hard."

Snapping back into reality, I began to get ready for my trip to Chicago. For some reason, the night before I was in a spiritual funk. Emahn and I were home alone, and I just felt the need to call someone. On whom could I call who would not think I was crazy, though?

Several weeks earlier, I was at a local café with some of my girlfriends at our monthly book club meeting. I was running behind, so when I entered the establishment they were talking to a local author who was originally from Chicago. Having been brought up to speed and hearing that piece of information, I immediately began to share my latest testimony about discovering Miss Amanda Smith. Since the author was from Chicago, I asked him if he had ever heard of her out of curiosity. He gave me my first yes, but quickly admitted he didn't know very much about her.

As we all continued to chat, the author sat there and said, "My mother goes through stuff like that. She has these visions, and she'll be talking and go into a whole other language." I laughed, because I knew he was referring to speaking in Tongue. Then he continued with, "Let me give you her number, and maybe when you get to Chicago she can help you with something."

I held on to her number for a while and decided to call her the week prior to leaving. I just wanted to touch bases with her in case I did need some assistance. At first, I wasn't so sure about calling her because I didn't want to say what I was thinking which was, "I met your son in a local bookstore and he gave me your number." *How crazy does that sound?* Fortunately, for me, she wasn't home and I was able to leave a voice message.

In my spirit, I felt I should call this woman again. I contemplated and went back and forth for about ten minutes, and then I finally decided to follow my gut instinct and just did it. The conviction in my stomach would not stop, so I felt I should just call her and get it over with. When she answered the phone, I went on to introduce myself and told her how I'd gotten her number. I continued with, "Well, I'm headed to Chicago tomorrow. I don't know why. I'm just coming." She stopped me mid-sentence in one of those "concerned mama" tones that asked, "You don't know why you're coming to Chicago? You're just coming?" So, I laughed and said, "Let me start from the beginning."

Once I filled her in she immediately said, "Let me pray for you." Now, that was the reason I'd called her in the first place. How would she take the fact that I felt the need for someone to pray for me and ended up calling her in Chicago was my question, but man did that woman pray! She went into a moment of Praise and Worship, and took just as long to simmer down as she had getting wound up. Of course, I didn't mind because I understood.

As we talked some more she said, "You remember the will of God will never take you where the grace of God can't keep you." *See*, that's what I needed. All I knew was that I was on a spiritual journey, and I was content in knowing that the will of God would not lead me anywhere the grace of God could not keep me. She then said, "The spirit of the Lord is here. I know when He's present, and I know He's here." I didn't even question it, because that's how I am. She later said in a calmer tone, "I thank you for calling me, and I'm glad I picked up. I will thank my son for giving my number out this time." After that, she told me she was glad to have been spiritually connected to me and that God had prompted me to call her, and I'd obeyed.

As she spoke, I listened to her talk about Paul and how the Spirit, or his anointing, was transferred to a rag or cloth he'd once possessed. She told me, "I don't know why you're coming either, but I can tell you that you're connected to somebody and you're going to the South side; even if it's nothing more than to go so that there can be a transferring of the Spirit." Now, this was getting deep. I then expressed I had some fear and she said, "You are a child of God, directed by God, and there is no room for the devil. He has no dominion over you."

I thanked her greatly as we ended our conversation, and hung the telephone up. I repeated to myself a good ten times, "I am a child of God, directed by God, and there is no room for the devil. He has no dominion over me." After that, every bit of negative energy left me. I continued to wash dishes, and then I heard Emahn say, "You got to go," with such power for a 3-year-old.

I remembered teaching her that when she feels afraid to say, "Oh, no! Mr. Devil, you've got to go." In hindsight, I never should have taught her to respect him by saying, "Mr. Devil," because he sure won't be so courteous to her. Emahn had no idea who I was talking to or about when I told her that, or at least that's what I'd assumed. She had been playing in her room and came out to enter the den. That's when I heard her say, "You got to go." She had enough sense herself not to address the devil as "Mister." We were the only two home at that time, so I believe on her way past me in the kitchen she saw, heard, or felt something just like I had. Whatever it was, it left.

The next morning, while riding to the airport, there was a sermon playing of a local bishop on one of the Gospel radio stations. Why did he say, "The next step you make will take you completely out of your element, circumstance, environment… right into your destiny?" My next step would be arriving at DFW Airport and getting on an airplane. How "ironic" was that?

At the airport I began to pray for a section of seats to myself, because I wanted to be seated alone. I simply wanted to pray, study, and meditate, but I needed to relax. When I boarded the plane peacefully, I thanked the Lord no one else had joined me in my section. He sure took care of that one; must've known I had plenty to talk about. As I prepared to go over my devotion, I reminded myself that these next steps would literally launch me into my destiny.

Upon my arrival in Chicago, I wrote down all the things I felt I should do like visit Harold Washington Library, the city records building, the gravesite of Miss Amanda Smith, etc. I also made a few phone calls to Quinn Chapel AME Church and other establishments mentioned in her autobiography for any information pertaining to what I was looking for. The problem was: *I didn't exactly know what I was looking for.*

I was in Chicago from February 19th-24th of 2003. During those days, I researched, researched some more, and prayed. I had to learn what I could about Miss Amanda... learn what I could about the orphanage... and learn what I needed to do in order to foster/adopt a child when I returned home. I was able to spend some time with a few old high school and college friends, but this trip was clearly about business. What would have been Miss Smith's 166th birthday had just passed, and the 88th anniversary of her death was quickly approaching. *Why would God send me here now?* I wondered.

As I continued to go through my To Do List, I constantly ran into dead ends. Most of the years I needed in Chicago history were burned, lost, or just missing. Everything was gone; I could find nothing. I was looking for something *big*; something that would tell me all that I was experiencing was really happening. I was so frustrated that there was no information on this woman who had an international ministry and ran the state of Illinois' only orphanage for African-Americans during her time... a woman whom the Chicago Defender hailed as "the greatest woman that this race has ever given to the world" at the time of her death in 1915.

Later, I decided to return to another library in order to look for more newspaper archives. When I asked an older Caucasian woman for assistance with the years in question, I was told all of the information on a Colored would have been in the *Chicago Defender*. *A Colored?* I'm sure what I was thinking showed all over my face. I wanted to say, "*She* was Colored *then*, but *we's* African-American *now*." I then took note of the date to confirm that I had indeed made the trip in 2003.

Anyhow, the *Chicago Defender's* archives did not go back farther than the 1980's at that time. My search was a lost hope; although, I did eventually stumble upon one thing. It was Miss Smith's actual census record, dated 1890. I left with a photocopy of a document where she acknowledged the orphanage, but my search ended there. I could not believe all of the information regarding it burned with the building. I started to feel like my efforts were hopeless and decided to stop. I couldn't even find any information on her only surviving child, a daughter named Mazie D. Smith.

Before I left Chicago, I decided—in spite of everything—the trip was still worth a visit to the cemetery. Continuing to make my way through Miss Smith's autobiography, I discovered from Quinn Chapel AME (the oldest African-American church in Chicago) where she was a member that Miss Smith was buried at Washington Memory Gardens Cemetery in Homewood, Illinois. Located on Chicago's south side, this was exactly where I was told I would be going by the lady who prayed for me over the phone just a day or so earlier. Having later phoned the cemetery, they faxed over a map of their burial grounds with a circle around Miss Smith's exact grave marker. When I say that's *all* the information they gave me, I mean that's all they gave me—no names, no addresses, no relatives to trace, no nothing.

Sunday, after accompanying my friends to their church, they took me to visit the site. *Man*! The sense of power that came over me! I marveled at the beautiful bronze and gold grave marker that was placed on her headstone by the House of Representatives of the State of Illinois, of Chicago, on April 23, 1991. I took in every word as I read: Amanda Berry Smith 1837 – 1915 World Renowned Methodist, African-American Evangelist and Missionary. It *was* possible. *That* was the something big I'd sought.

There I was, standing at the gravesite of this woman, feeling as if God wanted me to find something, but what? I couldn't even explain how or why this all happened in the natural, but in my spirit I felt a small, yet significant connection. Feeling somewhat overwhelmed, I also felt a huge loss as I wept softly like I had known this woman; like she was part of me. What was God trying to tell me? What did He want me to see and/or do pertaining to Miss Smith?

There was definitely a spirit of peace when we left and later headed to O'Hare International Airport. I had made the journey, although I questioned where it would lead me. As my mind tried to figure out what all of this meant, the Spirit of the Lord was with me. However, God reminded me that His ways are not my ways, nor are His thoughts my thoughts (see Isaiah 55:9). All that He is was greater than I could ever imagine. So, relieved in knowing that I was definitely walking in my purpose, when I settled on the plane to return home I proclaimed nothing would happen to me (like dying in a plane crash) until my destiny is fulfilled.

HEED THE VOICE

11 Having grasped that God is definitely in control of my very being, I decided to study the eleventh chapter of Romans. Because God had ignited in me a passion to work *in Him*, I was determined to follow through until my destiny is fulfilled. I was so on fire that I began asking people are they saved. If they answered yes, then I immediately asked how they knew. One of the persons I called on the phone myself, but two others called me, so I brought it up.

Me starting a conversation about salvation rarely ever happened. I was full of joy because one person prayed the Sinner's Prayer. I told him if he meant it, the key word being *meant*, this was the assurance of his salvation if anyone should ask and gave him scriptural references like Romans 10:9 which says, *"That if you confess with your mouth the Lord Jesus and believe in your heart that God raised Him from the dead, you will be saved."*

Later, I was blamed by his ex-girlfriend for the demise of their relationship. I wanted to call her crazy, but understood her pain and confusion. All-in-all, I told her that if the man had ended the relationship because he was sincere in his prayer and being with her didn't glorify Christ, she should be glad he was now saved and seeking to grow. She didn't quite get it, because she'd been an immature Christian for so long their carnal actions were normal to her. Eventually, after much intercession on behalf of myself and others, she came around.

As I shared the events of that initial day with Derrick, he asked an interesting question. The issue was if a person does not confess their sins, are they saved? I thought about that for a minute and, based on my experience and present revelation, I answered yes. At the age of five, I had confessed with my mouth the Lord Jesus and believed in my heart God raised Him from the dead. According to scripture, that was all I needed to do in order to be saved. Nowhere in there did it say confess your sins. It said confess Jesus is Lord. That's when it dawned on me how so many people simply get saved *by* Jesus, but not sold-out *to* Jesus.

The Bible tells us in the previously referenced scripture we are to confess with our mouths that Jesus *is* Lord (Savior of all) in order to be saved. Most of us believe that; however, we are to *make* Jesus Lord (Savior of our own personal lives) in order to be sanctified. This is where most of us drew the line and continued to struggle: failure to render, as in *surrender* (give up) control.

Salvation, in my mind, was Jesus dying for me and my *acceptance* of it enough to *believe He arose*. Sanctification was totally different, though. It was my dying for Jesus and *appreciating* it enough to *arise in Him*. It was the confessing of sins, the repenting of a heavy heart, *and* the sincere attempt at growing in Christ and living holy.

I didn't truly repent of my sins until the age of twenty-five. Before then I had been confessing them, but would turn around and do the same thing all over again. It was as if I lived to sin. Whether I planned to or not, I just allowed a lot of stupid stuff to happen. Jesus had a hold on me, but I *hardly* had Him.

It was on the night when I gave in to the conviction of the Holy Spirit stirring inside of me, after my date from hell, that true repentance took place. That was when I made Jesus Lord of my life and gave Him complete control. I was saved at five because I believed, but I was sanctified at twenty-five when I gave up.

Truthfully, looking back on that night, I honestly believe I dined with the devil. That date was the strangest I'd ever been on, and that guy was *scary*. We met once, dined once, and that was all I needed to determine something just wasn't right with him *or me*. Seriously, he reminded me of a black Al Pacino in the movie "The Devil's Advocate."

So, to answer Derrick's question, in my opinion and according to Romans 10:9, yes you could be saved and not confess your sins. However, based on personal experience, you could not be unrepentant of your sins and be sanctified or expect to mature spiritually. That's because sanctification is a cleansing process, and in order to be cleaned you had to first get it out by way of confession.

Upon our salvation, *each of us* (everyone who has believed in their hearts that God raised Jesus from the dead and confessed with their mouths He is Lord) received the gift of the Holy Spirit, who is our Comforter. Now, that didn't mean we all started speaking in Tongue and jumping pews, but that each of us knew Light from Darkness, which went deeper than knowing right from wrong.

For me, right from wrong was natural. Light from Darkness, on the other hand, was *super*-natural. It was a greater knowledge of good versus evil. Natural said, "2 + 2 = 4 is right," but the equation itself is neither good nor bad. On the flip-side of that problem however, super-natural said, "Alcoholism is an evil spirit," which clearly separates Light from Darkness, as well as good from bad. Natural was day-by-day *reality*, but super-natural was divine *revelation*.

At that point, I remembered how the choices I had made to live life as a sinner, as opposed to a saint, contributed to most of the drama I experienced when I was an immature Christian. I had confessed with my mouth Jesus is Lord, but I professed with my actions He was not *my* personal Savior. Reality said, "Girl, you're saved, but Revelation questioned, "Girl, are you safe?"

The moment I made Jesus *my* personal Lord, the Holy Spirit shifted from an afterthought to a priority and took up permanent leadership status. That's when I knew I had been nowhere *near* safe! As long as I was in the driver seat I had no clue where I was going, what I was doing, or what was lurking on the road ahead. But, when I allowed the Spirit to take total control, all I had to do was buckle up and let Him drive. I could not have been safer then!

The difference between Jesus being in the driver's seat and me being in the driver's seat quickly started to show. I got out of bed daily with the intention of living a righteous life. I knew from the jump I had immediately been set free from a number of things that had me bound when I repented. Some things I just knew I wasn't going to do anymore, because the desire was gone *instantly*. Just like that, He washed them away! Now, I didn't mature overnight, but I did start to do things differently. Instead of simply giving into the remaining temptations, I struggled.

I use the word "struggle" loosely, because I also learned that to struggle is to say I'm not doing it and to actually turn and walk away, only to find yourself fallen in the midst of turning away. To not struggle, or to run to the temptation (which isn't even a temptation but an addiction if it's that bad) is giving in. That's why it bothered me that others got up daily to purposely do the same thing day in and day out to their own glory and satisfaction. It was very different for me to get out of bed in the morning praying, "Lord, help me to do everything I need to do today, and on time," versus getting out of bed and saying, "Lord, I'll start when I start." One clearly acknowledged dependence on Christ with an attempt to do better, while the other clearly acknowledges dependence on self with an attitude to remain the same.

Thinking about this more seriously, I realized it wasn't even that those who are sanctified think they are better than everyone else, which I had often heard. They were just determined to be different *from* everyone else, or at least I was. After that assessment, I made a conscious decision to strive for holiness. Since God had brought me into that truth *for myself*, to live any other way was simply unacceptable. After God gave me divine revelation of my own, there was not an excuse in the world that would suffice my continuing in a lifestyle of sin.

1 John 3:6 says, *"No one who lives in Him keeps on sinning. No one who continues to sin has either seen Him or known Him."* I knew I had seen Him when I had my out-of-body experience on the night of my rebirth. I was standing next to Him, looking at myself. I was later informed that was my "dying to the flesh" moment. I *had* been reborn! I was living and breathing Galatians 2:20-21… I don't live, but the Spirit of Christ lives *in me*.

Ever since then I had known Christ and strived daily to surrender my will to His. From that moment, I willfully chose not to be comfortable in making sin a normal part of my daily routine, *regardless of what was taking place around me*. From time-to-time I may slip, but if every time you see me I'm slipping, then that would prove something is wrong with my testimony.

Instead of testifying, I'd be just a lying!

With life's ups and downs, highs, and lows, I continued to have issues with my patience. These little "attacks" usually came around the beginning of the month. It was no mystery why. Bills were due and monies were short. God had already told me to wait; I only wondered how long. On this particular night, despite our budget, I wanted Chinese food. Eating usually put me in a better mood, so we drove to a local restaurant. As I got out of the car, I said, "Lord, if only You would send me some assurance."

After we had eaten our dinner and the check came, Derrick paid the bill and we left. I held on to our carry-out bags, and on the ride home from the restaurant mentioned how funny it would be if God spoke to my patience issue through the cookie that was in my bag. I was thinking that is so *not* like Him. So, it would really have to be an act of God for something in that cookie to touch me. Normally, I didn't even get into that type of stuff because to do so is a form of witchcraft, although I always eat my cookies simply because I like them.

Now, any other time, I would have pulled that little piece of white paper out and placed it on the table. On this night, as we drove into the garage, I opened the wrapper, pulled it out, and read it—probably because we were still in the car. Had we been in the house already or still at the restaurant, I would have trashed it. At any rate, when I read the paper I started dancing and screaming. *I kid you, not.* It read: He who has not tasted the bitter does not understand the sweet. How wild was that?

Yes, I know someone had preprinted millions of those things but, to me, once again God had met me right where I was... in the valley, waiting for a mountain to appear. He was saying had we not gone through the harshness of the desert, we wouldn't be able to appreciate the serenity of the field coming over the horizon. That was all I needed. It was on the way! That experience brought truth to Matthew 7:7 which says, "Ask and it shall be given, seek and ye shall find, knock and it shall be opened unto you."

The very next day I was talking with and listening to the Lord when He answered an old question. I had to be careful though, because sometimes He just said stuff and I had to remember what it pertained to. Whenever the Spirit spoke, It hardly picked up where we left off. Each time it was something different. On that day I received the words, "Just because some call me Prophet doesn't mean my Father didn't make me Messiah."

When that thought registered, I remembered a conversation I'd had with my Father a long while before about interpretations. It had been at least two years prior. God normally responded to me faster than that, but I believe He took His time in responding because I felt that our chat about interpretations wasn't of any grave concern. However, God knew the answer to that particular topic of discussion would be for the book, so He answered when He knew I'd need it most. I remembered the discussion like it was just yesterday. I was talking to God about other people's interpretations one day after guests showed up at our house once we had eaten dinner.

On that particular night, I prepared tuna casserole as the main dish. As our guests entered, some of them opted to pass through the kitchen, as opposed to staying in the main hallway area on their way into the family room. Then, they began to joke about me *trying* to make Chicken Tetrazzini. Although I knew what I had made, I didn't say anything and chalked it up to their ignorance.

Well, during the group's latter conversation, someone mentioned that a very prominent, female, Gospel artist had crossed over. I heard someone say, "She sings other music now." Then I heard, "She sure does," in the background. I just hushed up because for one, I refuse to argue; and two, it annoys me when people are adamant about something they know nothing about. I knew the song they were referring to and had also heard the singer interview on one of the local Gospel stations with my own two ears, in her own words, and say she doesn't write secular music because she is a Gospel singer. Suddenly, it made sense.

Looking back, God was using both of those scenarios to tell me it didn't matter what people's perceptions were. Just like I knew I'd made tuna casserole and that singer knew she sang Gospel, certainly Jesus knew He was the Messiah. Knowing that, He continued in His God-given purpose and each of us is expected to do the same, despite nay-sayers.

As time progressed, it was hard to believe only months had passed. It was now May of 2003, and Derrick and I were informed that we were three months pregnant with our second child. Having started thinking about having another baby after our meeting with Pastor Bailey, I didn't start praying for another one until Emahn turned two. It was now a year later and she was three. Before we'd conceived, I would pray to God for Him to specifically allow conception when I was able to handle it mentally, emotionally, physically, and financially. Even though I had set aside the information I'd found earlier regarding the Department of Family and Protective Services, I still hadn't released the idea of foster parenting. Still, I hadn't expected to get pregnant the night I returned from Chicago either. Surely, God couldn't possibly be getting my hopes up to adopt, and then let me give birth. But, I was sure He was laughing… *hysterically!*

In the months prior to finding out our family was expanding, I had been asked to join a second book club—this one just for wives. I graciously accepted and purchased my copy of the first book. It was *The Power of the Praying Wife* by Stormy O'Martian. The group decided we'd read the first chapter of the book, then come together to discuss its contents in one month. Well, the most interesting thing happened when we got together a month later. One of the ladies announced she was pregnant, a second announced she might be, and another laughed because she couldn't be.

When we met the next time, in order to discuss chapter two, the second lady confirmed that she was indeed pregnant and would be joining the first, but so did a third and a fourth... me. We never figured out what happened, because nowhere in that book was there a prayer for a baby. As a group, we never finished reading it either.

That was our last meeting and for good reason. Four out of five members were pregnant. The second lady later admitted that as soon as she suspected her pregnancy, she prayed to not be pregnant alone. I then questioned what kind of girlfriends I have. I'd never prayed for anyone to get pregnant without them asking me to. *What kind of mess is that?* I figured God must've been having Himself a good ol' knee-slappin' laugh.

Later on, only two days after finding out we were expecting, Derrick received a phone call regarding a job offer. It was nowhere near what he was used to, but it was enough to help us while he continued to look for something else. This was definitely beginning to look like our Exodus. We both already knew God as the God of wrath, but we had to come to know Him as a loving God: the God of provision.

During this entire process of lawsuits, lay-offs, and simply struggling, I realized I also had an issue with trust. God had already exposed my faith and patience issues earlier, and now I was graduating. I had worked from the time I was sixteen years old until I left Corporate America to stay home with Emahn. At that time, I didn't know the Lord as Jehovah-Jireh, My

Provider. I knew I worked, and every two weeks *I* received a paycheck. Since, at that time, there was no paycheck to earn anymore, the reality sank in that we are nothing in and of ourselves. It was then that I began to reflect over my professional career.

When I became a stay-at-home mom with Emahn, I had decided that once she got older I would try various things. I even became involved with multi-level marketing. Most of the things I found to be good opportunities, just not good for me. I then recalled a message I had once heard a local minister preach where he said your success is not contingent upon what others do, and that what you do should come naturally *to you. Ding, ding! That was it!*

Writing had always come easily and effortlessly to me, most of my life. All I needed was a piece of paper, not even an entire notebook, and something to write with. Once in high school, during my senior year, one of my English teachers told me I had the best paper in the entire class. It was a compare and contrast essay on my two twin friends. The teacher said that not only was my essay the best, but it was also the hardest type to write. I kept that paper for a long while afterwards, because there was a perfect score of 100 percent on it. Reflecting on that incident, I knew I had a natural ability to write, but I was starting to believe I also had a super-natural ability to pen a story. I definitely had a passion for it!

It was upon realizing that writing is "the thing" which comes naturally to me and is not contingent upon what others do or don't that I began to really focus on it as a career and not just a pastime. I was convinced that God was definitely in on this some time ago, but I believe it sank in when the other book titles and overviews began to come. I asked God to bless me with a successful writing career for my upcoming 30th birthday. Up until that this time I would say I was a writer, but now I had started to speak that I'm an author. It was as if I was getting the clarity I'd been seeking, as well as God giving me just the right confirmations, at just the right times. For instance, later I had another dream.

This particular one involved another attack from a family member over something I'd said to them regarding scripture. I had no idea why these dreams kept coming up, but trusted God would eventually shed some light on it for me. When I awoke from that dream, I had another, more pleasant one that tied into the first.

Now in the initial dream, one of my grandmothers told one of my younger cousins to do something that was blatantly wrong. I don't remember what, but I do recall not being able to sit idle and do or say nothing about it. So, I stood up and told the child not to do what she was just instructed to do. I informed her to listen to me (*which was the first indication that I was dreaming*). Well, my grandmother pulled a knife on me as I was telling them what thus said the Lord regarding the matter, and then I heard someone say something about me always having something "holy" to say. My feelings were hurt. I awoke from that dream during the middle of the night with uneasiness. This was not the first dream I'd had where my grandmother had attacked me.

In the second dream, I was taking some type of writing course. I saw myself in a classroom, sitting behind a desk, and all I remember were two things. First, the instructor said, "Let your writing be the conviction," and second, that the statement was so profound I wanted to journal it even in my dream.

The next morning I told Derrick I wasn't sure what to make of it. He simply said, "Let your writing be the conviction." I asked him if He thought God was telling me to hush up and write, or to stop preaching and start pushing pens, in a sense. He *had* to be saying something with my family members always attacking me in my sleep. Derrick said he didn't know, but told me I needed to heed the voice.

The Clock Stopped Ticking

12 After hearing God clearly when He told me to let my writing be the conviction, I took it upon myself to follow Derrick's advice and heeded the voice. At least I had an answer concerning whether my writing was blessed and had been anointed. If it meant enough for God to give me direction pertaining to it in the midst of sleeping, then He obviously meant what He'd said and also had plans to bring it about.

I continued to read the Amanda Berry Smith autobiography and she mentioned several times that she faced discrimination as a female minister. I had begun to pray over this as well, because of some of the same issues regarding female ministers today. God chose to answer this particular question on Resurrection Sunday of 2003 while back at home. As I sat in church the words "Why seek ye the living amongst the dead?" resounded in my ears. Oddly enough, the minister wasn't even preaching on that particular text, so I zeroed in on the voice inside of me.

Prior to this experience, I always reverted back to

Romans 8:30 where God says, *"I've predestined you; therefore I've called you."* I never really went into any specifics concerning my call, because I knew I was called *by God.* The problem I had with other people was that most of them still believed God didn't call women to minister which contradicts: *"And afterward, I will pour out my Spirit on all people. Your sons and your daughters will prophesy, your old men will dream dreams, your young men will see visions."* (Joel 2:28) I felt that if God would cause a donkey to talk, then surely He could use me (see Numbers 22:30). Besides, He had already said that just as Jesus knew He had created Him to be the Messiah, I had the same assurance God had called me to be Voice of Power. So, having prayed about it myself, God saw fit to answer.

While visiting another church back home on that Easter Sunday morning, I flipped through the various scriptures regarding "Seek ye the living amongst the dead." I found a couple of passages where women received a message from on high and were told "Go and tell the men." The one that stood out the most was the following: *"So the women hurried away from the tomb, afraid yet filled with joy, and ran to tell his disciples. Suddenly Jesus met them. "Greetings," he said. They came to him, clasped his feet and worshiped him. Then Jesus said to them, "Do not be afraid. Go and tell my brothers to go to Galilee; there they will see me."* (Matthew 28:8-10) *"Then the eleven disciples went to Galilee, to the mountain where Jesus had told them to go. When they saw him, they worshipped him; but some doubted."* (Matthew 28:16-17) Now, whose fault was it that "some" did not believe? *Not the women's, for sure.*

The fact that the disciples did not believe Jesus had sent the women carrying *His Word* nonetheless, did not negate the fact that He had. It was all a matter of personal perception. At that point, I could not wait to get out of church. I grinned from cheek-to-cheek and I had my own Resurrection Service, right there, all by myself.

When we made it back to the house, as usual, Derrick asked me what I had gotten out of the message. I shared what I'd learned was that Mary and 'nem (yes, I said it) had delivered the very *first* Resurrection message. I guess he wondered what sermon I had been listening to. I then told him, from the beginning, what had taken place with the "Why seek ye the living amongst the dead?"

Shortly afterwards, Derrick replied in response to his original question regarding what I'd gotten out of that day's sermon. He said, "Wait a minute. Weren't these same men who Jesus told the women to go and tell men of authority and leadership?" I smiled, because my husband knows me. He was reading my thoughts, and this was about to get deep. "Yes!" I exclaimed. "These men were apostles who walked with the Lord and knew Him. They heard Him say He'd return, got the message He had, and didn't receive it because a *woman* of God, as opposed to a *man* of God, had delivered it." My husband sat up, then looked at me and said, "Looks like you had a better service than the rest of us." I sure had, because God had come through *again!*

As I continued to read Miss Smith's autobiography, she went in depth about her ministry and her salvation and sanctification experiences. She highlighted what I know to be true, which is that some people don't understand the difference, while others don't believe there is one. She then gave an account of a minister who was in one of her camp meetings one evening. This experience was similar to my own rebirth, except my habits were different.

In her autobiography, Miss Smith explained the following incident of Bro. Sharper, a local preacher: *"Sister Smith, I want to tell what the Lord has done for me. I have had an awful struggle for days over this* question [of sanctification]. I thought I would stay away from the meetings, but that didn't help me. And you know the Sunday you were around to my house, and caught me with the Bible and my pipe?"

"Yes," I said.

"Well, there was where I stuck because I thought if I did everything else alright, the Lord would not require me to give up my pipe. No, I did not know it was such an idol until I tried to give it up. Oh! How it held me. You know I love my wife and child, but I felt I could give up either of them easier than I could give up my pipe. I would smoke the last thing before I went to bed, and the first thing in the morning; and sometimes I would get up two or three times in the night to have a smoke, and if there was not a match, or fire, in the house to light my pipe, I would walk a mile to get it."

"The other night I lay down and fell into a doze of sleep, and I dreamed I saw a great host marching. They were divided into two companies. Oh! Such a singing I never heard. It was wonderful! The sanctified host was ahead, and out-sang the justified host. As they marched, they sang. I stood and looked at them. I said, "Well, I will join the justified company. They will get in too, just as well as the others." So I joined in the song with them, for I wanted them to keep up with the host ahead. Oh! How I sang with all my might, but the sanctified host seemed to out-sang us."

"In our march, we came to a culvert in the road, and I thought, 'I will watch and see how they get through there.' I saw when they got up to it, they all, with one accord, bowed low, and went through, and struck up their song on the other side. And when the justified company came up to the culvert, they stopped, and there seemed to be quite a contention about how to get through. But not one of them stooped. After a while they divided, and walked around on either side, and went on.

When I came up to it I started to go round, first on the right; but a voice confronted me and said, 'but you must go through.' Then I made an effort to go to the left; and again a voice said, 'but you must go through,' so I tried the third time, and again the same words, 'but you must go through.' And glory to God, the tobacco is gone, and I have got through!"

I could almost shout with him when I read that. It's because I knew what it felt like to go through! That's what had happened when I rededicated my life to Christ and had my out-of-body experience back in April of 1998. I had gone through. I was then reminded that Luke 13:24 (KJV) says, *"Strive to enter in at the strait gate: for many, I say unto you, will seek to enter in, and shall not be able."*

Later that week, I had another dream which terrified me. My dreams bounced back and forth from being scared by demons to being attacked by family members. Some of the thoughts I dismissed, because there was no way they could have ever been of God. In some of them I just knew the devil was out to get me. I learned that because He knows he can never overcome me in my consciousness, he began to torture me in my subconscious. The prophetess was right. I had reached a level where I had no fear of the devil at all (when I was awake). However, in my dreams he was wearing me out.

On many nights, I could not bring myself to sleep. And, on many mornings I dreaded waking up. During the nights I actually slept, I tried to pay close attention to what the enemy was up to. Sometimes I couldn't tell if I was asleep or awake, for instance on the night of a storm.

First, I awoke to a loud thunder and asked Derrick to go and check on Emahn. I knew if she was awake, she was also afraid. Being that it was during the wee hours of the morning, he did and something must have been up. He stayed long enough to fall asleep. Tune in for the rest.

I doze off and recall awaking to another loud, thunderous sound. I open my eyes, and I know I see a shadow of something move in the house, right outside of our slightly opened bedroom door.

Unaware that I am dreaming, I then see Derrick sprint into the bedroom and sit on his side of the bed. He is panting and shaking, and I know if he is terrified, then I have good reason to be alarmed. I look at him, and when he turns to look at me he is not my husband. I know that.

As I reach to turn on the lamp, he grabs my hand and we begin to wrestle in bed. He then starts kissing me vigorously and gropes me in a frenzy. As I struggle to get free, so I can turn on the lamp, I catch a glimpse of him and his eyes are huge. His face is disfigured and I am scared. I know that whatever I have seen run through the house isn't good and has taken over my husband, because when he sat down on the bed his body jerked in response to something. I try to pray, but it won't let me. Every time I open my mouth to pray or try to praise the Lord, anything to usher the Holy Spirit into the room, it puts its mouth over mine while holding me in an attempt to silence me—just like I had done Quad when she was praying for me in the other dream.

Well, having watched plenty of Christian television, even in my sub-conscious I recall hearing the testimony of a man who said he was lying in the hospital unable to speak. He said he wanted to praise God and pray, but was unable to because of his condition. He then said, as he lay on his back, he remembered that he could pray in Tongue under his breath. I wonder why am I thinking about this in the midst of a dream and don't know, but it is timely. I begin to pray and praise the Lord under my breath. Believing that it will work, I am able to get a hand free and click the lamp switch on. As this thing looks me dead in my eyes, I look at it and say out loud, "I *rebuke you in the name of Jesus!" I keep saying it until something snaps and my husband comes back. He then just lays limp in bed.*

I then heard a third loud, roaring thunder sound and awoke again. I reached for Derrick, but he wasn't there. He was still asleep in Emahn's bedroom from before the dream started. I flipped the light switch on and ran to get him. All I knew was the house was in the same setting as it was when all of that had just taken place in the dream. There was thunder, it was dark, and I was in bed alone. I was not about to lie there until I saw a shadow of something outside my bedroom or for Derrick to come sprinting in.

I didn't know if God was preparing me for something or not, but I went and got them both. I woke Derrick up and told him to come back to bed, and to bring Emahn with him. That next night before we prayed, I told him I wanted another house. I was serious, too. Because of our floor plan, I was ready to move so that my babies would be closer to me.

Not really thinking about any of that when the house was built, it dawned on me then that may have been the reason Emahn would often come running into our bedroom on some nights. There were nights when she slept until sunrise and would walk into our bedroom to say she was hungry. Then, there were other times when she literally ran in during the wee hours of the morning. I would always make her go back to her own bed, thinking she was just trying to be a baby. After that incident, I didn't do it anymore. As a matter-of-fact, I started praying over our house, specifically in Emahn's bedroom, nightly. I figured if I saw a shadow, then she could've seen an imp or something. The last thing I needed was the devil messing with my child.

After that bad dream with Quad, the one where the

demon was pacing at the foot of the bed, I was in the habit of falling asleep with the CD's playing. However, during the middle of the night they would often stop. So, by this time, I not only made sure the CD player was full, but that it was also on random repeat. I told you whether awake or asleep, someone was going to be calling on the name of Jesus in this house, and I meant that. *In fact, Christian music is the first thing we turn on when we leave the house.*

It was later when I told Derrick about the dream and he said, "Shaundale, I don't think that one was about anything. That one could've just been the devil." Although I didn't dismiss it totally, I told him he might be right. I was considering the fact that nothing felt right in our own environment and his face was disfigured. I did know he wasn't my husband, though. Thinking back, I guess I felt like *"Oh no! Ain't no anti-Christ being conceived up'n here."* I prayed over my marriage bed, as well, that night. I took a stand and said, "Nothing unrighteous will be birthed in here! Not in this heart, not in this mind, not in this bed, not in this body, not in *this* temple!"

As I usually did after I had a dream—whether bad or good—I talked to God about it. Sometimes then, sometimes I waited. He often answered through scripture or by dropping His response into my spirit. And, this was no different. I felt He was saying that sometimes the devil doesn't have to take anything from us because, oftentimes, we give to him freely. As I thought back over my previous "I'm living for Jesus *for real* days," I realized He was right.

There were many instances in my life when sin was so familiar to me, I unknowingly allowed the devil to literally climb into bed with me, lay-up, and have his way—to put it bluntly. Every time I gave in to whatever had been hindering my seeking Jesus, or growing in Him, the devil took full advantage. Whether it was one too many drinks, an overnight guest, or simply gossiping at work, every time I gave in, he held his hand out. It was no secret he came to steal, kill, and destroy. By the same token, he stole our bodies, killed our souls, and destroyed our minds all in one shot. He did exactly what he came to do, which was to keep the sinner from getting saved, and to hinder the saint in being sanctified. That was it, *flat out*. The reason he'd fought me while trying to turn the lights on in the dream was because he knew I'd expose him and see him for what he is: a liar and a thief. That told me some of us need to simply reach for the Light; Jesus will shine all by Himself.

I remembered that the digital alarm clock remained on during the storm, even when all of the other power in the dream was out. Even though it was pitch black, the red numbers continued to change. It was weird because instead of them increasing for minutes, they decreased rapidly for seconds. That was because God was trying to show me time is running out. Either I was going to take a stand and fight back, or I was going to lie down, once more, and take it. I declared that nothing unholy would be birthed in me, and I meant it. I took a stand, but my heart went out to all of those who had not gotten it yet.

In this case, the evil spirit that took over my husband represented familiarity. It was comfortable enough to just walk in; however, what it didn't know was that the old me had already walked out. I was a new creation in Christ—uncomfortable enough to care who or what he pretended to be, and bold enough to take a stand against it.

What God was showing me is that some of us have at least one open door the enemy uses to dash in and out of our lives from time-to-time, from anger to adultery and then some. Then, for others of us, he's taken up permanent residence by way of a person, a passion, or a position. In the dream, my open door was exposed as fear. The enemy dashed in and tried to have his way, but I declared "not this time." James 4:7 references resisting the devil and he will flee from you. "Come near to God and He will come near to you." God was showing me that He's waiting to see who will gather up the strength *for a purpose* and say, "Not in here," allowing Him to close the doors, one at a time, before the clock stopped ticking.

Dwelling: The Testimony

Thou preparest a table before me in the presence of mine enemies; Thou anointest my head with oil; my cup runneth over. Surely goodness and mercy shall follow me all the days of my life; And I will dwell in the house of the Lord forever. (Psalm 23:5-6, KJV)

"Commit your way to the Lord; trust in him and he will do this: He will make your righteousness shine like the dawn, the justice of your cause like the noonday." Psalm 37:6

"Wait for the Lord and keep his way. He will exalt you to inherit the land; when the wicked are cut off, you will see it." Psalm 37:34

"Trust in the Lord and do good; dwell in the land and enjoy safe pasture." Psalm 37:3

"Delight yourself in the Lord and he will give you the desires of your heart." Psalm 37:4

"Be still before the Lord and wait patiently for him; do not fret when men succeed in their ways…" Psalm 37:7

"Taste and see that the Lord is good; blessed is the man who takes refuge in him." Psalm 34:8

"For the word of the Lord is right and true; he is faithful in all he does." Psalm 33:4

"He guides the humble in what is right and teaches them his way." Psalm 25:9

LET IT FLOW

13 Having been made aware that the clock is about to stop ticking for some, God continued to keep me up at night. He was talking to me which I didn't mind, because it didn't happen too often. When it did, I had grown accustomed to getting excited. I was like a little girl who waited patiently for her father to get home from work. I didn't know when God would come in, but believed He'd stop by my room once He did.

Still waiting for the Lord to answer previous questions, I wanted to know about my personal path. God had already shown me that at the age of twenty-five I had been baptized of the Spirit, or gotten what Miss Amanda Berry Smith referred to as "the blessing." It was what she'd told God to give her or kill her for. I thought, *as Christians we should all be so desperate to know Him.* You couldn't hunger or thirst after righteousness anymore than wanting to *die* for it. It was then I knew I wanted to do what God truly intended for me to. It was also then that I really focused in on all that could possibly lie ahead for me, as well.

In that, I realized what Miss Amanda was saying is

this: give me holiness or call me home. I believe she recognized, like me, that in her own strength she wasn't going to be able to walk in salvation alone, so if God didn't grant her *righteousness*, He may as well call her on [home] to Glory because she'd fall short every time. In essence, I believe she was saying don't leave me down here to keep messing up, to keep falling, to keep *intentionally* sinning. I need holiness to keep me walking upright! I'm tired of crawling back to the altar for forgiveness of this same 'ole *elementary* stuff. Yes, I'm saved. But, I want to be *filled*. Give me holiness to the maximum capacity or kill me, 'cause I can't do it by myself. I don't want to be short-changed either. I want it all… salvation, holiness, anointing, and my inheritance! All of it comes from You, so if You don't give it, I can't have it. And, if I can't have it, I won't make it. So, give it to me or kill me. Miss Amanda meant it and God did it! I meant it and He did it for me, too! So, guess what, if you mean it He'll do it for you as well.

    I awoke the following morning reflecting on the 23rd Psalm. It was a perfect way to begin the day. Knowing it could only get better, later Derrick, Emahn, and I headed to one of the local Christian television studios because my favorite female televangelist was in town again and was scheduled to be there.

    When we made it to the station that Sunday evening, the seats had already been filled. I was not hearing that. Derrick then asked me what I wanted to do. I guess he thought I was going to tell him "go home," but he didn't know I *really* wasn't hearing that. Not that I'm more special than anyone else, I just knew we had not driven all that way to have to go home. I know, I know, like everyone else had? Well, what some of those people didn't know is that when you're blessed and highly favored—not when you *act* like or *look* like, but when you really are—things have a supernatural way of "just happening."

Being in my "condition," I told Derrick I was going to the bathroom. At the top of the stairs where there was no one visible except Emahn and me, I confessed, "Now Lord, You're going to have to work a miracle for me. I did not ride all this way to get turned around." In my mind I thought, *I probably don't deserve one*, but with my mouth I said, "Now, I *know* I don't deserve a miracle, but I've grown to expect them." I wasn't arrogant; I was simply confident in His provision. I continued on to the bathroom and when we came back out and started down the stairs, Derrick was waiting for us. I was about to peek my head inside the doors when I noticed him ushering for us to come down.

Once at the bottom of the staircase, Derrick called me to the side and introduced me to the pastor of a local church. He said, "The pastor says he has reserved seating and we can be their guests." The biggest smile came over my face. I knew, but I just had to ask *how* that happened. Derrick said, "When you and Emahn walked away to go to the restroom, others began to leave. The man then came over and asked if I was waiting for someone."

Derrick told him that he was waiting for his family to return, and then we would decide what to do. That was when the pastor introduced himself and extended us an invitation to be seated as their guests. When the event hostess asked the pastor for a final count of visitors he included the three of us, and we were instructed to follow them in. We ended up front and center on the third row! I learned a valuable lesson that day. God *always* has the final say, and my soul waits only upon Him for my expectation (see Psalm 62:5).

Derrick, Emahn, and I had a blessed time in the studio audience for that taping. In fact, this was how timely God is. The first person to speak was exactly who He'd sent me there to hear. I didn't even know who she was, but she commented on women who are dependent on men, or something of that nature.

Derrick knew I had been having issues with being a "Domestic Engineer," probably since the second year of our marriage. Emahn had been born, and he was working while I was home. Although I did not complain as much back then as I had recently begun to, the internal issues held the same weight. The day it finally sank in that my problem was depending on a man, Emahn had already turned three years old.

The plan was for me to stay home with our daughter until her third birthday, but even the excitement of the *sound* of that had worn off when she turned 18-months-old. I could not believe I had actually agreed to forfeit my career for any length of time beyond the normal six weeks, and now I was long overdue for a return. To help make the transition smoother, when Emahn was two and a half years old I started out-sourcing myself with hopes of transitioning right back into the workplace six months later. God obviously had other plans, but I wasn't recognizing it at the time.

I also wasn't able to just bounce back into my career as easily as I had hoped, and Derrick had recently been laid off. Just getting over what I finally figured out was post-partum depression, this really wasn't good. One day I got so tired of looking at and getting bills, I started a fire in the kitchen sink and burned them all. I positioned the faucet (just in case I needed it), said a prayer pertaining to the financial burden we were under being lifted, and declared freedom from debt. Then, I struck a match. After that, I watched with *sheer joy* as every item turned to ash.

It had now been almost three years since I'd left my career, and I had begun to rant and rave about almost everything, especially finances. There were days when I thought Derrick obviously didn't know money is the number one cause of divorce. Then, I found something constructive to do and tried to figure out what my options were, at that point, other than seeking full-time work (which God seemed not to be honoring), divorce (which God would not honor under the circumstances), or worse... murder (which God could not honor at all). It amazed me how I'd gone from being adamant about not talking about divorce to aggressively thinking it over, only three years later.

I could not believe I had fulfilled my end of the bargain but wasn't being allowed to continue with my career. Then, I remembered I'd made that agreement with Derrick; although, God was the reason my plans had failed. *Hum, what then?* Would I continue to be angry with *my* lord, Derrick, (in biblical days women referred to their husbands as this), or would I get angry with *the* Lord, my Savior, Jesus Christ? Since neither was producing the desired results, neither was acceptable to me.

I grew so tired of people telling me Emahn wasn't ready for school yet and to stay home with her until she was five. *Five!* That was *really* not part of the deal. One, I started school at the age of three and anticipated her doing the same; and two, I didn't know if these people were paying attention or not, but my husband had been unemployed and I was doing part-time contract work. There were bills we were still trying to maintain and others that we needed to get caught up. *"Is anybody out there listening to me?"* was what I wondered.

Well, one day while having one of those "This is not what I bargained for" fits, I was walking through the house with a basket of folded laundry in my hands. I stopped dead in my tracks and said, "Lord, I don't understand." Emahn was napping, so I was able to carry on the conversation uninterrupted. Otherwise, she would ask, "Mama, wha' you praying about?" I prayed she keeps watching and listening.

On that particular day, I referenced the scripture regarding "leave and cleave." I said, "Lord, You are my Father, my Provider. When I married, I left my house and am now under the lordship of my husband. Derrick is my provider and head of household, yet You are my Provider still. How can that be?"

At the Christian network station, the lady who spoke before the minister we originally went to see said, "Some of you are looking to men for what you should be looking to God for," referencing women. There it was again. *How can that make any sense?* I thought. I mean, I wasn't single with a sugar-daddy or rich boyfriend. I was a wife with a husband who was *ordered* by God to provide for his house. How could he do that when doors had not been opened to him in the area of employment, *and* what was I supposed to be looking to Derrick for anyway? More importantly though, what was I supposed to be looking to God for? I tried to answer it myself, because I needed an answer before I had another bathtub breakdown.

The first three years of our marriage, Derrick and I concluded that if it had not been for legal problems we would not have had any issues at all. Now, I concluded if it wasn't for money, we'd have no issues still. The comment was once made that had we done what we were supposed to with the money in the beginning (which was presumably give the other person the half they sought), we would still have it. I refused to believe that and prayed about it. God responded by telling me that if this was about money, then we would not have been victorious. I figured He was saying if it *was* about money, then we would have more than likely lost the first time. I knew then this entire situation went much deeper than the natural eye could see, and there was a spiritual lesson to be learned in it all.

There were plenty of times I wanted to say I'd rather re-live the earlier years. I didn't, only because I feared sounding like the Israelites when they started whining about being brought out of Egypt to die in the middle of the wilderness (see Numbers 14:3-4). I felt it, but decided to just get on to Canaan as best we could *together*.

As I stated earlier, I tried to answer the question what was I supposed to be looking to Derrick for first, then God second. I had surmised that I was to look to my husband to provide my every natural need, and God to provide my every spiritual one. You know, Derrick was responsible for shelter, food, utilities, clothing, and so on... all the basic stuff. Then, God was responsible for giving revelation, guidance and direction, and answering tough questions (like this one). *Boy did that theory fall apart.*

"But my God shall supply all your need according to his riches in glory by Christ Jesus (Philippians 4:19, KJV)," I heard in my spirit. So there we went again, back to square one. "But God," I asked, "if You're going to supply all of my needs, then what is Derrick for, my wants?" *Wrong!*

"Delight thyself also in the LORD; and he shall give thee the desires of thine heart (Psalm 37:4, KJV)." Okay, so now we were getting *somewhere*, I thought. As long as I obeyed His Word, God would give me what I wanted that was in His will for my life. I had that part. So, I imagined if I wanted something outside of His will, then that's where my husband would step in. You know, if I wanted a trip to a Dallas Maverick's game knowing we couldn't afford it. *Booommm!* It was as though I could literally hear a door slam. I guessed I'd messed that one totally up. No, God didn't leave. He could never break a promise, which He made when He said, *"I will never leave nor forsake you,"* in Hebrews 13:5. He just pushed mute because, apparently, I wasn't saying anything.

In the midst of all that silence I got some of it, though. Don't talk about what you want; be content with what you have. It went back to that old song "Just Give Me Jesus" or Kirk Franklin's "Silver and Gold." My paraphrase was: If you have Me, you have everything, and if you have everything, then you need nothing. *Interesting huh?* It was to me, but that still didn't leave me with an answer to what was I to look to my husband for.

Truth be told, it was really starting to boil down to "What do I need him for?" That was also probably why God hadn't released me to work just yet. He knew, despite my spiritual growth, in the natural I was still so career-driven, headstrong, and independent that if He had blessed me with a job I would have more than likely signed the employment contract and a divorce petition on the *same* day.

To justify my thinking of "self-survival," I later noted that God said in Genesis 2:18, *"It is not good for man to be alone."* Call me crazy but I thought, *now, He really has something here.* God never said, "Woman, it's not good for you to be alone, so I'm going to create you a man." *No*, it was the other way around. He created us for man's sake, and gave us children for own. Did you see that? He gave man a jewel, and gave the jewel a polishing cloth!

Having grown up around lots of kids, I realized early in life that children will either keep you bright, or make you dull. However, I learned later in life that a man who finds a virtuous woman had acquired far more than rubies (see Proverbs 31:10). Although that seemed like cruel and unusual punishment to me, I did acknowledge that children are definitely will-breakers when we allow them to function in their God-given roles. I might have thought I wanted out, but the will of my child broke mine to keep me in. Then, there were other times when I wanted to go off, but the will of my child broke mine and helped me keep my tongue.

When I received that, I knew I was making progress. God may have given Eve to Adam, but He gave *them* children to hold *them* accountable *to themselves, to each other, and to Him.* That's why they're gifts. They're to be used as little mirrors that help us see ourselves as God sees us, and remind us to reflect Him when we otherwise choose to look a hot "sinful" mess.

After that, I reminded myself of Romans 8:28 which reads, *"And we know that in all things God works for the good of those who love him, who have been called according to his purpose."* That was also why I focused so heavily on finding my call and fulfilling my purpose in Him. I was determined to get to Canaan in order to make a better life for Derrick and me, but I was especially thinking about my children... the reflectors of my soul. They would either expose the Light in me, or they would expose the Darkness; however, it was up to me to decide. At that point, they would have taken in whatever I had portrayed most often. *Light yields Light and Darkness yields Darkness.*

Having come home from the television studio with plenty to think about, it was later that week when I was in my prayer closet again and got the rest of what God had attempted to tell me regarding contentment. The Spirit of the Lord came upon me and I burst out in song. I didn't even know all of the words, but I sang it anyway. It was *My Help [Cometh from the Lord]* by the Brooklyn Tabernacle Choir. I sang the chorus repeatedly, because I didn't know the verses. That's when God dropped into my spirit the words "issue of blood faith." He was telling me I simply needed to endure.

For twelve years, the woman with the issue of blood suffered physically, mentally, emotionally, and socially. She had to have. You didn't bleed for twelve years and not suffer physical weakness, as the bare minimum, from the loss of blood. She had to have suffered mentally and emotionally over what could be done next, or what was really going on in her body. She definitely suffered socially because it would appear that she was isolated, but for twelve years she endured it. I didn't say she enjoyed it, but she dealt with it. Having spent all of her money, she accepted it until the day she heard Jesus was in town. All of a sudden, that was the day she chose to risk it all and made her way through the crowd.

God wasn't telling me to suck it up or asking me to grin and bear my burdens. He was simply saying to stay put until He arrived. It struck a nerve because it was an issue of me being my biggest enemy. I was the root of my own issue of blood for the past two years, clogging up the flow of the Spirit in my career, my marriage, my finances, and my home. I was so consumed with what other people were possibly saying or thinking that I became consumed with the "I have to go back to work now" syndrome, God's will or not. Yes, I was making my way through the crowd, but at what cost and for what purpose? Jesus was nowhere in sight, and there I was ready to risk everything I held dear.

Derrick had been taking odd jobs here and there until that job offer came through when we learned we were expecting again, and my contracts had come to as much of an end as President Clinton's term in office. We still were not making ends meet at all, because he'd literally taken a $200,000.00 pay cut. I was frustrated, disappointed, angry, bitter, resentful, hurt, and tired. No one knew all of that except God though, and nobody saw that side of me except my husband and child. I think that's probably what led me into my prayer closet that day. I looked at my daughter while she was asleep and resolved that she would not have to carry all of my emotional baggage throughout her life. The question was

"What was I going to do to unpack it all? So, I started singing that song from Psalm 121:1-2.

Well, later that day, as I was now refreshed, I turned on Christian television. I saw a pastor who comes from a family of Gospel musical geniuses sitting down as he interviewed his parents. Now this family, in my eyes, appeared to be a modern day Abrahamic Covenant family. The anointing simply seemed to be on everyone within the visible eyesight of them. In fact, I had even started praying, "Lord, bless my house like that!" Now, once again, I didn't want anyone else's drama ('cause everybody has some); I just wanted a blessing to fall on me and my descendants on down to my great-grand-babies' great-grand-babies. However, it wasn't until I began to pray specific blessings over my own children that I started to feel guilty about the rest of my family.

I found in my studies that God separated us by house, or lineage. He blessed the house of Noah right on down to Abraham, Isaac, and Jacob, when He blessed Shem and Jepheth. They were two of Noah's sons who did not look upon his nakedness (see Genesis 9:25-27). This was the same line Abraham descended from, and just like God blessed Ishmael and Isaac (Abraham's sons) He also blessed Jacob and Esau (Isaac's sons). They were all connected to one another's righteousness from one generation to the next, starting with Noah and Shem, and then on to Abraham, Isaac, and Jacob who was father to the Twelve Tribes of Israel.

Naturally, there were some generations skipped between Shem and Abraham, but you can only imagine that if Noah walked upright before God and was blessed, followed by Shem who walked upright before God and was more blessed, then there had to be at least one person in each of the next few *generations* to walk upright before God in order to be even more blessed. This continued on down to Abraham, Isaac, and Jacob, who were all ultimately blessed. Now, I wasn't praying for another Jesus, but a Dr. E.K. Bailey, Billy Graham—well, since I had a daughter—Amanda Berry Smith, Paula White, Juanita Bynum, Joyce Meyers, or *somebody* along those lines would do! I'd even take a Yolanda Adams, CeCe Winans, or one of the Clarke Sisters as long as the fruit of the Spirit was equally evident.

Looking at Abraham's genealogy, I thought about my own. A minister once told me a person could ask forgiveness for the sins of their ancestors, so having learned that I did. Afterwards, just like Job had sent up burnt offerings to cover his children, I was willing to sacrifice for my own. I also added a request for God's continued hand of mercy on my extended family. While it was clear that we could pray blessings over others, Derrick is only responsible for *speaking* blessings over our own. And, I wanted God to see fit to boldly and supremely bless *our house*—the house of Derrick C. Johnson and every person, dog, or even plant that is part of it.

Needless to say, the television interview with this modern day "blessed to the thousandth generation" family was a great and uplifting show. The father was busy telling of how he taught all ten of his children nothing but Gospel music, which was all they had a choice to sing. He later shared that he and his wife taught them nothing but holiness. The children didn't even get to go on sleepovers. I definitely wanted to hear this because Emahn was almost four, and that was her question when she played with other kids by now. She always wanted to know could either she, or they, spend the night.

I hadn't decided to let our daughter start going on or having sleepovers just yet, because I wasn't sure it was something I was going to be willing to continue. Then, the father made the most profound statement. Profound to me, that was. He said, "Every house has spirits. The only way to know what spirits are influencing your children is to keep them home." That was the *same* thing I had been thinking, and now I could actually say it. *Why?* Because, it had worked for them.

Listening to the remainder of the interview, I was still thinking about my earlier prayer session in the closet. Then, to close the show out, the pastor began to sing the words to *My Help [Cometh from the Lord]*. As I chimed in with him and the words penetrated my soul, I burst into tears. God instantaneously ended that previous conversation. It was then that it all made sense. That was it! *All* of my help comes from the Lord. I was looking to Derrick to meet needs I should have been looking to God for. That was *exactly* what the lady had said at the Christian television studio. Well, what needs were those? *All of them.* Any need I had looked to Derrick for was an insult to the Lord God, Jehovah Jireh (My Provider). God wanted me to trust *Him* to provide for me. This had nothing to do with Derrick.

Remembering when I was questioned earlier regarding whether I thought it was fair that God went through Derrick to get to me, I shuddered. No, it wasn't. My husband had lost his job, his social status, and his financial well-being all because God was calling me. That didn't seem fair at all. I had once said yes, but that was when I didn't understand the depth of what was taking place. It was my thinking that if Derrick is the head of household, then he is also the first line of defense. *So why not go through him first*, I thought. Now, it seemed God was using a whole new type of Math. How in the world did He figure that subtracting my security, my sanity, and my sin *from myself* would add to my spiritual growth or development?

It was after my confession of the sin of not trusting God that Derrick received the actual call for the best job offer to come (which came in May of 2004). Because I had wavered in my faith, it really made me wonder whether I was the hold-up. After that "issue of blood" thing, I truly believe I played a major part. I had been talking about going back to work for at least two years, even after God had told me to write this book. No job offers were coming, and my contracted clients had slowed to none. I had even decided to work up until the birth of this new baby, if I could just find something. All this was going to do was provide me with the security and sanity I felt I needed as a woman, a wife, and a mother to keep me from further sinning and throwing in the towel. I lacked faith, so God withheld favor. It wasn't until I started weighing the risks that He began to heal me.

Being unemployed myself had begun to irritate me, because I was doing absolutely nothing outside of the house. I could only do so much cleaning, laundry, cooking, household shopping, reading, and/or lounging. I had also stopped calling myself a stay-at-home mom because I was trying to return to my career. So, I resented being a housewife and all it entailed. Then, I realized that although my head was at home, my heart was not. There I was trying to go to work, when my girlfriends were trying to come home. We each thought the other was crazy.

Nonetheless, sitting around playing house while the real world went on was not kosher for me. It also wasn't as fun as sitting at my grand mama's playing house with Barbie and Ken. In the real world words like "bills due," "late fees," "disconnect notice," "mortgage foreclosure," "property taxes," and "liens" existed. In Lala Land there was only Barbie, Ken, a pink house, a pink car, and you. In fact, I didn't even remember my Barbie having a mailbox, let alone a bill! So feeling more and more relieved and becoming relaxed and refreshed in the presence of the Lord, I began to slowly unpack some of that baggage. Loads and loads of pressure were lifted from my shoulders when I sang the words "all of my help cometh from the Lord."

The following Sunday was Mother's Day, which we enjoyed at Concord that year. In three and a half years I had never felt so affirmed and reassured, or so validated as a woman and a mother. God had definitely shed His light on me. The pastor preached, and when he stated that mothers do their best work behind the scenes and our children are our greatest investment, for the first time since walking away from my career, I felt okay about giving it up and totally letting go.

It had been almost four years, and close to two babies later, when I finally recognized that if I never worked outside of my home again, then so be it. In all of that time I had never officially said my professional goodbyes, because I was always looking for an opportunity to go back. I felt I'd made my greatest sacrifice ever by giving up my career, income, independence, and space—*my life*—for my family.

I soon started the process of walking in my destiny and living out my purpose *for real*. I realized this wilderness was just a pit stop I had to go through, and it would shape my every future thought and desire. It was this transformation that made me realize I didn't want to be a parent whose child reflected her darker side. I had given in and of myself to my family, and with that baggage steadily being removed, I was ready to give unselfishly to God.

As I prepared to move ahead into whatever new endeavors He had awaiting me, I knew I could walk boldly in the assurance of knowing it was not in His will for me to be working, because I was supposed to be writing. This was the season He needed me at home, taking care of *His* business. He needed me to stop thinking about whether other people thought I was just sitting around playing with Emahn while my husband carried all the financial concerns on his shoulders, and He wanted me to stop wondering whether I would ever get the life I so badly wanted for myself back. It was in His will for me to recognize that all of my help would come from Him, to touch the hem of His garment, and to simply let it flow.

TEACH THE WORD

14 Since I had turned up the desire to walk the path of righteousness and all it entailed, God was on a definite roll. After Him shedding light on me that He was basically everything to me, it seemed all I ever asked or thought He answered; and I had no complaints. I did just what He'd asked, I let it flow. I was just fortunate I had already bought a backup journal. It had been a year since my first entry, and during that time I went through two journals and had recently opened a third.

One day while getting some ironing done as Emahn napped, I decided to take the time and have my devotion. As I settled down, I said, "Lord, take me where you want me to go this time." As I flipped through the pages, the Bible fell open at 1 Samuel 1. I asked, "1st Samuel? What's in 1st Samuel that You want me to get?" So, I began to study. I knew the very next day I was exactly where I was supposed to be as I read chapter two. It regarded Eli's punishment, as priest, for doing nothing about his sons and their behavior (see 1 Samuel 2:12-3:18).

God was answering the question I'd posed a year or so earlier about people in leadership positions *in* the church, who don't have the same values *as* the Church. Maybe that wasn't it at all, though. It could have been that their conviction was just low due to a lack in their relationship with Christ. Well, whatever it was, shortly after reading that passage all I knew was God took care of it. He took 'em all out, including Eli, because He knew about various situations regarding his son's inappropriate behavior and chose to do nothing about it.

Suddenly reminded that as parents we are the priest of our homes, I had to declare that my life and destiny are under the influence of the seed of the prophet *again*. I didn't see that, but I knew it was just over the horizon. Things were getting tighter and tighter, even with the increase in income. Bills were so far behind that we couldn't catch up and move forward at the same time (unless I got a job). I had to quickly dismiss that notion though, because I refused to stay in this pit any longer than I had to. So, what did I do? I burst out in song, because I felt better after singing a good Praise and Worship song every time I did. Singing always did wonders for my soul. That was probably why it's been said that it's good to keep a song in your heart... depending on what it is.

While singing I realized the phone hadn't rang all day, so I got up and checked the dial tone to make sure it wasn't disconnected. "Hum, it works," I said aloud. I could very well get used to this—no telemarketers and no bill collectors. So I prayed, *"Lord, please let this peacefulness continue. Don't let any unnecessary calls come through. Every time the phone rings, from now on, I want to know it's somebody I'm supposed to talk to. In fact, don't let anybody ring the doorbell, either*—no solicitors. *Bless this house and all who enter. Let no evil enter into this house. Let it not ring the doorbell. Let it not even make it to the doorway, in Jesus' name, amen."* Seriously, I prayed that.

It was a week later, and the phone had not rang prior to 6:00p.m. when Derrick walked in. In fact, the first three days after I prayed that prayer it did not ring at all. Of course, we made calls out but none came in. I thought *I could really get used to this.* I had quiet time, study time, prayer time, listening to God answer time, and on top of all that I had writing time. Heck, I would give up Caller ID if I knew it could continue. That was so simple I decided to try it again.

On another day, I imagined a life without worries. Not without problems, but without worry regarding a specific dilemma. Then, it dawned on me, *"Do not be anxious about anything, but in everything, by prayer and petition, with thanksgiving, present your requests to God."* (Philippians 4:6) I sat up and said, "Lord, I want to live an anxiety-free life." Then, I laughed at the foolishness of that statement. After that it was as if I heard, "So, you think that's funny?"

I stopped laughing and remembered God doesn't tell us to do anything He has not enabled and equipped us to. So, then I got serious. I said, *"Lord, You said be not anxious for anything. That's what I want. I don't want to worry about nuthin'. I want to have, and not just know of,* Your perfect peace. *So, I'm just going to by prayer and petition, with thanksgiving, make my requests known unto You from now on. I'm not going to be anxious over anything, amen."* I snickered again. The thought of that was so silly.

It was coming up on the end of May and first-of-the-month June bills had already started to arrive. Remembering that originally it was my choice to be a stay-at-home mom, I weighed my decision against the pleasure I used to take in paying my bills. I'd enjoyed it when I was single and even during the earlier years of our marriage. Nothing felt better to me than writing out a check in the full amount of a bill and marking it paid. Lately, it seemed everything I once loved had become a much-hated burden. Everything from paying bills to watering my plants, I had started to despise. There were days when watering, feeding, and polishing my plants was far more important than making sure Vanity, my dog, had water. I would just water and talk, or polish and sing.

Well, on this particular day, Derrick checked the mailbox and brought in bills. I opened and looked at them, and to my surprise didn't huff or puff as usual. I didn't even exhale, which was totally unnatural for me. Usually around the first of the month I would go into depression and start having semi-anxiety attacks. Just because I'd had a bonfire in the kitchen didn't mean they would stop coming, but somewhere between that episode and now I had grown in faith and in patience. I'd trusted God to do something, but didn't have a clue what. Regardless, I recalled my previous prayers and started praising Him. He had reminded me, once again, to trust in Him with all my heart. *There is power in an humble prayer, I tell ya!*

Since I was taking everyday as it came and not worrying anymore, I started to look towards Canaan eagerly. I even said, "Lord, either You're going to deliver us or kill us. Either way, I'm ready." I was serious. Either we were coming out of this thing, or He was going to just reel us on home to glory. *You see we're still here.*

On another morning, having already gotten the day's devotion out of the way, I was showering and received the words "the Church is like children" in my spirit. I said, "Okay, Lord." (Pretty much in a "What do You have for me today?" tone.) We had already gotten the preliminaries out of the way the night before, so I had grown accustomed to getting up and talking to Him just like I'd get up and talk with Derrick or Emahn. So I repeated, "The Church is like children." I then thought about Emahn, who does so much simply because I do it.

Before Emahn could hardly talk, we were all having dinner one evening when she said, "Alleoojuh." *Alleoojuh?* I looked at her, then at Derrick. Then, he looked at her for himself. She was no more than a year old and still in a highchair. I looked her in the eyes and asked, "Hallelujah?" She repeated, "Alleoojuh." So, then I asked again, "Hallelujah?" Then she said, "*Aalleeoojjuuhh!*" as if to ask, "What's wrong with you? Can we eat now?" I was ecstatic! Derrick and I looked at each other smiling. I *really* prayed that she stays on the path back then. She was so young, I figured the firmer the foundation, the stronger the finish. Then, I thought about the image of my modern day Abrahamic Covenant family.

Returning to my original conversation, what God was saying and filling in the blanks with was that, like children, the Church needs to be taught. I wrote it down and dismissed it the rest of the day. I later received a message to pray for someone who didn't want a divorce, but it looked like the end was inevitable. I didn't remember to do it until later when I continued my study of 1 Samuel.

While praying for this particular person, the Spirit spoke and told me to ask him why he didn't want a divorce. I thought that was a strange request. It was my thinking that someone not wanting a divorce was a good thing, right? I said, "Lord, what difference does that make? You're not for divorce, so if he doesn't want one, for whatever reason, let's just work this thing out." Once more, I heard, "Ask him why he doesn't want a divorce?"

It was because God was trying to tell me if the man said he didn't want a divorce because of natural needs, He wasn't particularly interested in working that situation out just yet. It was a self-serving request.

However, if the guy said he did not want a divorce because it goes against the very will of God, or he wants what the Father wants, then that was a workable and *selfless*, or spiritual request. If he did not want a divorce for *selfish* reasons, God wasn't particularly interested in his *self-serving* happiness. He wasn't necessarily saying to tell him to accept the divorce; however, He did want to be worked into the equation because of a spiritual, selfless need *first*.

Although "Okay," is what I said, I thought *Lord, You know this person, and You also know he is not going to receive me saying the Lord told me to tell you so on and so forth.* The truth of the matter was it wasn't even a direct prayer request. It came from someone else regarding this person. He hadn't specifically even asked *me* to pray for him. I got the message from someone else who thought to ask me about praying for him. I continued to say, "Lord, what if he doesn't receive what You've told me to tell him?" He said, "Stop praying." Then I asked, "What if it's for selfish reasons?" He said, "Stop praying." I thought, *man, I always get the hard jobs. Why do I have to tell the man this?*

I then opened my Bible again and continued to read. Before I went too far into the chapter though, I stopped somewhere around the second verse of 1 Samuel 22 and said, "Lord, give me a fresh, new, creative revelation." Then, I read on beginning with verse three of 1 Samuel 22 and moved on to verse four. For some reason, I was able to complete the other chapters in one sitting. However, something was happening here that was slightly different. I didn't want to say "not right," but definitely different.

I then re-read the two verses again. As I tried to continue on to the next verse, it was as if my eyes would automatically shift back to the beginning of verse three. I asked, "Okay, what is it about these verses You're trying to show me, Lord?" I could not read past verse four. It was as if once verse four ended, the remaining verses faded from the page. I must've re-read those two passages ten or twelve times. I knew God was trying to tell me something and, whatever it was, I was determined to get it then. I grabbed my journal and pen, and began to dissect the verses because God wasn't revealing the rest of the text to me at the time.

As the message unfolded before my eyes, my heart raced. "Sometimes you have to leave those closest to you behind until God has revealed your purpose to you." I wrote. But, that wasn't it. *Too broad.* Then, "As a child, sometimes it may be necessary to make other arrangements for our parent's well-being until God has revealed to us our well-being in Him." *Nah, too shallow.* Then, word-by-word, so- He- left- them- with- the- king- of- Moab. *Question: Why? What for?* Well (syllable-by-syllable, by now), for pro·tec·tion and se·cu·ri·ty. *Answer!* Sometimes, we have to take our parents to the King (Jesus), for protection and provision, while we wait on God to reveal to us *our own purpose.* That was it! Something went at peace inside of me, and I knew I was right.

Afterwards, I felt this urge to pray and said, "Lord, I know what You're saying." That night I had to place the bulk of my baggage on the altar. I knew exactly what God was telling me based on past prayer requests. It was probably also based on the fact that I was now anxiety-free and said I wasn't worrying about nothing, and that included *nobody.* So, I guessed He was saying that since I was still unpacking baggage to go on and put those in a safe place, too. I was all for that, because then I no longer felt obligated to lug them around anymore.

That night, I put the heaviest bags of all on the altar. I got so much stuff out, I ended up crying again. I didn't even intend to go there, but as a picture of almost every living member of my entire natural family, known to me, flashed before my face—saved and unsaved alike—I really knew what God was saying then. This did not feel good at all, but I had to start praying all over again. Eventually, I gave God my entire family and left them all in His care, so He could tell me what He was going to do for *me*. As hard as that was, it was an eye-opener. God still wanted to know, regardless of what was going on around me, was *I* going to play the game of life by His rules, or would I allow the enemy to have his way *by relation*.

As I continued to skim this text with a fine tooth comb, my soul filled with joy. God had definitely answered my prayer for a new revelation. I journaled a minimum of four pages that night alone, but for some reason got tied up with the word "stronghold." It was as if it kept bulging from the page. What was it about this word that desired my attention? Then, there in the middle of the lesson, it sprang forth. I saw the words "If you want to save them, save their children." Remember, those were very first words I ever heard God audibly say, to my recollection. It had to tie in somewhere with this lesson, but where?

I sat up again, as opposed to lying down. The words "children have to take their parents to the king and leave them there, while they wait on God to tell them what He's going to do for them" came to mind. I thought back to that original experience. It was after a trip back to Dallas, from Bunkie, when my heart was heavily bleeding. I was so upset by the things I saw some of the adults doing, that I cried out for them that night on my knees. I was hurting for the children, because they were watching the adults through spiritual eyes. It was after that incident when God responded audibly. Then, the message burst forth: if you want to save them (parents), then leave them with the King of Kings and save their children.

Having gotten that, it was interesting to me how

David's stronghold represented a place of survival, or refuge, as he sought safety from King Saul. But, somehow, somewhere along the lines where it related to our children, that very same place of security had become the enemy. I wept for joy and sorrow, but I prayed the following *Prayer of Purpose* because, once again, I had gotten it.

It wasn't about me, and it wasn't about Bunkie. It wasn't even about my family. It was about God and *His* family, the Church. If I was so concerned about the Church doing right, then He was saying save the children *of* the Church... the carnal or spiritually immature Christians. If I wanted to save *them*, then I would have to save their children (the future of the Church) *from them*, because some parents *are* their children's stronghold. The scary part about that was: anyone who is in charge of another, acts as a parent or guardian of some sort—pastors included.

Prayer of Purpose
(Rejuvenation)

Father God, I forgive every adult in my life who had the responsibility of training me up in the way I should go as a child of God and sowing into my spiritual being, but did not. I forgive them for not being the Godly example they were created and called to be (see Proverbs 22:6). Despite how old I am now, I release them to You and move myself out of the way, asking of You to keep them in your care while I wait on You to tell me what You will do with me, especially as I am going through (see 1 Samuel 22:3-5). I rejoice in knowing, as Your child, You have a purpose and plan for my life, and You are in favor of my success and not my failure (see Jeremiah 29:11). You have restored me! You love me! You take delight in me, and You alone validate me! Help me to seek to please only You, not even myself, from now on, in Jesus' name, amen (see Galatians 1:10).

Then, the tears flowed again. God was telling me if I wanted to save the parents, then I needed to save their children *from them*. That's what my burden was; knowing that God was getting ready to reverse the curse and cause the children to lead. As tears filled my eyes, yes again, fear tried to creep up on me. I exhaled, put my head down, and praised and thanked God anyhow. God spoke those words to me in the early morning hours of the Monday following Mother's Day 2002. He completed this puzzle in the early hours of Memorial Day 2003. One year and exactly two weeks later, it all started to make sense.

As painful as it was for me to look at that problem head-on, what God was showing me did not negate that it existed: Spiritually immature parents are their children's natural-born enemies. *When we choose not to protect them in the love of Christ, by default, we hinder them from the truth of Christ.* Jesus said in John 14:6, *"I am the way and the truth and the life. No one comes to the Father except through Me."* In most cases, we, as parents, choose for our children based upon our understanding of that truth, or the lack of. We protect them in what we *perceive* as the love of Christ through others, oftentimes without actually *knowing* the love of Christ for ourselves. That simply means, being mature in one area does not mean we've got the other areas covered.

After all of this, I noted that God placed David in his wilderness experience in order to help others. 1 Samuel 22:2 mentioned that about 400 men were with David who were in distress, in debt or discontented, and David became their leader in the midst of his own brokenness. David went through for character-building, but he came out for kingdom-building! That was what I gathered God was getting me ready for, as well. Just as David had access to *a* king, I have access to *the* King! Even in the midst of my own wilderness, Jesus had given me favor. All He expected in return was that I help those who seek His refuge in my spiritual strength, and listen for Him to give further instruction regarding His plans for my life, just as David did. Because, ultimately their deliverance is linked to mine.

I then asked the Lord how I was supposed to do all that He had just revealed. For the past year I had been praying for clarity on what I'd previously heard and later saw in that very first vision. I knew then *for whom* I was supposed to be doing, but I knew now *what* exactly it was. So, I started praying about *how*. It came so quick and easily. My ministry was really about deliverance. The woman of God had already spoken that in the prophecy. How did I come to that conclusion for myself? Because at one time my stronghold, like so many other young people's, was some of the adults closest to me.

Like David, I had carried the burden of running from dream-killers like Saul. On one hand, I knew what God was telling me about what the Christian life *was supposed to look like* (hot or cold), but I also saw what others who had gone before me were showing me *it could be like* (lukewarm). I started this study at 12:05a.m. It was now 1:47, but I wasn't about to stop. At the rate I was going, I could have stayed awake all night. *Heck, maybe even for days!*

As I continued reading the lesson at hand, God began to give me supporting scriptures for all I was being told. The question was "How was I going to do it?" I knew I could because it was in my power to do so under the authority and anointing of the Holy Spirit, but how could I physically? My heart raced as I envisioned myself, with outstretched arms, shielding a group of young children behind me from parents who lashed out at them and me as well. It didn't feel good to be put in that position, but God was saying it had to be done. So trusting in His will and His Word, I suited up.

When I read on into the next chapter, *how* was laid out right there for me. I could do it in the spirit of the children. In the spirit of the child whose face reached out to me in that earlier vision and asked me with his eyes, *Why did you run away? Why did you leave me?* I could also do it with the power and strength that was shown to me in that same vision when evil surrounded us, and I raised my right hand and with the authority and anointing of the blood of Jesus rebuked the devour from myself, my friends, my extended family and my child. I could do this! Not because I said I could, but because God had already shown me I could.

In the conversation that took place between Saul and David in 1 Samuel 24:9-15, I envisioned David as a child. This was the first time that had ever happened to me. I'd never previously imagined him as such, even when Samuel went to Jesse's house to anoint him (see 1 Samuel 16:11-13). As I read the scriptures, I knew after all of this I wasn't crazy. I couldn't be, not at this point. I then channeled all of my energy into that conversation and what was taking place. I imagined a child, any child if he had a voice of his own and courage enough to do so, sharing his feelings with his parent(s) in the same manner as David did.

By simply asking the question David asked Saul, "Am I nothing to you?" I could hear the heartache and cries of my inner child wanting to know the same thing. Am I nothing to you that you would dare defy God and attempt to destroy me for no reason? God said to train a child in the way he should go in Proverbs 22:6. To train meant to teach or to show, not just to tell. It meant to model or exemplify, demonstrate, or epitomize holiness. He did not specify parents. He just said, "Train."

In the English language, it is understood that the subject of the previously mentioned sentence is "You." Therefore, God said, "*You* train up a child in the way he should go." *You* reading the scripture, preaching the Word, teaching the lesson... *you* with custody... *you* with visitation rights... *you* guardian... *you* neighbor, counselor, coach, doctor, lawyer, neighbor, nurse... *you* in the general sense of the word—*parent or not*. Make it personal and teach the children *by example*, regardless of what is going on around you.

God then said in Mark 9:42, "*And if anyone causes one of these little ones who believes in me to sin, it would be better for him to be thrown into the sea with a large millstone tied around his neck.*" That meant to train natural children, or even spiritual ones, in godliness or suffer the consequences of not doing one of the many things we were *called* to do. Because, as Christians, we are all ministers above being parents or professionals, first. I thought about children everywhere, and God laid the following *Prayer of Hope* on my heart.

Prayer of Hope
(Restoration)

Lord, I apologize for not always being the responsible Christian You created me to be. I failed You and I failed the children. I confess that because I lacked faith, those You left in my care lack faith, and because I was spiritually immature, they are as well. Please forgive me for the negative testimony I have lived in front of them, and free me from being a spiritual hindrance and stumbling block to any child, natural or spiritual. Help me to walk in righteousness and to honor You always. Enable me to be a positive witness for Your glory. I pray that (each child's name) will find and know You, and that he/she/they will forgive me for where I have fallen short of their God-given expectations. Forgive me for making excuses and living a lie. Help me to be a Godly example. Help me to start anew with a greater respect of You, so they can have greater respect for me, in Jesus' name, amen.

It was now 4:00a.m. Naturally, the tears flowed once more. Looking back, I was just as guilty where other people's children were concerned. Somewhere, someone was watching me before I decided to live right, which also meant that somewhere, someone's child had been misled by my word or actions and lost their Kingdom position, or the favor of God. I was responsible for that, and at one time there was a huge rock with my name on it waiting to be attached to my neck as well... all because no one had taught me that to be double-minded is to be spiritually unstable. *Either we're going to transform the world,* or *we're going to conform to it* (see Romans 12:2)! *We can't do both!*

Growing up, I heard carnal Christians say one thing, then saw them do another. Being that I lived what I saw and not what I heard, that prayer was for me also. I prayed it so that my own children would have hope of a better spiritual example as my walk *and* my talk lined up, but that I would also be a better role model to others, like my cousins, nieces, nephews, neighbors, friends, etc.

Jesus said in Matthew 28:19-20, "Therefore go and make disciples of all nations, baptizing them in the name of the Father and of the Son and of the Holy Spirit, and teaching them to obey everything I have commanded you. And surely I am with you always, to the very end of the age." He never put an age limit on discipleship, and teaching others to obey what was commanded meant I needed to know what thus saith the Lord for myself. That was the only way it would work, and the only way I could responsibly teach my own and others. I had to learn the Word, to teach the Word.

HIS WAYS

15 Owning up to my part in deterring others from seeking the Light, I accepted the responsibility that was before me in getting them back on track. I immediately realized this would not be an easy task, but was determined to help those who wanted to be safe with the King get there. The others, those who did not, would be against me and I knew it, but I had a responsibility to uphold. God wanted me to teach the Word.

It was great that Derrick and I attended the eleven o'clock Sunday morning worship service, because even though I stayed awake most of the night, my soul was stirring when the sun came up. I awoke energized and refreshed, as if I had slept comfortably all night long. My prayer was, *"Lord, no matter what, in all things keep me humble."*

Although my original objective was to save the children in order to save their parents, I knew I would rock the boat. I had been given the lesson on compassion, and soon the test would follow.

That Sunday morning our associate pastor

conveniently spoke on "Praying for Your Enemies." *How timely*, I thought. The main thing I got was that before I did any of the things God had revealed to me, I needed to release the old and let go of the desire to get even. *Just get Godly*, I heard in my spirit.

The Lord was telling me to stop holding grudges. After that, I needed to let go of the desire to keep count. That was it for me. I had homework to do. Of course, I wrote the other steps down, but since I knew what my issues were I needed to work on those first. Especially, since I also knew what my purpose was. The last thing I needed was the devil beating me up with the same old spirit of unforgiveness. How could I teach it if I couldn't *do* it? There were children of all ages, natural and spiritual, awaiting the promises of their own purpose at stake, and I wasn't about to mess that up for them *or* myself.

Later, I was watching Christian television again and there was a pastor on whom I didn't recall seeing before. He said, "The devil can take you to the edge, but he can't push you over." That was so true, especially in my experiences. *That certainly wouldn't keep him from trying though*, I thought. As I listened to this man speak, he encouraged me. He simply said, "In this life, bad things happen to good people." *No kidding.* "But, right at your lowest point, God will send you somebody with a word." I knew that to be true for a fact, as I remembered the other minister speaking directly to me the day I stepped out of the bathtub.

It was the next day, after hearing this man speak of the devil taking you to the edge, that I just felt like it wasn't going to be a good day. I was in the shower and said, "Lord, I wanna feel like a little girl who knows her daddy will make everything alright." I said, "I've never experienced that, and I want to feel like I have a father who is Superman and will take care of everything. I don't want to have to be concerned for anything on today." I forgot shortly and began to lather up. Well, my Father didn't forget.

When I was dressed and stepped into the bedroom, Emahn was sitting down with the Bible open. She had her finger pointed and was looking in the Book while talking and shaking it. I just looked at her and smiled. I asked, "Are you preaching?" She said, "Yes." I then promised myself not to do that again, because I didn't want her to assume she was supposed to be doing anything simply because someone said so, *especially me.* When I walked over to her, she pointed to a verse and asked me to read it. I said, "Okay."

I was still watching Christian television at the time, and there was a lady on talking about how at three months pregnant God had gotten her attention. Her water broke and she was put on bed rest. She said the only way she made it was with the Word of God. Daily, she had to think that her baby had a 50 percent chance of living or dying, based on whether she made one wrong move. As she spoke that I said, "Oh, God! Don't test me like that." Then, I began to read, *"The earth is the Lord's and the fullness thereof."* (Psalm 24:1) Emahn said, "No, this one," and pointed to Psalm 23.

My heart was filled and my soul rejoiced, because the first thing I read aloud was, *"The Lord is my shepherd I shall not want."* I had forgotten just that quickly how I had asked God to feel like a daddy's girl, and He remembered and let me. All day I reflected on Psalm 23. It was becoming my new favorite scripture. Most of my life it was John 14:1 (KJV), *"Let not your heart be troubled: ye believe in God, believe also in me."* I had no idea just how soon I'd need it all over again.

One Sunday after church, while washing my hands in the ladies' room, I felt a gush of water running down my pants' leg. I rushed back into the stall drenched. There was both water and blood flowing down my right leg. All I could think was that I was going to mis-carry my baby. This couldn't be happening to me. On the ride from the church to the hospital, I sat quietly. Derrick didn't utter a word. What could he say? I didn't think any natural man could ever be prepared to comfort a woman in that situation. I understood that, and was fine with it. Besides, I would rather he say nothing than to utter the wrong something anyhow.

Once in the emergency waiting area, we sat for two hours. I knew then I had made a mistake. Instead of taking the additional thirty minute drive to our usual hospital, we went to the closest one and waited all afternoon to be seen. I started to get restless, because all I could think about was something happening to my baby while I was sitting there in the waiting area. I didn't know how I would have reacted, but I do know I prayed.

The first time I talked to God about this matter was when I went to the bathroom again while at the hospital. I said, *"God, haven't I been through enough already? When does it end?"* The next time I went to the bathroom it was, *"Lord, I'm sorry. I brought this on myself, didn't I? I'm supposed to be sitting down somewhere writing. This is all to Your glory. So whatever Your will is, it's fine. Just prepare me for the worst, but help me to expect the best, in Jesus' name, amen."* The third time I said, *"Lord, thank You for whatever. Thank You for getting my attention. I'll finish the book."*

I later went home at $14^{1/2}$ weeks pregnant with what they termed abrupto placenta (a tear in the placenta). I was informed there was a 50 percent chance of the tear healing on its own and me carrying full-term, or I had a 50 percent chance of it further ripping and mis-carrying. Having already received Word from the most accredited Physician, I followed the doctor's orders and left for home on bed rest until my obstetrician could see me.

That following Monday morning I scheduled the earliest appointment my OB/GYN had, which was that upcoming Friday. My doctor not only confirmed their information, but also saw a fibroid on the sonogram just about the size of the fetus. It had been discovered right after I'd given birth to Emahn four years ago by her doctor who had recently retired, but had been no threat. Now, it appeared to be a hazard to the baby I was currently carrying. She placed me back on bed rest and scheduled another appointment the following week.

Thinking back to the lady I saw on television, who had been put on bed rest at three months pregnant, I also thought about Miss Amanda Berry Smith and Dr. E. K. Bailey. Both had been ill when they began their writing careers, and both had impacted my life.

Just as God had caused them to sit and be still, He had done the same for me. I believe it was His way of getting me to personalize the severity of acting outside of the anointing. He was showing me that if I did not sit and be still, I might deliver out of season and risk the birth of my child in the natural and others in the Spirit. Did I want this baby to be a sacrifice because of my own stubbornness? *Not!* Did I want the book to be a sacrifice because of disobedience? *Definitely not!*

Over the initial shock of the pregnancy complications, one day while sitting in bed watching a great televangelist in the Atlanta area, I heard him say something that captured my attention. The sermon topic was about God speaking audibly. I recalled my own experience and listened intently as he ministered on. He said, "When God tells you to do something do it, because He won't make another move without that one. Don't worry about the person not receiving it. God knows how to make Himself heard." *Uh oh*, I thought. I knew exactly where this answer had come from… the "ask him why he doesn't want a divorce" response. I still had not acted on sharing God's answer with the person, because I was waiting on Him to do something else.

Between the Lord telling me to ask the man and the minister saying to tell the man, I said, "Lord, if he wants his answer, let him bring it up. That way I'll know he's ready to receive it." (Just for the record, that didn't work.) God had told me to tell the man. It wasn't up to me to determine whether he received it. I just hoped he would in the spirit in which it was being given. I later called him and left a message for him to phone me back. When he did, I just spit it out. He listened, but made a joke. Nothing like the response I'd expected from him, though.

When I mentioned the part about being *selfless,* as opposed to *selfish,* the man said he wasn't the one who needed to change. I said, "Marriage is not about the person who *needs* to change. It's about the person who *wants* to change. It's about sacrificing for the overall good of the marriage." When the conversation was over, I thanked God and said, "Lord, I told him, now it's out of my hands. I did what I was supposed to do." I then prayed that God would simply begin to change them both.

During the next day's devotion while reading a book entitled "Living in the Presence of God… The Works and Life of Brother Lawrence with Devotions by Steve Troxel," I flipped to the day's topic and read an overview of the sacrifice of Isaac. I didn't know how to take that one. Would this baby be a sacrifice for something else, or would there be a ram in the bush? I decided right then and there to continue not being anxious for anything. God already knew I wanted this child, and I had no problems telling Him again with a prayer of thanksgiving. Still on bed rest, it was then that I made up my mind to accept whatever God saw fit to do. Besides, the people around me made it extremely easy.

During my season of bed rest I felt "much love."

Everyone was so nice, there wasn't one thing I needed that wasn't taken care of—including entertainment for Emahn. Sis. Robbie T. Byrd, our former Women's Ministry Director, even sent someone over to sit with me from the time Derrick left for work in the mornings until he returned home in the evenings. For that, I was especially grateful.

Being that I wasn't able to attend church just yet, the following Sunday you already know what was on TV—Christian television. The minister I was watching asked this question, "What are you testifying to, the good life or the bad life?"

I realized then either you're a saint or a sinner. There is no in between. We are not sinners saved by grace. We did not fall down to get back up again. If you're covered by the blood of Jesus, you are a saint who sins from time-to-time. Not the other way around: a sinner who is free to sin, daily, because grace allows you to be a saint on Sunday. That is simply carnal foolishness! Now, whether you believe that and walk in it is optional. But, you are one or the other. And, if you fail to recognize that you're a saint, by default you admit you are a sinner. And, the wages of sin is death. So, you're hell-bound (see Romans 6:23).

Listening to the man of God, I recalled the comments of an older woman I'd once looked up to. Her complaint was that witnessing wasn't her thing. I thought, *hum, witnessing for God is not you, but sitting here with a beer and a pack of cigarettes (advertising for the enemy) is. How interesting?*

I was fully aware by that time there are some who still do not realize our lives *are* our witness. If you're living, you're testifying—even if your mouth is closed. I agreed with the man of God; the question needs to be answered. What are you testifying to? Is He dead or has He risen in your life? If He has walk like it, talk like, live like it, and act like it. If He hasn't, let me serve notice... *He has!*

While still watching Christian television another minister appeared. He said, "The difference between heaven and earth is that on earth we like full bellies and full bank accounts. However, in heaven God likes us empty and broken, because brokenness is attractive to Him." I thought about how true that statement was in my own life. To me, it was symbolic of God looking down from heaven and being much more pleased that I was down and out, while looking up to Him, as opposed to being on the up'n up and being content in my own natural ability.

Shortly after that, I listened as another outstanding woman of God testified about the time she and her husband were on government assistance. *There it was,* I thought, *another "mountain high, valley low" experience.* I'd heard so many of those testimonies, I had a mental library. They were filed in my brain under "From Homelessness to Holiness." At that time, I couldn't even imagine writing about us being on government assistance, and there she was on national television telling all her "business." That's when the Spirit reminded me that I had to be transparent. I couldn't tell anybody half truths if I wanted them to be fully delivered. It was then that I couldn't imagine *not* writing about it.

During this time, Social Services was always considered a last resort for us. We were well on our way to not needing government assistance too, until things drastically changed. There were too many consecutive days when we paid all the bills, but there was no food. Then, there were too many days when we had food and the bills suffered. I was sick and tired of people telling us to have the cable and cell phones disconnected because, once again, I felt no one was listening or paying attention to me.

Derrick and I hadn't had cable or a cell phone in almost three years. At that point, we were struggling to simply keep the lights and water on, or put $5.00 worth of gas in the car to go look for a job. So, I made the decision to go to the local Social Services office. It broke my heart. That was my lowest point in all of this, without the added frustrations of unhelpful or ungodly advice.

Derrick didn't seem to understand why I hurt so badly. The truth of the matter was I felt like Social Services was the last step we would take just before we went completely under, as opposed to him seeing it as a time of regrouping and staying afloat. So, I came home and cried. Never mind we would have a full refrigerator again with other benefits. I only thought of all the shattered dreams and lost hopes I had that were brought to an unexpected halt. Life just wasn't fair.

I could not believe my reality had come to such ruin, so I said, "Lord, I would be better able to handle this if I was by myself." I didn't understand being married with a child and in this situation. He said, "If you were single, you'd be dead." I didn't understand that comment then, but later when I felt I couldn't be any more humble, it dawned on me He was right. If it wasn't for Emahn on most days, Derrick on others, and then the both of them in between, I would be dead. He knew one, I'd feel like I had no reason to exist; and two, that feeling would be too much *for me* to bear. That's why He didn't allow it to happen any other way.

I later reflected on a sermon our pastor once preached. He spoke about the number two. I vaguely remember it, but he referenced several scriptures regarding the number two. One was Matthew 18:20, *"For where two or three are gathered together in my name, there am I in the midst of them."* And, the other was Ecclesiastes 4:9-12 which states, *"Two [are] better than one; because they have a good reward for their labor. For if they fall, the one will* lift up his fellow: but woe to him [that is] alone when he falleth; for [he hath] not another to help him up. Again, if two lie together, then they have heat: but how can one be warm [alone]? And if one prevails against him, two shall withstand him; and a threefold cord is not quickly broken." Oh, how those helped me most.

Definitely stronger in my faith by this time, things were progressing with both the pregnancy and the book to the point where I vowed to take up my bed and literally walked after my last doctor's visit. Although the bleeding had started to lighten up, I was still expected to make my weekly appointments in order to check the baby's heartbeat. Everything eventually started to make sense, because I knew the problem had started due to the fact that I was being disobedient and not writing, or walking in my calling. Soon, the more I wrote, the better things got. When I was on a roll again, I was placed on partial bed rest. I was actually able to walk around the house and did so.

In spite of everything going on, I finally adjusted to being different. Scripture did say that those without the Spirit do not accept things of the Spirit (see 1 Corinthians 2:14). That should have been common sense to me. Nevertheless, I finally became aware that if your relationship is surface deep, your convictions are surface deep. However, if you have a daily walk with God, then you know Him well enough to know His heart and won't jeopardize breaking it. The deeper your heart ties to Jesus, the deeper your convictions run to avoid a tear. It was easy addition. Who, in good conscious, would purposely hurt someone they truly love? So, if that made me different, then different I was.

As I thought more about my spiritual growth during this valley experience, I realized I was nearing the completion of the book and the tear was being healed. It was revealed to me that the dreams concerning my older family members constantly attacking me were taking place because I couldn't perceive being rude or disrespectful to them. I had never been one to talk back, yet that was what always started the situations in most of the dreams where conflict arose. I had spoken out against them in defense of their children… something, up until this point, I'd never be able to imagine.

Unable to relate to being ill-mannered toward my elders, I questioned God once more about how I would be able to encourage children to take a spiritual stand. In one dream, my grandmother represented her generation fighting to maintain its rendition of power, or influence/control. As fear tried to come over me, I thought back to Ephesians 6:10, *"Put on the whole armor of God."* I remembered hearing another minister say, "You're either going to choose character, or you're going to compromise." Just what I was thinking when I said I wouldn't prostitute my principles, and God was challenging me not to forget.

By that time, I had been on partial bed rest for almost two weeks. I could not believe the second draft of the manuscript was almost complete, because in the past five days I had written an average of five chapters. I was excited about it too, because I had not written anything since my trip to Chicago back in February. It was now July. God certainly had His ways.

Shut 'em Down

16 During the time when I was on bed rest, God continued to remind me that He had His own agenda. His ways were truly not ours, and He certainly had His own. Letters began to come from the lady I had hit in the car accident. Then, additional letters came from the city of Dallas. The lady was suing both the city and me as joint defendants. I said, "Now Lord, I thought you took care of this."

As my nerves began to get uneasy, I remained faithful, but on edge. I prayed and prayed. Then, I waited and waited. The letters continued to fly back and forth to the plaintiff from the city. Because I was a third party, I was copied on almost every document. As I read, I continued to trust that God had taken care of this matter two years ago. In the meantime, I spoke with numerous attorney-friends concerning the situation. I also made various phone calls, as I prepared myself for court. I knew full well if that stop sign had been in its proper place there was no way I would have hit anyone, and I was readying myself to prove it if I had to.

On June 29, 2003, I turned 30 years old and felt

confident the manuscript was complete. However, God kept the story going. I had finalized it a second time, yet whenever something else happened I knew it was to be included. I convinced myself the book was finished time and time again, only to pick it up months later to start writing where I had previously left off. It was as if God was saying, "In My time, not yours. Don't rush Me."

I remained on bed rest for exactly four weeks. I continued to pray and lay hands on myself. Every time the pain from the fibroid would begin, I prayed. As I touched every inch of my stomach, I said, "You are healed by the blood of Jesus." I called those things that were not as though they were *for my good* (see Romans 4:17). "The tear is healed. The bleeding and the spotting are completely gone. You will give birth to a happy, healthy, beautiful, and normal child," I whispered as I rubbed my belly and talked to Eian (Ē-ŏn). "You are healthy and you are strong," I continued.

As the pregnancy progressed, things got better and better physically, although everything else was still in chaos. For the first time, I could not imagine bringing a child into the nightmare we were living. Previously, it had yet to dawn on me the level of catastrophe going on. I mean I knew, on some level. I guess I was partly in denial, on another. Where was a foster/adoptive child going to fit into this, and why would a natural one be sent down from heaven in the midst of it?

By August the household wasn't anymore stable than it had been, and to top it off we had to deal with the severe illness of our founding pastor, Dr. E. K. Bailey. Now, add that to receiving a letter regarding an established court date about the auto accident. I was at my wits end again.

The only thing that kept me going was that the Lord had ordered my steps to Chicago and back, and He'd rewarded us with the conception of a child when I returned. My prayer after we'd met with Pastor Bailey years earlier had been to conceive when I could handle every aspect of a pregnancy, so I had to rest in the assurance that this too was working for our good.

Continuing to pray and trust God for miracles, by mid-August the city of Dallas and the plaintiff were in their own legal battle. I never went to a hearing after I was released from bed rest because this case was between the two of them. The plaintiff accused the city of negligence, and its defense was there was no knowledge of the missing stop sign. Therefore, the city was not to be held legally responsible for the sign not being put back.

As I tried to put the whole thing out of my mind, in order to get ready for Eian's arrival, I thought this couldn't get any worse. By October 2003, it had. One, Pastor E. K. Bailey passed away. Two, we hadn't completely named the baby yet. All I knew was, boy or girl, it would be Eian. As we played with numerous names and their different variations, Derrick and I finally decided on Eian Kinsley at Pastor Bailey's funeral, having seen the program. Not only did it sound good, but it looked good too. Baby E.K. Johnson; it was a natural fit. Besides, had it not been for Pastor Bailey convincing me to have another child, she might not be here.

With my due date quickly approaching, I prepared myself for the finalization of the second draft of the manuscript. During this time, I heard a televangelist say, "If you can't decide what side you're on now, you won't be able to decide what side you're on then." He was referring to the rapture, which was something I didn't learn about until years after my rebirth. Yes, I knew Christ would return for the Church. I just didn't know there was an actual name for it and what would actually occur.

I realized then God had definitely used that point to teach me how to feel the passion I felt for Bunkie in relation to the rest of the world. I decided I would stand for Jesus. All children had to be saved before it was too late, and it was high time I got off the boat in order to help them decide now. It wasn't just about Bunkie anymore. It was about children everywhere, in every sense of the word "child," be they natural or spiritual.

I thought about the time I'd sat in Tuesday morning Bible study and shared portions of one of my recent testimonies. It was the one regarding the vision with the little boy and the fireplace and how, later on, God had audibly told me to save the children. After listening intently, one of the members said, "That's why God told me 'Some children are grown.' It was for you."

After class, I headed straight for the lady. I wanted to know more about the comment she'd just shared. When she told me the details of how she had walked into her house one day and sat on the sofa, then heard out of the clear sky what she had spoken, I froze. She said she could not figure out why God had said it, or what it pertained to, but she knew He had spoken it.

Prior to that conversation, I continued to pray about exactly who God was talking about. Was it children in the natural, or children in the Spirit? This confirmed it. He was referring to those who were immature or carnal. Some children *are* grown in the flesh, even though they *act* like babies in the Spirit. I had decided long ago to save whoever, but my heart was burdened over actual children in the natural connotation of the word, not spiritual ones—the babies, not their parents.

To me, the children could not fend for themselves *and* take on the spiritual responsibility of their guardians too. Like David, they would eventually have to take them to the King and leave them there, as they sought God's purpose for themselves. Realizing all of this was actually starting to sink in, I thought, *but they have no voice.* "Oh, really, voice of power?" I heard in my spirit. My heart trembled.

Later, a man I didn't recognize came on the television saying, "God is looking for crazy people these last days." Well, that was certainly me. "He wants to do something so big in your life, you have to be crazy to believe it," he said. He had my vote on that one, too. I believed if I had not been crazy already, then I was soon to become crazy if I had to endure anymore in the natural scheme of things.

As God would have it, I continued to dream, listen, and journal. You know, life continued on. I then heard it said, by someone else, "All hell breaks loose when you're going into your season." "Well, praise the Lord!" I said. There was going to be a silver lining to this nightmare after all. Since God had already shown me Canaan, I believed Him telling me to go and get it was just around the corner, but I still had to wait.

Having called those things that were not as though they were regarding the pregnancy, I was up and at 'em inside the house *regularly*. I even attended church in a wheelchair. At that point, the doctor said I could stand in ten minute increments, but I could not pick up, clean, etc. She did not say I couldn't go, so on Sunday I rode to the church and was wheeled into the service. As our church members encouraged me and told us they were still praying, my heart rejoiced. I told them the next Sunday I'd walk in, and I did.

After that, I was constantly on the go. Derrick even allowed me to ride with him to the grocery store, providing I used the electronic buggy when we arrived. I complied and, needless to say, it never happened again.

Unable to control that little scooter, I rolled right into the soda (or where I'm from, soda-water) display. He just pointed me in the direction of the cash register and started re-stacking the overturned sodas as he shook his head. I knew he was laughing at me, because he didn't look up. Of course, I grabbed our drinks from the stack that remained in place before I took off. I did not want to get home and open a can to have it splatter!

Working hard at being a good steward of my time, I continued to fine tune the manuscript and had gotten to a satisfactory conclusion. So, I headed to our local print shop to produce hardcopies when I fully recovered from the tear in my placenta. Because the first store could not offer me what I needed, I left and went to another.

While at the second copy center, as I waited I noticed another lady ahead of me in line. She was waiting for a print job, as well. We started talking, and when her copies were finished she showed me the items. She "just-so-happened" to be printing some information regarding her book. So, suddenly aware of what seemed to be a "coincidence," she introduced herself and added that she was a Christian author and a member of The Potter's House. To my surprise I responded, "I'm a writer, too!" I then let her know I was a very active member of Concord.

The lady and I continued to talk about various things pertaining to writing, particularly ours, and knew both our steps had been ordered right into that print shop. We then exchanged contact information and departed. Later that day, she e-mailed me and said how delightful it had been meeting me and, having viewed my website, she knew there was a spiritual connection. I agreed, and we later saw each other at a local support group meeting for writers and continued to stay in touch via e-mail.

With a tangible, *evident* manuscript in my hand, I thought more about taking possession of the promises God had made me and decided to let everything totally go. I was preparing to start phase two of the publishing process, still I was hurting in more ways than one. I knew I had to let it all out in order to move forward, so I did.

By this time, we were still struggling in our finances,

Pastor Bailey had passed, and Eian Kinsley was on the way. I felt all of these different emotions running through me from shock to sorrow. It was as if I had a permanent lump in my throat. Only a week or so earlier I was out-and-about running publishing errands. On this day, I sat down with a heavy heart and journaled. I just wrote whatever came to mind. Although I was saddened, I tried my best to remain upbeat for the sake of the baby when I concluded with:

Come Home

What's wrong with leaving early?
What's wrong with going home?
What's wrong with seeing the face of God
And shouting, "Holy" all day long?

What's wrong with dancing amongst Jesus?
What's wrong with having joy?
"What's wrong?" I ask the question,
"With being there when I come?"

"What's wrong?" I ask the question,
"With leaving this place behind?"
"What's wrong?" I want to know,
"With having perfect peace of mind?"

What's wrong with seeing mansions,
and walking on streets of gold?
"What's wrong?" I ask the question,
"If God says it's time to come home?"

And there it was: the peace of God that surpasses all understanding (see Philippians 4:7).

Pastor Bailey's death hurt Derrick and me badly. He had invested in our family in more ways than we could count. When I told him Derrick had been laid off, he actually called him *himself*. He didn't have his assistant do it. He didn't leave us a message. He didn't even drop a card in the mail. He called our house from his house, number on Caller-ID and all, and brought a joy to our house that was indescribable—even in the midst of his own storm.

Dr. Bailey talked to my husband as a man, as a friend, *and* as a pastor. Derrick had a smile on his face that spoke volumes without ever opening his mouth. I couldn't put a price tag on that. In the end, it seemed all that was needed was a "proper" thank you and good-bye. The poetry tribute did it, and two weeks after experiencing his death, we embraced baby E. K. Johnson's birth. God had not only come through for us, but had brought us through *with Him* as well.

Over the next few months to follow, I continued to watch Eian grow. That's when it dawned on me if Emahn never matured, Eian could never get to where she needs to be in this world. What was my point? "I'm glad you asked," as Pastor Bailey would have said, because some of us are simply holding up one another's progress in the Spirit. If Emahn was still nursing at age four, then Eian would not be here. *This might be "TMI" (Too Much Information) for some of you, but normally when a mother nurses her menstrual cycle temporarily stops. Without a cycle, there can be no conception.* I said that because, at some point, we must all seek to *eat* the Bread of Life for ourselves.

I noted then that since I understood my purpose, I was now able to get out of bed more frequently on the offense and not on defense of the devil, because I was full of *spiritual substance*. It was like I knew I had work to do and, no matter what, he was going to try to stop me in some way, shape, form, or fashion. Regardless, I was going to be ready for him—when- and however he came.

He wasn't even fighting me, but who I am supposed to be in Christ.

I had finally gotten that this whole battle was all about my purpose in God's plan and the devil trying to discourage me. But, do you know what? God convinced me that *"Neither death nor life, neither angels nor demons, neither the present nor the future, nor any powers, neither height nor depth, nor anything else in all creation, will be able to separate me from the love of Him that is in Christ Jesus my Lord."* (Romans 8:38-39) I learned this first-hand when I publicly announced my *now* apparent call into the ministry.

Having acknowledged and accepted my call, well over a year now, things began to heat up internally. Physically, I was still dealing with the pain from the flare ups of the fibroids. Emotionally, I was constantly wrestling with the same old spirit of unforgiveness. Although I'm not proud of it, I was really good at holding a grudge. At any rate, one afternoon I went online with The Board and shared some things with them regarding my latest incident. It was so bad that day I went into the closet after hearing some truths they shared with me about my attitude. It all started because we had extra people in the house and, as usual, something got broke. It was always my stuff, too. From furniture, to accessories and office equipment, or whatever... something of mine always ended up broken. On this particular day, I snapped.

From time-to-time Derrick and I would usually have guests, and it always seemed no one had any regard for *our* house rules. From telling unmarried grown folk they can't share a bed in *this* house, to telling kids not to touch this, that, or the other, somebody always tested me. By the time The Board and I stopped shooting e-mails to one another about my latest loss which, at that time, happened to be my All-in-One printer/scanner/copier/fax, the phone rang. It was Quad. As soon as I answered, she called my name and I bawled. All I heard was, "Girl, you *must* be upset."

Well, by the end of the conversation I was heading for the closet. I sang myself into a praise break with *I Love You Lord,* and went into a medley of *Bless the Lord Oh My Soul.* I had already rendered disciplinary actions, but was still livid. Here I was trying to finish a book and became severely crippled within an instant. Plus, it wasn't like I could just run out and buy a new one. I think that's probably what angered me most about the situation. We were broke, and there wasn't an option to replace *anything*—especially something someone else had ruined. I figured if something was going to be destroyed, then me and/or mine should be the one(s) to do it.

When I made it into my closet, I began to pray and said, *"Lord, I know You didn't make me this way. You didn't make me with a heart this cold. I know You did not make me with an unforgiving spirit. I know You didn't. Take it and all other unrighteousness out, and put Your righteousness—Your fruit of the Spirit—in."* As I continued to pray about the one thing that had me the most bound (unforgiveness) and the causes behind it (mainly my ability to remember every bad thing that has ever been done to me and the need to get even), I got an immediate revelation.

I realized the devil had that hold over me for years and just how brain-washed I was. It wasn't me not being able to forgive. It was him who had me not *wanting* to forgive, and The Board saw through it. I gave in to my flesh, because I felt more comfortable holding on to the hurt and anger. It felt more natural, if that makes sense, and I thought I was justified for holding onto it. Oh, but when the spirit man begins to fight back, he suppresses the natural man. Then, all of a sudden, that which used to be an enjoyably *natural* experience is intolerable. While in the closet praying for myself and regaining my strength in the Lord, I came out of bondage with the Light on!

Later, I immediately got an image of what used to be one of my favorite television shows awhile back: WWE Smack Down. I'm talking way back when it used to be WWF. Sometimes our spirit man and our natural man went at it so hard, it's like the spirit man had to take a chair, *or something,* and whap the natural man upside the head to knock him out long enough to make it a little while longer. I used to think if The Rock ever got put out of commission, in my opinion, they might as well have cancelled the whole show. Just like if I hadn't let go of that evil spirit and got back *on mission,* I might get cancelled too. I was so glad I got that when I did.

Being that I had accepted my call to the ministry, I had begun to take a "Ministers in Preparation" course at church. It was on July 20, 2003 that Pastor Bailey announced his acceptance and support of women preachers after a long struggle in that area. Had I ended the book that previous June when I thought it was finished, you and I both would have missed what came from that latest closet experience.

I realized God hadn't let the book go to print two years prior, because on Monday, March 1, 2004 our ministry leader taught on ministry hindrances. Unforgiveness topped the list. Having already accepted that I was being broken and there wasn't anything I could do about it, except give in, I accepted the next step in the process.

Since I had already prayed about the spirit of unforgiveness and released it *specifically* where it related to particular people, what I needed to do next was to pray some more and release it *generally.* I was way past broken furniture, office equipment, broken hearts, failed relationships, lying, and deceit. I was even past issues from my earlier years and had forgiven myself for my part in most of the drama. What I wasn't past however, was being taken to court for two years while trying to build my own house, raise my own child, and live my own life. I didn't learn the difference until then.

This particular lesson came from Genesis 50:15-21, and regarded Joseph and his brothers. As I sat in my Ministers in Preparation class that Monday night, I thought, *here we go again*. The ministry leader asked the question, "Why didn't Joseph hold a grudge?" Well, you know me, or at least you should by now. I thought, *Lord, it was easy for Joseph to forgive because they were his brothers. It didn't take too much to do that*. Thinking I had just said something, I heard God clearly say, "That's how you're supposed to be towards others." I understood exactly what He was saying. I was supposed to see others as my own brothers and sisters in Christ, even when they mistreated me.

On the way home, I talked to God and told Him to take all this stuff away once and for all. Just strip me and let's get it over with. See, I didn't really follow through that day after I got my earlier revelation in the closet, because partial obedience is total disobedience. And, obedience is better than sacrifice (see 1 Samuel 15:22). When I walked out of the closet I had a fresh, new per·spec·tive, but I wasn't willing to put in the par·ti·ci·pa·tion. God told me to apologize, and I was told by The Board to embrace, but I did neither.

I did feel the need to apologize to some of the individuals, though. I just couldn't imagine why. Yes, I was holding a grudge, but I was also the one whose things were ruined, feelings were hurt, and so on and so forth, in either instance. Now, I was expected to apologize to the ones who broke it, for holding a grudge over them breaking it; or apologize to the one who hurt me for holding a grudge over them hurting me? What was that about? Didn't I deserve an apology of my own?

There God was trying to set me free, and I was still holding on to the net. It didn't even have me anymore; I had it. *What a shame?* So, you do realize I prevented my own deliverance in the area of unforgiveness the first go 'round, right? I did. I *broke* through in the closet, but because I wouldn't *walk* through (when I came out) I missed the boat—all because I was still holding on. This was even after I asked Him to help me let go. "What happened?" You asked. *Plain ol' stubbornness!* I felt justified, remember?

Well, when I was in the car on my way home from class, I *talked* with the Lord. I said, "I'm not going around this mountain anymore," and began to praise and worship Him at that instant. Lo and behold, when I made it to the red light near my house, I began to cough up something that was in my throat and reached into the glove compartment for a napkin. I could feel whatever it was in my esophagus and began to gag. I could not breathe and immediately wondered if the devil was trying to choke me to death. I looked at the red light and suddenly those were the longest few seconds of my life. As I struggled to breathe, I thought about what I'd do when the light turned green. If I drove forward I could wreck, because my hands were wrapped around my neck. I could see an accident just waiting to happen as the line behind me at the intersection grew.

As soon as the light turned green, I gagged and coughed up whatever it was in my throat. Since I already had a napkin in my hand, I used it to catch what I'd spit up. Within minutes I was hacking and continually spitting wads into the napkin. When that paper towel was full, my mouth continued to fill. I couldn't wait to spit again but had nothing else to use—and I *hate* spitting! As my jaws continued to fill, I turned into the alley behind our house and headed for our garage. As soon as I turned into the driveway, I swung the car door open and spat right there. *Ugh!*

There I was sitting in the driveway behind our house, coughing and hacking out of the car door. I simply couldn't understand it. I then clicked the remote control garage door opener and pulled into the garage. As I sat, I wondered if I had just choked on something, or if the devil had choked me himself. In shock by this time, I went into the house confused. It must have shown all over my face too, because Derrick asked me what was wrong. After washing my hands, I said, "I think the devil tried to choke me!" He looked at me, and Emahn repeated what I'd said in the form of a question. "The devil tried to kill you mommy?" she asked. Derrick then told me to watch what I say and that we'd check it out later on.

When the girls went to bed that night, Derrick said, "You could have been purged." Immediately, I felt that could have been it. I had *just* prayed to God about deliverance of unforgiveness in the car and I was willing to par·ti·ci·pate this time. He could have very well been purging me *just* then, which meant He wasn't only cleansing me, but was also extracting or digging out some stuff, as well. Cleansing was surface deep, but purging happened from the inside-out.

After that conversation, I felt relieved. It was as if another weight had been lifted or another bag emptied. I was getting lighter and lighter, while preparing to soar higher and higher. God is so good that, on that particular night, I was able to release things which had been holding onto me, as well as me holding onto them. I let the net go! The devil *really* wasn't prepared for that.

I had been told earlier by The Board there were others I needed to forgive, as well. Once I understood who, I then questioned why. God was showing me I had to forgive the plaintiffs in those lawsuits for all those years of drama. If for no other reason, I rationalized it was because He said in Proverbs 28:25, *"A greedy man stirs up dissention, but he who trusts in the Lord will prosper."* So I had to forgive for myself and God's perfect plan for *my* life. God was confirming it when He said that's exactly how I am to treat others… like Joseph treated his brothers.

That's when God told me, *Shaundale*, I had to take on the Spirit of Joseph. So I released it, all of it, just as Joseph had. *And do you know what else?* As I read and re-read that section of scripture in Genesis 50:19-21, which says, *"But Joseph said to them, 'Don't be afraid. Am I in the place of God? You intended to harm me, but God intended it for good to accomplish what is now being done, the saving of many lives,"* I realized God had a message especially for me.

That passage of scripture had my attention to the point where, even now when someone wrongs me, I stop and check my Spirit of Joseph. It's not always instant, but I guarantee you it comes before I lay down to bed at night. Then, I asked myself, "Am I in the place of God?" That's it, my simple remedy for loosening the chains of unforgiveness. Ask yourself, that *one* question. "Am I in the place of God?" *Why?* Because when the light was flipped on for me, I knew the answer to the question had to be "no." *No*, I am not in the place of God. Therefore, I have no right to decide whether He should punish anyone or how, if so. On that evening, I made myself a reminder with an index card. I wrote the following note:

"I Don't Have the Right to Hold a Grudge"
Am I in the Place of God? (Genesis 50:19-21)

Because I am not in the place of God, I only have the right to acknowledge that the situation has occurred and move on. It is for God to decide what to do about it, if anything at all. I don't have authority over anybody but myself, and therefore cannot make anyone pay for anything by themselves. They need Jesus, too! So learn to let go of the hurt, of whatever depth, and let God... for the saving of many lives! -Voice of Power 03/04/2004

To this day, I *still* read my card and I *still* ask myself that question when I lay down at night, depending on the day's events—sometimes more than others. Although I am easily frustrated, I am not easily angered; regardless, I am not in the place of God.

Joseph taught me that it is okay to acknowledge that what was done was intended to hurt (and probably did), but because God is going to use it for good *in me* (for the saving of many lives), to let go the notion of getting even. Our new pastor had already preached the same thing. It just took God getting me to the point of par·ti·ci·pa·tion in the process of *His* program.

After that purging experience, every other day I started asking God to turn on the vacuum. I said, "Lord, whatever memories I'm holding on to that mean me no good, take 'em out... shut 'em down." It doesn't even have to be a memory of something that was done to me. It could be something I've done in the past that the devil tries to use against me in the present to hinder the future. I know life is a journey now and traveling the road is a process. Sometimes stuff tries to creep up from behind, but as soon as it does I keep on moving and say, "Shut 'em down, Lord; just shut 'em down!"

Having dealt with the obscure issues of my life, I still had to work through the obvious ones. Dealing with the pain of the fibroids had begun to take its toll on me. I was hurting in my abdomen and awoke screaming during the night from sharp pains shooting through my stomach more than enough times. When I started having to empty my bladder every ten to thirty minutes, I knew something had to be done. I couldn't accomplish anything during the day because of my frequent bathroom breaks, nor could I sleep at night because one wrong turn could summon that pain.

One night, I awoke screaming so loudly Derrick jumped up. Usually, I just moaned. But, recently I'd started to scream. I went to the bathroom and cried. All he could do was hold me. Nights prior to that one, I remember grabbing my stomach and praying. "Lord, I'm tired. I've been dealing with this too long. I know You can heal me if You want to. Even if You don't, I'll still love You. I'll still praise You." After that, I started to speak that I was healed according to the power of the Holy Ghost already at work within me. Still, I made an appointment to gain the knowledge I'd need regarding my options if medicine came into the picture.

I'd never considered a hysterectomy, because I'd always wanted a son. However, I felt like I'd already given birth to dozens of them and had never seen the reward of all the nights I'd spent balled into a knot crying from the heightened pains I experienced. I prayed about that one night, as well. "Lord, it's not fair. You said a woman's curse is to experience painful childbearing. My menstrual pains and my labor pains feel the same. I never screamed one time while in labor with Emahn for 24 hours before they called for a C-section. I now scream for abdominal pains. Where is the justice in that? What is my reward? Where is my child?"

When I finally made it to the doctor and plead my case, I was crying for whatever she thought was necessary. A hysterectomy would hurt my heart, but those fibroids were sending chills through my entire body. Not to mention that I thought it was resting on my bladder and causing all those bathroom breaks. She ordered a sonogram and I had to come back for it the following week. Until then I waited and continued to expect my healing, believing I wouldn't need any of the options she had suggested—including the laser removal.

The day I was scheduled for the sonogram came and I went emotionally expecting the best, but mentally prepared for the worst. As the nurse prepped me we chatted about nothing I particularly remember; however, I couldn't miss the way she asked," Who told you that you have fibroids?" I replied that my first OB/GYN told me, and then my second confirmed it. She then announced, "You don't have fibroids." I squinted my eyes and wrinkled my nose. "What do you mean, I don't have fibroids?" I asked.

She turned the monitor towards me so that I could see the screen for myself and proceeded to trace the lining of my uterus onscreen with her index finger. "Do you see how smooth this area is?" she asked. When I nodded, she continued, "Well, if you had fibroids this is where they would be. It appears that you've never had fibroids. I can't find them. They must be gone." Then, she pushed some button, saved the images, and turned everything off. "Gone?" I asked. "Is that possible? Can they just be *gone?*" After wiping off her utensils, she looked at me. "No, it's not. That doesn't just *happen,*" she replied.

I was elated. *Oh, my God!* I'm sure you could imagine the rest of my day. When I followed up with my doctor again, she further explained that fibroids don't just dissolve and go away like that. I wondered if I needed a second opinion, but I just knew Jesus had lent His hand in this one. The doctor said when the pain was at its worst, there's a slight chance the fibroid was shrinking with each contraction. Over time while I was screaming in a fetal position, unaware, my body was healing itself. To this day the fibroids are gone, but I was temporarily placed on water pills because my body was retaining water. That's when my doctor mentioned putting me on high blood pressure medicine, because over the course of the visits my blood pressure had maintained 141/80, 144/100, 150/111. My brain seemed to leap out of my head, because my thoughts were coming too fast for me to form words. I was *not* receiving that. Not after all I had been through. *Are you kidding me?*

I left that office and ranted and raved. I empted all the cabinets of my seasonings and salts, and replaced everything with low sodium/no salt ingredients—which, by the way, are horrible. I drank more water. I walked. I changed my diet a little, because I only weigh 124lbs at 5'4" (with shoes on). And, I prayed. I was like, "Lord, You know I am *not* trying to have anything; especially, high blood pressure. I don't care if my family has a history of it. I prayed all that stuff off when I was pregnant with Emahn. That's been over five years, *at least*. I cancelled everything from begging to bankruptcy! This falls in there! I'm not receiving this. I'm not accepting it. The devil is a liar and he's gonna stop messing with me!"

Well, a few days later I had a physical scheduled and had been praying for my blood pressure to return to normal. Over the past two weeks, it had increased significantly and I didn't know what I would do if it was higher. As I nervously took my seat, I awaited the nurse's assessment. I was concerned that I might make the numbers higher simply because I was so worked up already, but the results showed 140/70 and the nurse said, "You have perfect blood pressure, ma'am." *Praise the Lord! Hallelujah!* I was ready to sing like Andrae Crouch, "Can't nobody do me like Jesus!"

My First Ministry

17 Having realized the devil had switched lanes again and attacked my body, I was ready to "push the pedal to the medal." I was in full-fledged "road rage" mode. I felt like I was really headed somewhere. I later found out I was. I just had to know when to hit the brake and send his butt sailing. And, now was the time.

One day when I was sharing the experience I'd had in my deliverance of unforgiveness with a lady from church, I told her of the events which had led to my current revelation. After listening carefully, she told me I have a problem with restoration. I was stunned. I had been doing well and was on a roll in forgiving, but she was absolutely right. I wasn't seeking to build relationships with any of the individuals. It was because although I could now forgive, I still wrestled with forgetting, which meant to embrace and move forward. I had gotten the Spirit of Joseph in forgiveness, but hadn't quite grasped the Spirit of Joseph in favoring.

While Joseph forgave his brothers, fed them, and opened his home to them and their own, I struggled with the very thought of even holding a conversation with those who had wounded me. Nevertheless, I was able to finally forgive the plaintiffs and see them as family in Christ, as God had suggested from the beginning of the text in Genesis 50:19. "Why didn't Joseph hold a grudge?" I was asked. "Because they were his brothers," I answered. And God told me that even those who are my brothers and sisters *in Christ* will sometimes cause me the greatest pain, but I was still expected to treat them as such, for the saving of many lives. Now, He didn't expect me to throw a tea party and invite them over, but He did command that we not withhold good from those whom it is in our power to help when they deserve it (see Proverbs 3:27).

Honestly, my only concern with that scripture was figuring out who is to determine the level of worthiness. *Surely, not me!* I had already started to think how if it was left up to me, hardly anyone would ever deserve any good in my eyes after seeing some of the people closest to us go from laughing *with us*, to laughing at and talking *about us*. Then, I realized if that's my attitude, maybe I really hadn't been fully delivered of unforgiveness after all.

I figured a mature believer would trust his gut for the spirit of discernment to measure for him and offer favor *through mercy*. So, I knew then that's what is expected of me and what I started doing… showing grace. One was not giving someone what they *really* deserved (mercy), while the other was going the extra mile for them (grace). You know, for instance, instead of going smooth off, you give a compliment. Not only did they *not* deserve to be let off the hook, but you turned the other cheek and blessed them.

Having finally learned this truly had nothing to do with stock options, the layoff, the lawsuits, the people, or any other negative experience in the past few years, about a week later, while studying my devotion, I read in

Numbers 11:11-15. Here, Moses was questioning God about his call. This was the very same call he'd received after his own period of brokenness when he found out the family he'd always known wasn't his family at all. Then he became a fleeing murderer, married and lived amongst another people and, above all else, heard a voice speaking to him in a burning bush. *Talk about a valley experience.*

One day, Moses was a prince and the next a peasant, in a sense. He went from being surrounded by simulated friends and family in a palace, to being taken in by strangers in a desert. Then, *all of a sudden*, He heard the voice of God. When he did, He later raised some serious concerns; as did I. "Lord, who am I and what did I do to displease You that You would put the burden of all these people on me?" was our mutual question. Seriously, I began to say, "Lord, You don't intend to use me. Where is everyone else? What are they doing? What have I done, Lord? What have I done?" Why did I *ever* ask that? God let the scriptures speak.

In Numbers 11:25-26, God poured out His Spirit upon the leaders (even those who did not go to the Tent, but remained in the camp), because they had been previously set apart and established *as leaders*. It didn't matter that they didn't want to receive It (Holy Spirit) and didn't go into the Tent to get It. They had already been set apart by God, and *It* found them! *Now, how 'bout that?*

One week later, I went downtown to the hearing scheduled between the plaintiff in the car wreck and the city of Dallas. Having prayed, I decided all I could do was to make sure our household was in order and let God handle the rest. I had trusted Him for two years to take care of the auto accident and all of its consequences, and this was going to be it. As it turned out, the plaintiff didn't even show. As a result, the city attorney filed for a dismissal.

Later, during the same week, I was walking through the house and heard the voice of another woman of God's on television. I recognized her immediately as the same person who had said, "Arise Joshua," but wasn't really watching. I had reached a point where all I needed to do was be open to the Holy Spirit, and I kept either the television or the radio tuned to Christian media when I wasn't reading inspirational literature, studying my Bible, or praying. I had gotten listening in my spirit, and I was open to however He saw fit to enter in.

As I made my way into the den I heard, "God is getting ready to close some doors in your life." I stopped instantly. When I turned and looked up, she was looking directly into the television at me. As I looked back at her she continued to say, "You're ready to move forward, but not until God has closed some doors that no man can re-open." Was she talking to *me*? Could be, but I didn't want to go assuming she was, so I started praying… a prayer of thanksgiving as a matter-of-fact. I sure did! I said, "Lord, I don't know if she's talking about me this time, *but* I sure do thank You for closing doors in our past and opening them to our future!"

Well, believe me when I write *within days* God closed the doors to both the auto accident *and* the stock option lawsuits! He sure did. I hadn't been to court for the auto wreck on behalf of myself at all, and we hadn't been in a year and a half for the $500,000.00 dollar lawsuit (not since before the day I prayed to never go back again).

Three days after receiving that prophecy, on a Friday, I appeared for court, even though the plaintiff in the auto wreck had missed the first trial. If I had not shown and she did, she would have been granted her petition by default. Trust me; I had learned that lesson the hard way. When our names were called, both of us went forward and we each explained what had happened from our own perspective when asked. So when my turn came, I expressed to the judge that although I did not deny hitting the plaintiff, I did deny the responsibility *of* hitting her. Whoever was responsible for that missing stop sign was also responsible for the accident and her injuries. I believed that and had the faith of God... strong enough to move mountains. After that, I said nothing else.

I felt like God was telling me not to say another word, so I just listened to the judge and the plaintiff go back and forth. The lady referenced the city and the judge informed her that because she had missed that particular court hearing, the information was inadmissible. Liable or not, the city of Dallas was no longer a party to the court case.

After a brief conference to determine the extent of each of our damages, the case was dropped. *Can you believe that? I can!* I shouted! I danced, too. I probably even cried. It had been two years and it was finally over. I didn't even have a *natural* attorney, because we couldn't afford one and I didn't know anyone who practiced civil law. Oh, but I now knew what people meant when they said, "He's a doctor in your sick room and a lawyer in the court room!" He'd been both to me. And, I knew it well from my own experience.

On that following Monday, Derrick met Monique at the courthouse. Neither of the plaintiffs nor their legal representation showed. So, guess what happened this time? In short, Monique was able to finalize the documents without a dispute. I danced, shouted, and probably cried some more. *All* of our legal drama was over.

The televangelist *was* talking to me. Or, was she? Maybe or maybe not, all I know is I received a blessing that possibly had not originally been intended for me. However, because I received it in faith and gave thanks for it in advance (like it was mine), I got the blessing—or someone else's overflow, *again!* The televangelist could have very well been speaking to someone else, just like Jesus was headed to heal Jairus' daughter when the woman with the issue of blood touched Him. Her faith interceded and stopped Him dead in His tracks! In other words, a child of God showed up with a need. I hope you didn't think the Lord could be present and ignore one of His own *without cause.*

Listen, when Jesus walked down the street, some of everybody touched Him. The disciples said, "You see all these people and You're asking what *somebody* touched You. (Mark 5:31, Shaundale Johnson paraphrase)." Well, that led me to believe some of those people, including believers, were only interested in being able to say they touched Jesus, and so was I at one point. However, by now, like the woman with the issue of blood, I was more interested in saying, "Jesus touched *me!*" Why else would she have been recognized? Because, like Jairus, she sought His power, and so had I!

I was no longer simply making my way through the crowd *just like everyone else.* I finally had "issue of blood" faith and was pressing with praise and with purpose. That was when He touched me and closed doors that will forever remain unopened to man.

Hebrews 11:1 (KJV) says, *"Faith is the substance of things hoped for and the evidence of things not seen."* That's why when having been touched again I read the next day's devotion in Joshua 24:2-3. It was revealed to me that God skipped completely over Terah (father of Abraham and Nachor) and blessed his descendants. This happened because Terah worshipped against God. God then took Abraham and blessed him *and* his descendants. That was the kind of generational blessing I was seeking.

As I dug deeper, I prayed, *"Lord, I can't undo what my ancestors have done, but I'm trying to live holy and want you to break generational curses off of me and my children, down to my great-grandchildren's great-*

grandchildren, *for a thousand generations. I don't mind if you skip on down to me and mine, or the house of Derrick and Shaundale, at all!"* Then, I remembered Deuteronomy 7:9, *"Know therefore that the LORD your God is God; he is the faithful God, <u>keeping his covenant of love to a thousand generations of those who love him and keep his commands</u>.* By placing that scripture on my heart, I believed His answering that request was guaranteed. As long as I upheld my part to love Him and keep His commands, He would uphold His and keep His covenant of love to my descendants for a thousand generations!

For some reason, days after that I had the words "Journey to Journal," as well as "I can only be me" in my head. As the Ministers in Preparation class progressed and I prepared to publicly announce my call, the devil tried to do a number on me through my very worst enemy… *me!* I had tried several ways, in my head, to get out of publicly announcing my call, even so that I tossed and turned until about 2:00a.m. one morning. Then, having sat up, read, prayed, listened, and journaled, I got it. I could only be the "me" God said I am in Christ. Who He had called me was voice of power. Therefore, from my natural journey of living came my journaling, or my voice, but from my journaling has come my spiritual journey of ministry, which is His power.

With that revelation, the time came for me to share my call to the ministry with my church. Throughout the day, I had the same feelings in my belly that I did before the initial prophecy. I was nervous and felt closeness to God. Still, that didn't stop the devil from whispering, "It's not too late. It's not too late." Although I was "anxious" most of the day, I couldn't particularly place my finger on what I had been experiencing since about three days prior. My pelvic area hurt. I couldn't explain it. I just knew it hurt. It wasn't my hips or my thighs; it was my actual pelvic area.

When I tried to make it clear to Derrick, the only words that came to mind were, *it feels like I'm getting ready to give birth*. Thinking back, honestly, I had gone through enough contractions to enjoy this moment. The only thing was, when I sat down, the most comfortable place was the toilet. It was as if all of my pelvic area was expanding, so there I sat—fully dressed—resting on the toilet throughout the day over a two or three day period. It seemed the opening in the toilet seat provided me with the most relief, because I needed the support under my legs. The joints where my hips and thighs connect were the most sensitive. I wished I still had my boppy pillow from when I was pregnant to slip around my back.

As I sat waiting, for what I didn't know, I tried to relax. However, my current circumstances had me trying to make light of the situation. I had started to waddle. I knew I wasn't pregnant. It just helped relieve the pain when I walked with a curve; a twist does not describe it. I also knew I'd have to be in the early stages of labor to be going through what I was dealing with, so I'd have to be obviously pregnant—as in noticeably big. Still, I couldn't shake the feeling that I was getting ready to give birth to something... something I did not conceive. I didn't even recall feeling my body get ready to birth my children, so whatever this was I knew it was something serious and something supernatural... so supernatural, it scared me. Yet, through my sobs I told the Lord, "Yes, I will save the children." When the pain stopped, the pressure was on.

Having been given the charge of II Timothy 4:2 (to preach the Word; be prepared in season and out of season; and correct, rebuke, and encourage with great patience and careful instruction), I had begun to research the five-fold ministry gifts referenced in Ephesians 4:11. I wanted a better understanding of each and to know where *exactly* did I fall. It certainly helped that I had been tested in the area of compassion and had passed, because I was to correct, rebuke, *and* encourage. However, as if that wasn't already enough, He added *with great patience and careful instruction.* I cringed at the thought of how many times I had done the exact opposite.

As I continued to pray for even more clarity and revelation, I realized my concern had actually shifted to the carnal, or immature, Christian at some point. It amazed me to see the hand of God at work so vividly in my own life. To be able to plainly see the transformation I had made in the Spirit from being a Christian concerned about my own well-being (like the woman in the vision with the big hat), to how Christ drew me with the child in the house, for others, was sheer joy. That's when I noted, although there were children on the train in that previous premonition, there weren't any being turned away. No, that didn't mean there won't be children in hell, but it does tell me if there are, it's because of the adults who were turned away as well.

I now just wanted to take each of the spiritually immature, or spiritually stupid, as I had once called them, into my arms and whisper, "Just grow." I wanted them to all know, as believers, each of us has already been planted. However, it was up to us, from the beginning, to decide whether we would ever take root. The Holy Spirit waters, but we determined whether we actually absorbed It, sprouted up and branched out, or rejected It, withered and died. Every time we took one step in the direction of the natural sunlight, we risked being over-exposed and burning, but if we chose to lean in the direction of the Son Light, we would branch out and bear much fruit (see John 15:8).

My purpose had finally come full circle. It was sharpening the Body of Christ, to do the work of the Lord, for the saving of many lives. I was concerned about everyone, but I was carrying the Church. No matter how hard I tried to shake it, God worked harder to steady me. Still being equipped myself, I continued to undergo some fine-tuning of my own.

One day, as I listened to a local minister on one of the neighboring radio stations, I heard him say something about if you don't tithe, then you're not giving. It didn't make sense to me then, but I later equated it to: If my tithes are $200, but I offer $20 instead, then it's not an offering at all, because the offering doesn't start until $200.01. The offering was *above* the tithe! So, the minister on the radio was right. If you don't tithe, you *don't* give. Then I thought, *so I owe?*

As I drove home, I was floored by the thought that I had been stealing from God. It took me all this time to really get that. I mean, sure I knew I was being disobedient periodically when I hadn't tithed consistently. *But stealing?* I thought I was at least doing something by offering *some* of it all this time. *Duh! How could I offer something when I hadn't even paid what I owed?*

I wondered if I could seriously get away with offering our mortgage company *some* of the mortgage payment, at that point. *Heck no!* I thought. They want their money, *all of it*, when it's due. *Then*, they'll take whatever you plan to *offer* above and beyond that amount. So, with a new revelation on tithing, I realized something had to be done fast. I had been wrong *again* for over twenty years. So, guess what I did? Well, first I apologized to God. Secondly, I talked with Derrick. We discovered where the problem was and understood it wasn't necessarily a desire *not* to tithe; it was more a lack of *prioritizing* the tithe.

From the beginning of our marriage we had tithed. It wasn't until we were expected to write out a five-figure check that we had a problem. We put God on hold, and

He turned the tables around and put us on hold. *Now, we're still waiting!* As we've grown through the years, although I put the tithe and offering in an envelope on payday, I would tuck it away in a drawer in the house or some secret compartment in the car. When it came time to put the envelope in the offering tray on Sunday morning, guess where it was. Still at the house or in the car! I had a desire to give, but it wasn't important enough to me to set the envelope out in a visible area prior to Sunday morning worship service.

As soon as the offering tray was passed I'd say, "Well, I'll bring it next Sunday." I guess you already know between that particular Sunday and the next one, dozens of *tithe-takers* came up. Either Emahn needed something for school, or Eian would run out of the one thing I forgot to pick up the last time I went shopping.

Everything from a flat tire to an extra dozen of eggs and a gallon of milk applied as a tithe-taker. You take a little bit here and, before you realize it, that $10.00 you *borrowed* from what you owe God already has multiplied to $100.00. Now, God was due for this *and* the next week's pay. "What are tithe-takers?" you asked. Well, tithe-takers are those unexpected things that come up and catch us off-guard. Beware though, because there's a difference between *a* tithe-taker and *us* taking tithes!

Taking tithes is classified as the following: We take our tithes and go out to eat. We take our tithes and buy clothes with matching accessories. We take our tithes and go away for the weekend. In other words we spend it, fully aware of what we're doing. *Get the idea?* So, not to even put myself in a predicament where I would cause *our house* to fall victim to another tithe-taker, and therefore shut up the window that God promises to open *Himself* and pour out a blessing I don't have room enough to receive (see Malachi 3:10), I developed a new strategy.

You see, I had been a tithe-taker for years because I

was offering God something on what I owed Him, as opposed to giving Him all He was due. That's what happened with the Montero. I took $18,000.00 and bought an SUV, and two years later God took it back when I had the car wreck. Having learned that lesson *the hard way*, I was determined to grow, and I did... some. That was when I fell victim to tithe-takers. I went from voluntarily spending all of it on myself, to unintentionally spending some of it on my family. *Now, I'm not trying to make excuses, I'm just trying to make it plain.* Regardless of the situation, I owed God an apology and my soul some repentance.

After I apologized and asked forgiveness, I decided to try a new thing at the request of my husband. One payday I was going to pay the local utility bills when Derrick looked at me and said, "Go pay tithes." "What?" I asked. "Go pay tithes? I'm not even headed anywhere *near* the church. That's on the other side of the city. I'm staying on this side of town today," I rambled. Still I said, "I'll wait until Sunday." Derrick continued his appeal for me to go and pay tithes. He said, "Pay God *first*." Then, like a light, it clicked. That was how to ensure you gave God your first fruit. You took it! *Duh, again.* That was so simple.

Just like we took everything else to the post office, the dry cleaners, the bank, etc. we should have been taking God His portion, *first*. So what did I do? I drove to the church, delivered our tithes (and offering), and then prayed in the prayer room that God would bless it *and us*. Well, when I tell you somewhere around two weeks later Derrick got two job offers and had a third one pending, you are going to think I'm making this stuff up now. I kid you not; it happened!

Derrick had been working for the Department of Labor right at a year or so by now, although he was still applying for better job opportunities elsewhere. This job was the one he'd gotten two days after we found out we were pregnant with Eian. She was now six months old, and during this time we had begun to pray for him to get a better paying position, one he enjoyed as well. I don't even remember the specifics of my earlier prayer request, just that I asked a special blessing for being faithful *this time* in bringing our tithes in. No, I didn't deserve one for doing what I was supposed to do, but He did say in the rest of Malachi 3:10, *"Test me in this and see if I will not throw open the floodgates of heaven and pour out so much blessing that you will not have room enough for it."*

Derrick was working one job and had three others waiting on him to respond. Now, if that wasn't "don't have room enough to receive" favor, then I don't know what is. All we had to do was decide which job was sent by God. By this point, he was just grateful for options. I was simply grateful for discernment.

Job one was going to pay more money now, but at the expense of him being away from home for weeks at a time. Plus, he had to cut 3-4 inches of his dreadlocks. Job two offered more stability with the possibility of increased earning potential in time; meanwhile, he would get to stay home and keep his hair length. Job three was only a tad bit better than his current position, so it didn't make the cut.

I thought back to when I had to remind myself, and Derrick, *What God has for you is for you... as you are.* I'd told him years earlier he would not have to get his hair cut off in order to get a good job, as he had been advised. Now, maybe it would not have taken as long in the natural, but in the Spirit we had no control over where God had us. Besides, I refused to believe he was not going to get his ideal job because he wears his hair in locks. Man looks at the outside, but God looks at the heart. And, I didn't see any natural man with enough power to stop God's spiritual plan for our lives or Derrick's career.

I continued to see a man who had been laid off from a job that had paid him in excess of $250,000.00 a year in salary and benefits. His resume' alone, in my head, could have gotten him any of the jobs he had applied for. My concern was why it didn't, and I refused to believe it had anything to do with his hair. It was *God*. He had dried up the well, and it was up to us to trust Him to replenish it *in season*. Believing that, Derrick accepted job number two. The seasons were changing. *Praise the Lord!*

When he phoned the other supervisor to decline job number one—the one that asked him to cut his hair—the man cussed at him and hung up the telephone. When he told me that, I said, "See, I told you only one of those jobs was from the Lord. You know that was nothing but the devil!" He had offered more money and wanted Derrick to conform by changing his appearance. Plus, he was going to have him traveling 60 to 70 percent of the time for a significant amount of money. But, you already know I wasn't about to prostitute my principles—especially not over the well-being of my marriage. I didn't even want to imagine the problems the enemy would have tried to throw at us over the distance. Right about now I'd be writing D.R.A.M.A. (Divorce Ready and Murder Anxious).

As Derrick transitioned from the old to the new job, I began to realize how much I had grown over these past few years, even though consistently paying tithes was still a struggle. (Yes, even after all we'd been through.) I had at least gotten to a place where I no longer wondered *if* the Lord was telling me something, though. I simply tried to clue into just *what* He was telling me. So, as I rolled up my sleeves, I went into my prayer closet. Praying that God's will continued to be done in my life and the lives of people I hoped to touch, in addition to greater discipline and strength, I prayed for you, the reader, and yours as well.

As I continued to journal my daily experiences and write the manuscript, God continued to show Himself. I even felt comfortable enough in my recent prayer responses to begin seeking employment again. I started looking into both technical and writing positions. One I was educated in, the other I was skilled at. Although nothing came, I continued to pray. I reached the point where I simply cried out all over again. I said, "Lord, the positions I'm applying for I don't even want. My background is in technology, but I want to write." I repeated that I didn't want to work on another computer. I didn't even want to see one unless I was typing on it. All I wanted to do was write.

Continuing to believe God was working something out in the super-natural, I kept searching for a job and waiting for Him to supply it. Well, as He is so all-powerful and all-knowing, He even showed me how most of the time, when we pray, we don't even know what to ask for. Having been simply praying for a job, any job, then going back and saying, "Lord, I don't even want to do what I've been praying You give me," He allowed me the blessed opportunity to become one of the newest members of our church staff.

God pulled that "exceedingly and abundantly above all blessing" out *again!* As the new Web Content Manager/Technical Writer, I would even be able to work part-time, from home, where I could continue to be accessible to my family… my *first* ministry.

His Word

18 Psalm 37:23 (KJV) reads, *"The steps of a good man are ordered by the Lord,"* and I knew it to be very true. Having surrendered my natural life back in 1998, I hadn't realized it would be an on-going spiritual process. Just in these last few years alone I had learned to surrender my financial will, my mental and emotional will, as well as my my social will. I had finally grasped "home is where the heart is," because home is where the Lord is supposed to be. My family would be my first ministry, because they saw the real me. If what I did would not line up with what I said, then Derrick, Emahn, and Eian would suffer naturally and spiritually. However, Emahn and Eian would suffer most because they would inherit my carnal nature and curse their own children.

Proverbs 13:22 referenced a good man leaving an inheritance to his children's children, and that the wealth of the sinner is laid up for the just. I wanted my legacy to include a strong spiritual foundation. That, to me, was a *real* inheritance. *"For what shall it profit a man, if he shall gain the whole world, and lose his own soul?"*

Mark 8:36 (KJV) asked. *Nothing!* That's why I desired for the fruit of my womb, for generations to come, to become like trees of righteousness, planted by the waters and bringing forth fruit in their season (see Psalm 1:3). We would have roots strong and deep in the Lord, starting here and now. It would be up to Derrick and me to make the initial deposits by teaching the Word of God, praying for and with our children, and making sure they heard more of *I'm a Soldier in the Army of the Lord* than they did of *Soldier* by Destiny's Child. With the world as distorted as it is it would be hard, but not impossible.

One morning while preparing to head to the church, the phone rang. I was on my way to attend several meetings with some of the members of the pastoral staff concerning their web page content, which I had been hired to work on. One of the ministers I had not scheduled to meet with was calling. He had been reading his daily devotional and felt the Lord had laid me on his heart. When I finished with my meetings, I stopped by his office and he shared with me part of his morning Bible study lesson. As I read through the paragraphs, my heart raced. Because I'd been constantly saying, "Lord, but I don't want to preach, I just want to write and teach," I was amazed at the accuracy of the text concerning my answer.

The passage referenced that when Peter preached at the day of Pentecost (here we go again), thousands were saved. However, when Paul preached for the first time a man went to sleep, fell out of a window, and died. The writer of the devotional pointed out that although Paul's speaking ministry never took off, his writing ministry soared and thousands are still being saved to this day. I wanted to shout right there!

Although Paul was *called* to preach, he had been *gifted* to write and teach. A call is an order or command, but a gift was an endowment upon, a bestowal on, or a donation to. I noticed then that even though we all have the natural ability to write, I, like Paul, possess a supernatural ability, which could be likened to the anointing. That's what happened when I allowed God to "turbo charge" me!

I had begun to say the responsibility of *every* Christian is to enhance and increase the Kingdom of Heaven. The question asked is, "Are you?" Are you walking in *your* call, in order to fulfill *your* Christian responsibility, by way of *your* gift? According to Matthew 28:19-20, we are to go and make disciples of all nations, baptizing them in the name of the Father and of the Son, and of the Holy Spirit, teaching them to obey everything God has commanded. Paraphrase: enhance (to go and make better, teach) and increase (to go and make bigger, add to). With that in mind, here we go!

Step one is to determine whether you've ever confessed Christ *is* Lord and were saved. Step two would then be to determine whether you've ever accepted Christ *as* Lord and were filled. Then, step three would be to determine whether you have a gift and/or calling within. *So let's continue onward. There's a kingdom waiting to be enhanced and increased, and guess what... you're a major key!*

Step one: are you saved? The Bible states in Acts 2:21, *"Whosoever shall call on the name of the Lord shall be saved."* Let's start there. If you are unsure of your salvation from day-to-day, then bow your head, quiet your spirit, humble your heart, and simply call on the name of Jesus. He will hear you and He will answer (see Acts 2:21).

"My First Prayer"
(Salvation)

Jesus, if You would help me, I will believe in my heart

that God raised You from the dead, and confess with my mouth that You are Lord (see Romans 10:9).

If you *sincerely* prayed this prayer, and as a result now *believe* Jesus was crucified for the redemption of your sins and God raised Him from the dead, *then you are saved*—no ifs, ands, or buts about it. Please join and actively participate in a Bible-teaching, Gospel-preaching church, and make your confession known through baptism and by maturing spiritually. *Now, let's proceed.*

Step two: Are you filled? Jesus said in John 3:5, *"I tell you the truth, no one can enter the kingdom of God unless he is born of water and the Spirit." Let's press, okay!* I have prayed for and with you. Know that in repentance it is very important to confess each sin as the Spirit leads. We overcome by the blood of the Lamb and the word of our testimony, according to Revelation 12:11, and God is about to give you one! Bow your head and lift your hands in total surrender for God's will over your life, as you begin to pray the following:

"Believer's Prayer"
(Sanctification)

Lord, I'm sorry. I know You were crucified and raised from the dead, by God, for the redemption of my sins. I know You are Savior, but even though I've known better, I haven't done better. I've made such a mess of my life, and I'm so tired of living outside of Your will. I'm sorry for (call sins by name as the Spirit leads). I now confess You as the Son of God and Lord of my life. I need You. I give You full control. Please come into my heart and make me new. I confess all of my sins right now and ask that You would forgive me, so nothing remains. I am a new creature. Old things have passed away. Come and abide in me, and help me to live the rest of my life to

Your glory. Please order my steps as I try to live right. Keep me on the straight and narrow road that leads to life, in Jesus' name, amen.

If you *sincerely* prayed this prayer and truly experienced *repentance* as a result of a *transformation of the heart*, my soul rejoices for and with you! Please join and seek to actively participate in a Bible-teaching, Gospel-preaching church, and make your transformation publicly known through growing and serving. *Serving where?* "That's a mighty fine question to ask," as Pastor Bailey would have said. Let's move on to step three then, shall we?

Matthew 22:14 states, *"For many are called, but few are chosen."* With that being the case, where do you fall? At this point, I encourage you to seek God for yourself in order to find out. All Christians are called to make disciples (enhance and increase), but only a few are chosen to lead the way. So, for myself, I petitioned God *specifically* to make sure I was still on the right path. After that, I thanked Him for bringing me safely to this point.

Well, one morning after that prayer request, I awoke with one of my cousins on my mind. The strange part was that this particular cousin and I aren't even close. She's really my third cousin who was born and raised in Texas, while I grew up in Louisiana. For whatever reason, when I strolled into the bathroom that morning and looked into the mirror, my cousin flashed in my mind. Immediately, I said to myself, "I've got to try to find that girl," and said a prayer for her. I then started getting ready to tackle that day's To Do List, because I was headed to the church for another meeting.

After those discussions came to a close, I sat down for a moment and decided to check my e-mail. When the application loaded, inside my Inbox was a forwarded e-mail from the Christian author I'd met in the local print shop back in 2003. It was now 2005, and we hadn't been in touch. The Subject line of the e-mail stated "FW: Book Club Symposium" and the body included a note to me, which simply asked if this would be something Concord's Writing Ministry would be interested in. I opened the attachment and read the words of someone who literally said, "Hey y'all, this is an invitation to a book symposium my "little cousin" is hosting. I read the name and thought, *I have a cousin named that, too.* What were the chances?

Now, purposely searching for additional information, I skimmed the remainder of the e-mail. Even though I knew there was no way I was going to make the event, because it was in Atlanta and we were on a tight budget, I continued to scroll downward. I always liked to see where my e-mails originated from because, by some chance, there could be someone on there I've been looking for. Usually, I only did this when I received something from family or old college friends, though. Who knew, this time, me and the lady I "just happened" to meet in the print store, two years prior, would possibly be linked? We knew there was a spiritual connection made on the day we'd met. We just didn't know what it was or how it would manifest. What were the chances *for real*? Well, once again, God in His infinite wisdom showed me.

As I continued to scroll downward in the message, I found an e-mail address on the "little cousin's" original letter. I thought this was wild because the e-mail actually originated from her just one day prior. My heart started pounding and my hands shook. I grew more and more nervous, as I contemplated whether to contact this person. Could she be my cousin? If not, would she think I was crazy? What would I say? How would I even explain this "twist of fate"? Well, I didn't know, but I had to chance it. I just *had* to.

Full of questions, I acted on impulse and replied to the original e-mail. This is the jist of what we typed. Of course, I included a little more personal information in the original message, and then she replied with more of her own.

```
-----Original Message-----
From: Shaundale Johnson
To: Undisclosed Recipient
Sent: January 19, 2005, 8:59AM
Subject: FW: Book Club Symposium
```

 Hi. This is interesting. I just received this e-mail from an author-peer of mine. However, what was interesting is the name from which it originated, because I have a cousin with that exact name.
 Long story short, my name is Shaundale (Hornes) Johnson. I'm originally from Bunkie, Louisiana and if this is Inga Lewis, grand-daughter of Lola Milo Lewis (the sister to my grandmother, Mittie Milo Hornes) then this is a strange "coincidence." Especially, since I was just thinking about Inga this morning before I left the house. God is so miraculous!
 At any rate, I do realize this is a mega-chance I'm taking (putting my family business out here), but if "by chance" you are the right Inga, my do we have some catching up to do and a story to tell everybody else. If not, my apologies and I hope that I at least brought laughter and humor to your day.

Be blessed,

Shaundale

I then continued with my day's activities. I didn't necessarily forget about the e-mail, I just didn't have it at the forefront of my thoughts. By the time I made it home, I was so swamped with other things to do that I didn't get back online until approximately 11:00p.m. that night. That's when I saw it... the reply from Inga Lewis. I was immediately sent back into that morning's earlier events.

Snapping back into reality, as I read the name Inga Lewis in bold lettering, I noticed her Subject line. She had replied with "Yes, This is Me" as her header. I *screamed*! I then ran to the bed and shook Derrick to wake him. I hadn't told him about the original e-mail, because I was busy and hadn't thought anymore about it until I saw the reply. As I brought him up-to-date, I went back to my desk and read the remainder of the e-mail aloud. Inga replied with:

```
-----Original Message-----
From: Inga Lewis
To: Shaundale Johnson
Sent: January 19, 2005, 11:34PM
Subject: Yes, This is Me!
```

Hi, Shaundale!!!

   Yes, I am your cousin Inga Lewis. Is this a small world or what? My grandmother IS your grandmother's sister. This is SO funny.
   Do you live in Atlanta? If not, I guess you won't be at the symposium... LOL!!! God IS a Miracle-Worker.

Take care,
Inga

Okay, could God have been any clearer than that in answering whether I was one of the few who are chosen?

I grinned from ear-to-ear *for days*! What was the likelihood of getting in touch with the right Inga Lewis, via a forwarded e-mail, who "just happened" to be co-coordinating a literary symposium? Oh sure, I could have made a few phone calls back home to find her but, at that point, I knew for a fact nothing in life happened by chance. I had not only a pile of journals, but a whole manuscript to prove it. The steps of the righteous *are* ordered by God (see Psalm 37:23), and He really meant it when He said, *"For I know the plans I have for you; plans to prosper you and not to harm you, plans to give you hope and a future."* (Jeremiah 29:11)

I learned from this experience that, as a Christian, to deal in coincidence, luck, or things "just happening" is the same as calling God a liar. If things "just happen," then why does He order our steps according to the plan He knows He has for our lives? *Whenever we say we're lucky, we make luck* a god, *but when we say we are blessed, we acknowledge that the blessing comes* from God.

Days later, Inga phoned me and we talked and talked, and planned to talk again. Come to find out (that's my Bunkie roots), she was the Event Planner for her book club's upcoming annual event which would feature, get this, African-American, Christian, female authors on their panel of guests. "Shut the house down!" as Quad would say. I knew then I was headed to Atlanta and couldn't anything short of death stop me—budget or no budget.

Although I had not been anywhere since Chicago, I readied myself to take another trip for the sake of the call. During that time, I continued to finalize my manuscript—yes some more—and gave God all the glory. Things came together better than I'd even imagined. Regardless, I continued to ask God for favor, not just for me, but for all who would be affiliated with this project.

I didn't know why, but I started to envision a CD—as in compact disc. I'm not a singer, but I can hold a note or two. I didn't know why God would be showing me a CD being released with the book, but accepted it. Unsure of how this would play out, I just continued to walk in what I knew I had been called to do—write.

As I continued on my journey, I was in awe of my accomplishments in both the natural and the Spirit. A girlfriend told me, actually she warned, "Shaundale, everybody's not going into your next season with you. Don't be surprised when people you least expect question the validity of what God is doing in your life." I then began to pray that God would continue to place people on my path who would help and not hinder me. I was getting too close to the prize, so not knowing what Atlanta held I asked God for holy connections. I asked *Him* to make all of the contacts both for and with me. When He did, I could not wait to get back home to tell it! You *know* I sent an e-mail when I shared the following testimony:

```
-----Original Message-----
From: Shaundale Johnson
To: Undisclosed Recipients
Sent: March 2, 2005 12:39PM
Subject: ATL Trip - All About Business

God is AWESOME!

    First off, I got in Thursday night and
that was the only time my feet touched the
ground.  I got  a good  night's sleep  and
Friday morning Inga and I headed to one of
the  local  universities  for  an  African-
American Author's Festival. Okay, HOW COME
I met  a whole  slew  of authors?!  I mean
met, as in chit-chat with, not just shook
a hand and said hello. One of them was Nea
```

Anna Simone!

Okay, now Saturday I was at Inga's event and was sick. I started praying, because I knew the devil was trying to keep me from a blessing. I put my good foot forward and said, "I'm going in there if I have to LIMP." Inga and I were sitting in the car praying, because we knew it was the devil. I got out and was SICK, but kept going. My head was not only hurting, but spinning.

When we made it inside, I sat and laid my head on a table. When I heard voices next to me, I looked up. I met Victoria Christopher Murray!!! When I met Mrs. Murray, I told her the story about finding Inga via e-mail and how I ended up there. Later, I was introduced to the president of the book club hosting the event. Okay, WHY were they kind enough to add me to the program?!

I ended up telling everybody how Inga and I found one another after all these years, which was an act of God in itself, and the rest was history. I then gave a brief testimony of some of me and Derrick's valley experiences. People were telling me how moved they were, which was very encouraging for me. It let me know everything is for a cause.

When I got back Sunday, y'all know I had that local event to attend Sunday for the author showcase. Well, then I got invited to do something in the fall where Nikki Giovanni and Eric Jerome Dickey are being featured. Also, I was looking for a way to make a contact with the bookstore in New Birth (Bishop Eddie Long's church) while in Atlanta, and God sent someone to the symposium on Saturday to meet me. Inga and I were riding down the highway when I told her I needed to get in touch with New Birth. As big as that church is, I KNEW they had to have a bookstore. Besides, I had been watching Bishop right along with everyone else on my Christian soap opera channels, and he'd blessed me just as much as the others had.

Well, lo and behold, this lady approached me at the literary event and introduced herself. She said she attends a "little church" they call New Birth. I got COUNTRY. I was like, "New Birth! Bishop Eddie Long, New Birth?" She LAUGHED at me, but she gave me the bookstore's information. I was SO excited! God is SO good y'all… TRULY GOOD!!!

Shaundale

Having returned to Dallas, I continued in my now "norm." I sought God more than I had previously. I started to affirm daily that I am Shaundale, voice of power—whatever that entailed. Motivational Speaker had lost its savor, because motivational speaking was *Shaundale* encouraging someone to *be* something. But inspiring, I'd determined, was the *Spirit of the living God* stirring someone to *do* something. That much I knew, and He was setting the stage for me to *do* my part.

Before I wrote that e-mail, I sent one to Inga's book club. I simply thanked them for a grand experience and a wonderful opportunity. I knew there was a blessing there for me, and I'm glad I went to get it! I also received an email from another author who was featured on the panel of the book club symposium, Marc Lacy. He had been so inspired by my testimony that he wrote a spoken word tribute entitled *Ode to Once Broken, Now Blessed*. The original piece follows.

Ode to Once Broken Now Blessed

Once broken, now blessed
Yes!
Embalmed with Psalms,
Letter 23 to be exact.
The fact remains plain
That my cup runneth
Over with blessings...
The touch and caressing
from The Almighty
Have made me and my family
Persevere and overcome...
Overcome walks
In valleys and shadows of death
And I can still breathe,
Meaning I have breath.
Fearing no evil
Standing tall
Exhibiting the wherewithal
My oily head has been anointed...
And I've been appointed
By my Savior as an exalted sheep
Fleece embedded deeply with
Surely goodness and mercy...
Blessed with libations from
A full well...
Forever in The Lord's house will I dwell...

I've just got to tell...
That Baby Emmanuel is the Composer
And Arranger of your and my
Salvation's greatest hits...
And when you feel the joy
You start to gleam by the bits,

Jumpin' up high, grabbin' the
Stratosphere, then landin' on the
Clouds and doin' the splits...
You can't deny that Jehovah Jirah
Sent us The Messiah who blessed the
Magi to bring gifts and frankincense...
Hence... conception immaculate
Mother Mary and Daddy Joseph
Had to understand that The Son of Man
Was birthed... died... for us, then
Moved the stone
And was unearthed.
Perfection in the resurrection...
The Christ
The Savior
The Holy Spirit
Ohhh, bless His name
Bless His name
The Most High
The Omnipotent
The King
"B' rump pump pump pum,"
Said the coy drummer boy.

B' rump pump pump pum,
Ahoy girls and boys.

Follow me as we're drainin'
From the land of Canaan
To a place exhibiting milk and honey
Oh, Nazareth
Oh, Galilee
Oh, Jerusalem
Oh, Calvary
Oh, Bethlehem.

Here I am...

Little light o' mine's a shinin'.
Little light o' mine's a shinin'.

Now I have the spirit to keep climbin'
From Genesis to Exodus and oh what a revelation...

I've now witnessed the passion
No income and family raisin' takes lashes
But each lash represented stages of evolution
Spawning wisdom, character
And oooh that intestinal fortitude
Grips tightly as we receive the
Blessings from The Almighty...
Pockets were broke
But spirit was never broken
Believin'
Being soakin' wet from
Having been anointed
Arms a' everlastin'...
reachin' out and touchin'...
Blastin' doubt into oblivion,
Now blessed is our dominion....

I can jubilantly rest
For I was once broken... and now I'm blessed... yes...

©2005 Marc Lacy
AVO Publishing

Marc based the poem on Psalm 23 and when I read the words, he'd captured the entire essence of the book—as well as my spiritual journey—after hearing a 10 minute testimony. *That, is talent!* I imagined his wheels were spinning as I spoke. I was truly grateful and deeply humbled. Immediately, I emailed him back to let him know.

After speaking with Marc over several weeks, via email and by phone, he was able to send me a compilation of tracks he'd laid of the poem to music. Derrick and I listened to every version and chose the most favorable to us. When we let Marc know our preference, he mass produced it and sent copies. This was the CD I'd envisioned being released with the book, but hadn't really shared it. I had learned, by then, you can't tell everybody everything. So, I knew to keep my mouth shut. I was having enough problems dealing with the book not being produced yet, so surely I wasn't about to add to the drama by saying a CD was coming with no clue from where or what type of project it would be. Although I had no idea, God is true to His Word.

FOR YOU

19 As time would have it, circumstances dictated that Derrick and I spread our wings and fly elsewhere. God had proven Himself faithful to His Word, so we responded. Concord had carried us through some major seasons of change; however, there was a restlessness that I continued to encounter at a heightened level from day to day—both on staff and in service throughout my many ministry objectives. Having been faithful, active members of Concord for nearly ten years, it was a very painful experience when the struggle ended and we were freed from the cocoon God had used to shield us through the storm. We were ready to flutter but had neither idea where to go specifically, nor inkling in which direction to head.

From my new perspective, the world seemed a bit larger than it had previously. We visited numerous churches throughout the Dallas/Ft. Worth area during the course of a year and a half. Every six weeks or so we ended up right back at the church of the minister who had spoken over the local Christian radio station about robbing God of His tithe, Dr. Tony Evans. I continued to stay close to Jesus during this transition, but my journaling slacked while my praying and writing increased.

With *Once Broken, Now Blessed* nearing completion, I continued to write and managed to start on more literary projects. I knew God was going to bring about my destiny; heck, I had literally given birth to it. I just still didn't know when I'd be able to name it "Author" and bring it home as a tangible manifestation of my delivery. It was if my baby was in an incubator, and I could do nothing but watch and pray for its continued health and strength to fulfill its own purpose and destiny someday. I was too brave to question God's sovereignty and too afraid to doubt it. So I watched, waited, listened and wrote, or tended to other "children." Even if the writing wasn't coming to fruition just yet, that didn't mean I needed to do nothing. The vision was plain, so I needed to *act* like I believed what I had seen. Especially, since I had learned from Dr. Evans that dreams happen when you're asleep, but visions take place when you're awake. The time soon came when I could hardly tell the difference.

On Saturday, June 16, 2007, I awoke from a dream that left me with answers to questions I hadn't asked. Once again, my grandmother was involved; however, this time, I was the only child. Tune in.

I am back in Bunkie, attending church with my mom and grandma, when a fire suddenly breaks out. The strange thing is that from the outside it appears to me that this isn't our church, but the one my grandmother attended before joining the one I grew up in. It's a huge white church on a hill, on the outside, but the floor plan is exactly that of the brick church I grew up in on the inside. And, it is packed with people from all over our community. Whatever is going on, it has brought everyone out.

On my way back to my seat from the bathroom, I see flames coming from the front of the church. Since the layout is that of my childhood church, the bathrooms are in the back, to the sides of the pulpit. Well, as I open the door to walk out, I see huge flames coming from the front of the building—in the small waiting area where the water fountain and offices are located. As other people start to turn around to see what has captured my attention, screams break out. Then, people start to panic as flames sweep across the ceiling and along the walls. From my location I am unable to see my grandma or my mom, and panic starts to immobilize me when a beam falls and lands across the section of pews I've left them in.

Continuing to helplessly watch the chaos, my feet don't move until a wave of screams echo throughout the building. It is as if the vibrations shake the floor beneath me and suddenly I remember I, too, am in danger. Then, a face I recognize appears. It is that of a man I knew as Uncle Vincent. He is the deceased father of one of my childhood friends. I ask him if he's seen my grandma and mom, and he assures me they made it out safely. As I wonder why a man who passed away years ago is there, he seems to read the expression on my face. Still, he doesn't stop or answer my nonverbal question. Instead, he ushers me to safety as well.

Once outside, Uncle Vincent points in the direction of a big tree and disappears. I look ahead to see my mom standing behind my grandma, who is resting in a chair. When I turn to look back at the church, it becomes engulfed in flames. I then walk hurriedly towards my grandma and my mom. As I approach them my mom is smiling, but she has this look on her face that lets me know there is concern.

The closer I get to them I can see my grandma's exact expression, too. She appears to be tired, if not exhausted. Immediately, concern grows inside of me and I walk to a slower, steadier pace. Just then, I realize one person is missing to complete this photo of our family—my sister. Then, it dawns on me that although my grandma practically raised my sister and I, we don't have one single picture with her and my mom. The entire scene now seems incomplete and a feeling of sorrow falls upon me. It's as though my grandma senses it too, because she lowers her eyes and sighs softly. When I am close enough to touch her, I stoop down and take her hand in mine. She looks at me as if she wants permission for something in such a childlike manner that it's humbling. Still, my mom stands behind her smiling as if clueless to what is transpiring between me and Muh.

In unspoken words, my grandmother speaks to me with her eyes and shares with me words I still hear in my heart today. It's as if she's longing to say something, but she never speaks; she just looks at me with the last expression I know—without a doubt—I'll ever see on her face.

Leaning closer to her, I break the silence. Allowing a smile to form on my face, I feel it is imperative for her to know not only does she have my full, undivided attention, but that she also has my full, unmistakable compassion as I speak, "It's alright. We'll be okay. You can go on now, you hear?" Just then, I rose up a little and gave Muh a hug. My grandma laid her head on my shoulder and died. I felt her spirit leave her body as I held her in my arms. Then, I raised my left hand, gave God praise, and cried.

After that dream, I woke Derrick up and shared it with him. Moments later the phone rang, and my mom informed me that Muh had been taken to the hospital a second time in a week and had a doctor's appointment on Tuesday. Hanging up the telephone, I told Derrick and the first question he asked was if I wanted him to drive me to Bunkie. My response, "No, she has a doctor's appointment on Tuesday. I'll wait to hear what he says before I decide to go. My only concern is she might not make it to Tuesday."

Over the next couple of days, my family was constantly on the telephone with each other. They were praying for one thing, but I was praying for another... for my premonition to *not* be true. My grandma could *not* be dying. And, God could *not* be letting me see it before it happened.

I wanted to gather my family together and let them all know what I had seen, but none of them knew the depth of my gift. Sure, they'd heard about some of the dreams I'd had over the years, but never had I prophesied before and I didn't want to get cussed out now.

Usually, I waited until something happened, and then I would say I knew it would happen and how. Part of the reason was because I still didn't believe God would trust me with something so precious, yet so powerful. So, with each manifestation, I needed more confirmation. Well, two days later, on Tuesday afternoon, my grandmother passed after I prayed to accept God's will and His gift, and that as He prepared me to receive her death He'd also equip me to be bold enough to speak life—even in the face of adversity.

Losing my grandmother took me on an emotional roller-coaster ride. She'd been mis-diagnosed years earlier with bone cancer, but she actually died of Melanoma—the most serious type of skin cancer. So, please know I'm very serious about my sunscreen.

The more I thought about the dream, the more I believed my grandma wanted both my sister and me with her and my mom, the way it used to be. She wanted to see us one more time, but I let fear paralyze me and never gave my sister the opportunity to go if she wanted to. One of my best friends reminded me that if I was supposed to be there I would've been, as consolation. Still, one of my biggest regrets is not getting on the road that Saturday morning when I awoke from that dream. It was almost if Muh had come to me to say good-bye, but needed the assurance that it was okay to leave. It was two weeks later before I had a chance to properly grieve. But, the day after she died I managed to pen the following tribute for her obituary. To this day, I don't know when I took the time to write this; I just know I did.

Then You Went to Sleep

In my dreams I saw your face,
And you seemed a little concerned.
You looked at me with weary eyes,
And my heart began to mourn.

Squeezing your neck, I gave you a hug,
And I whispered in your ear,
"It's okay. We'll be alright.
You can go on now, you hear?"

As I patted your back, you let out a sigh,
And tears escaped my eyes.
Still, I raised my hand and gave God praise,
Because in my arms you died.

I wasn't there when I wanted to be,
For whatever reason He deemed;
But, three days prior, I saw your face,
Because He speaks to me in my dreams.

In my dreams I saw your face,

And we were both at peace.
You relaxed your body and I held you close,
And then you went to sleep.

There were times when I wanted to throw in the towel or put down my pen during all this time, but my grandmother's memory has helped me persevere. As I have continued to "tarry" on the altar over my writing, I've been reminded of the children I fought so valiantly for in my previous dreams before she died. Then, I am challenged never to doubt my gift or my anointing… never to question my call… in her passing; to speak the truth in love; and, to let my writing be the conviction.

I don't quite know yet what else the meaning of the dream entailed, but I do know there was a sense of freedom I hadn't experienced before in my efforts to "save the children." Had my grandmother's death signified the tearing down of walls, the collapse of a system, or the freedom of strongholds?

Certain I had followed through on what I'd been instructed to do, for the longest time I could not understand why the publishing process had been halted for so long. The emotional and mental turmoil I went through, daily, as I tried to figure out why the book hadn't manifested caused me great pain. I went to bed some nights in tears, because I could only imagine what people were saying. But, in it all, I held onto the Word of God. You know, "As a man thinks within, so is he." (Proverbs 23:7) So, I learned to think like a *New York Times* Best-selling Author. Then, I pretended to be one. It was then that I was able to walk, talk, and act like I was one already.

Later, my mind raced back through all of my earlier attempts to publish over the years. I thought back to a day when I drove to Ft. Worth and noticed a billboard I'd never seen before, even though I had driven that route almost daily over the years when going to meet Derrick after work. The billboard caught my attention because the only thing on it was speak4achild.org. I had *never* seen that billboard, so when I made it home, immediately, I went online in search of something. Before I searched, I was like *okay, Lord, I don't know how that sign seemingly popped up between yesterday and this evening, but I got it.* Nothing came up for the website at all, but a bunch of other children's advocates' links appeared when I Yahooed it. I was like, *I know You're not telling me to start anything, because I just want to write. That's it.*

With speak4achild.org on my mind years later, I continued to pray. I prayed for clarity, for my call, for children, and specifically *for* my call to children. In the meantime, we joined Oak Cliff Bible Fellowship in August of 2008 and Dr. Evans started teaching a series on revival in September. This was confirmation that we'd found the right church home, because revival had become my personal mantra. It started with the prayer for my family in the beginning. Then, it grew to include my hometown, my country, and now the world. Throughout this series, Dr. Evans has mentioned numerous scriptural references that God used to speak various things to me in the beginning, like 2 Chronicles 20:15-17 which references this battle not being mine, but God's.

Joining OCBF back in August didn't just feel right—*it was right.* Dr. Evans unknowingly confirmed a multitude of things I have experienced over the last seven years, in the last seven months, that he could have no prior knowledge of without God. When I think about that, I am reminded that seven is God's number of completion.

I was rushing this book, because I didn't recognize in the natural scheme of things all that had to take place spiritually; namely, my family migrating to Oak Cliff Bible Fellowship and sitting under the tutelage of Dr.

Tony Evans, and the death of my grandma, for its release. For months, as I sat at home and wrote daily, I wondered what God had for me next. I still prayed over my writing, but with *Once Broken, Now Blessed* closer to publication I began to pray more fervently over the call to children's advocacy. I knew that's what God wanted, by now; I just didn't know where to begin. Then, one day, it happened.

I decided to try www.speak4achild.org again. I hadn't looked into the organization for quite some time being that I had returned to work after awhile. Still, the domain was available for purchase and the web search brought back several links—one of which was speakupforachild.org. I clicked on the link and then I read and prayed, all the while wondering whether I was supposed to actually register speak4achild.org or work with speakupforachild.org. I didn't know if God had given me one or wanted me to find the other, so I thought about registering the first and emailed the latter. Working with a pre-existing organization was best for me; however, God knew He had free reign over my life. Had He said start the first, I would have. Thankfully, He didn't.

At that time, I requested information from and completed an application for Court Appointed Special Advocates (CASA) of Tarrant County (http://www.speakupforachild.org) to become a volunteer children's advocate. After signing the forms, just when I was about to seal the envelope I Googled CASA Dallas County (which is closer to where I live) and found their link (http://www.dallascasa.org). Having reserved a seat in their next information session, only days before the December 2009 deadline for new advocates, I am excited about being able to do exactly what I was purposed for. The more I learned from the national CASA website, the more I knew this is what I am supposed to be doing—in addition to writing. However, nothing confirmed it more than my interview one week after the information session.

When I arrived, I checked in and took a seat in the waiting area. I was still unsure if I was supposed to be there or actually at the Tarrant County location, because the billboard lead me to Tarrant County first. Well, there on the coffee table, was a newspaper with the headline: the VOICE. I picked one up and read: Dallas CASA. A powerful voice in a child's life. Spring 2008. It was their quarterly newsletter. I became overjoyed, because I knew—without a doubt—this was where I was supposed to be. I brought that copy home and hung it in my office as a reminder that God created me to be Shaundale, voice of power. It doesn't get any clearer than that. Besides, although I'm no expert on the matter, I do think I know the hand of God when I see it!

Not much else has changed over these last eight years, except I recognized that 2007 was our year of completion, 2008 was our year of new beginnings, and 2009 will definitely be our year of gifts and harvest. The seeds have been planted, and the Spirit has watered. I have grown so much, in so many ways. Now, I am like a tree planted by streams of water, which yields its fruit in season and whose leaf does not wither. *I expect* whatever I do to prosper, from this moment forward. (See Psalm 1:3) *Amen!*

With that and everything else I have been through, I just wanted to encourage you in your trials. Heck, re-reading this final manuscript and making the necessary revisions have encouraged me! It may take awhile, but if you stay in faith, like Jeremiah 17:8 says, "*You* will be like a tree planted by the water that sends out its roots by the stream. It does not fear when heat [divorce, mental/emotional sickness, lawsuits, physical disease, death of a loved one, loss of a job] comes; its leaves are *always* [forever, constantly, endlessly, eternally] green. It has no worries in a year of drought [homelessness, unemployment, barrenness, singleness] and never fails to bear fruit [yield a harvest]." *(Inserts and emphasis added.)* I have been there, and you can tell from my story that I'm stronger, wiser, and better for it all. (Shout out to Marvin Sapp!)

As I started to feel as though I had learned all of the lessons I was expected to out of this season of what turned out to be preparation, just to make sure, I prayed some more. In fact, the closer I knew I was getting to God's true and accurate completion of this phase of our lives, the more fervently I prayed. I wasn't afraid of failure anymore either... and the enemy is? Well, let's just say what the prophetess spoke was true: I have no fear of the enemy. He is so small in the grand scheme of my life that I awake to wreak havoc on him; not the other way around. Still, to make sure I had done all I was supposed to for God and no one else—not even myself—I sought the Lord.

By this point in my life it was so *not* about me, if I shared anymore of my business *I* would be the book. So having already prayed, I grabbed my Bible and simply asked the Lord to really bless all of my efforts toward this project. I didn't want any of this to be in vain—the financial ruin, the sleepless nights, the loss of my grandmother, nor the tears.

When the Bible fell open to Isaiah 40:1-2, I read these words: *"Comfort, comfort my people, says your God. Speak tenderly to Jerusalem, and proclaim to her that her hard service has been completed, that her sin has been paid for, that she has received from the Lord's hand double for all her sins,"* I shouted because I felt God had redeemed me.

At one time I went through the thoughts that, once again, I had done so much wrong I'd deserved all that was happening to me and had brought all this "shame" upon Derrick and the girls out of pride. But, the devil was still a liar! He wanted me to think that no matter what God had not forgiven or forgotten. *But,* God said, "Her sin has been paid for *comma!*

That "but" meant He put a pause right there and had something else to say. He added, "[Tell her also] that she has received *from the Lord's hand* double for all her sins." *(Inserts and emphasis added.)* I shouted again! No longer for the gift, but for the Giver! I was reconnected, and it *was* worth it. I was safe again, and I was whole—completely and without void. I was new *again,* and my hard service had been completed and I could start anew. Not just with a testimony though, with an anointing too!

Throughout this journey God had washed me, filled me, blessed me, and anointed me over and over again. As I was constantly reminded, I constantly shouted. If I hadn't learned anything else, I *did* learn how to shout through the storm. So with that said, what else did I get from all of this? When in doubt, shout!

First of all, I didn't know what was going on with us; or secondly, what God even wanted from us. Nor third, did I even know what to expect. Through it all though, one thing remained: He wanted us to praise Him at all times. Not *about* the situation, but *throughout* the situation. Reflecting upon all I've gained in this "brokenness to blessed" experience, that's the one thing that stands out above all.

I learned approximately three years ago, through trial and error, God wasn't as concerned with my happiness as He was with my holiness. Sure, what we'd experienced hurt, but I found that when I praised God anyhow, He blew on it like a concerned parent over a scraped knee. He put a Band-Aid on it for me, and then He kissed it and made it better. *Oh,* but when I hurt and complained that was when He re-applied the pressure *every time.* I guess

He figured I wasn't healing properly just yet, so He had to break me all over again to reset my bones and straighten me out some more. That's because He wanted me to be happy and healthy, not happy and sin-sick. And, He wants the same thing for you!

EPILOGUE

You have no idea how happy I am; my baby's coming home! In April of 2001, I was convinced I had been victimized on so many levels. Yet, here I sit in April of 2009—eight years to the week of the car wreck, layoff, and lawsuit—a new person, with a new name, and a new purpose.

Somewhere along the road, I chose to start believing God and am now persuaded that He really does bless, and He adds no sorrow to it (see Proverbs 10:22). I'm almost sure it has to do with one Easter losing everything and another, eight years later, experiencing God on levels that made it all insignificant. For instance, on the morning of April 2, 2009, I laid awake in bed until 4:00a.m. I couldn't figure out why I was unable to sleep until it later dawned on me that I had culminated 11 years in the Spirit that previous day and hadn't acknowledged it.

Having praised and thanked God, I finally made one "birthday" request: Father, protect me from all of the people who are going to say I'm crazy; prepare me for the opposition. That's when in the stillness of the morning I heard, "Shaundale, you're not crazy; you're chosen. Don't let the few who are chosen be overtaken by the many who have settled for the call." That was all I needed, and it will remain my constant reminder and motivation simply because, if I have done what was required of God to pour out His spirit upon me, who can be opposed to that? You can't, in good conscious, hate the meek for being meek or despise the humble when He raises them up, can you? It was also very reassuring, because my devotion for the day was Job 8:21. "He will yet fill your mouth with laughter and your lips with shouts of joy. *Amen!*

I once listened to a writer I admire (and someday aspire to be like) interview on a local radio station. He made a great comment. "When you stop feeling like fighting, your dream will take over and fight for itself." That was how I had felt for the last six years while *Once Broken, Now Blessed* seemed to lie dormant. I no longer wanted to fight; especially, after God kept allowing stuff to be taken away. I was tired of fighting. Still, I *had* to write.

When I came across Proverbs 18:16 (your gift will make room for you and place you before great men), I understood. That's what the author meant; the gift *would* fight for itself. Now, I've got my seatbelt on, because it's about to take me somewhere, too! And, I promise you, if you'd trust God to work whatever you're going through for your good, then you'd quote me in saying, "Whether I'm up or if I'm down, wear a smile or even frown, I recognize—in it all—for my good and to His glory." *Hallelujah! Hallelujah! Hallelujah! Praise His name!*

During this last year, we had one more car accident. The entire family, including Vanity (the dog), was involved. I was behind the wheel as we sat in traffic atop westbound Interstate 20 at the exit of southbound Highway 67 on our way home from Dallas. I glanced into the rearview mirror to see an 18-wheeler, minus the trailer, coming at us full speed. All I could do was pray, "Help us, Jesus," and prepare for the collision as Derrick turned to see what I was looking at.

As I inched the car to the right, in order to get to the shoulder and avoid the accident I saw about to happen, the driver of the 18-wheeler veered right too. I then inched my way back over to the left, because it appeared he was trying to hit the shoulder in order to avoid the van that separated him and us. While he did that, I inched forward in order to try not to get the full impact of what was about to take place. Well, he hit both the wall and the van. Then, the van hit us. Fortunately, I had inched forward enough to avoid hitting the car in front of us. Still, the car was totaled but, thankfully, we were safe. We were stranded on top of a bridge. We went from being *in* traffic to being *the* traffic. I couldn't believe what had happened. No one in our car was hurt, but the girls were a bit shaken. Vanity just sat there looking at us like the one time we decided to bring her along we all *had* to get hit. It was almost funny.

Over the years, I have had everything from a Geo Prizm to a Jaguar XJ8… and none of them out-drove, out-road, or out-performed the other. They all got me from one destination to the next in the same amount of time—nothing supernatural about that. They all sat in the parking lot or garage until I moved them—nothing supernatural about that. Neither came and rescued me when I need it; of those I didn't sell/trade, neither was there for me once tragedy struck—*absolutely* nothing supernatural about that. But God, the author and finisher of my faith was, is still, and forever shall be. And, He says, "I am not finished with you guys yet."

I shake my head about that incident from time-to-time. I couldn't save us, and the Mercedes-Benz God had blessed us with by then couldn't save us either. Only calling on the name of Jesus saved us. That car did not matter. Our house did not matter. Our accomplishments or other worldly possessions did not matter. We could've gone flying off the top of that bridge into wherever the enemy intended when he tried to take my whole family out—including the dog. And, the only thing I thought about was the health and well-being of my family and the manifestation of my dream... *this* dream. There isn't a day that passes when I don't think back to several supernatural experiences which have taken place over the last eight years. Those are my mile markers; they give me comfort and reassurance. I recall every moment, as needed, and my fear subsides as my faith prevails.

Derrick and I have been married ten years now, and Emahn and Eian are beautiful girls who love the Lord. Yeah they're cute but, more importantly, their hearts are in the right place. I've told them a nice smile makes you pretty, but a good heart makes you beautiful. I tell them who (the righteousness of God in Christ Jesus) and what (princesses in a royal priesthood) they are, and will continue to do so until God changes their names and reveals more of their identity. Until then, it's our job to speak over them according to the Word of God and hold them accountable to His standards. But, the key is keeping ourselves aligned with His Word and His Way.

Derrick and I recognize that if we choose not to honor God, we cannot ask it of our children; neither can we expect it. And, even if they don't see us fall short, God still knows and will punish the children for the sins of their parents to the third and fourth generation (see Exodus 20:5). I personally don't want my children in bondage over my mess, so I strive to honor God and am quick to repent when I *think* I've fallen short.

Every now and again, I still think about adopting/fostering a child. But, having gone to the CASA meeting, I learned you cannot be on both sides of the legal system. God is so funny—*now*. That's why I kept getting pregnant when I was ready to pursue fostering a child. I couldn't be both a foster parent and an advocate. Although I believe Derrick and I have lots to offer any child at this point in our lives, I would rather stick to God's plan and speak4achild instead. Derrick happily agrees for reasons of his own.

As I have struggled with various aspects of this journey, like waiting, I have decided never to stop believing God for His promises—not even on top of that bridge. Sometimes, all I had was the assurance that He'd called my name or held me close. He taught me that dreams are His way of reminding us that we have a purpose greater than ourselves. I had to know what I knew to be factual; even if I was the only one who believed it to be so.

Sitting in that car, knowing we were about to be hit, my life never flashed before my eyes. I only wondered to what extent we would be impacted, on what level we would be affected, and how effective our family would be in the end. Upon impact, I knew the answers to every question: a little, a lot, and very much. This time, He was totally with me.

It was the lessons learned here in the wilderness, in this place of brokenness, which prepared me for the experience of a lifetime: the freedom of the bridge top… the freedom to walk by faith, not by sight (2 Corinthians 5:7); the freedom to stand firm with the belt of truth buckled around my waist (Ephesians 6:14); and, the freedom to hold tight to the promises of God even when I saw the enemy coming right at me. I didn't see him in the first collision back in 2001, but I felt the impact in every area of my life afterwards, including pledging.

After a 10 year haitus from my sorority, as I wrestled with the Spirit concerning all He had revealed to me concerning it, I was ready to walk away forever. Years prior, my financial membership had fluctuated. I was active, then I wasn't. Still, even then, I couldn't bring myself face the truth.

Over time, I was severely challenged by a non-soror but sister in Christ. She asked me if I wanted someone else's 19 or 20 year old daughter to duplicate my experiences. *Ouch! That hurt.* "No, indeed," I shouted. "If the trip can be made in 40 days, why take 40 years!"

I realized maybe that's why I'd desired to be an Undergraduate Advisor had I remained active. I wanted to be one of the sorors who was willing to put their faith on the frontline and gather to touch and agree that our next line of young women were going to uphold Christ's standards "so help them God" when they come in, undergrad or not, 25 or 50. If I had anything to do with it, we were *all* going into the promised land shouting what I tell my own daughters, "I'm your big sister *in Christ* before I'm anything else." That's why, parents, "do as I say, not as I do" *doesn't work!* And, truth be told, many of us can't hold anyone else accountable because we're not upholding any kind of standard ourselves.

So, with that, I've felt compelled to now take my rightful place and actively serve my sorority as a mentor in its mentoring program. If some *real* woman of God had gotten to me at 12 and shared with me my true identity in Christ, I would not have broken down at 21 in search of the enemy's lie. Besides, had I not pledged, I would not have a fraternity brother who was my Jonathan and gave up his seat in order for me to receive my reward the night of the prophecy.

I believe the Lord has released me for such a time as this, and my hope is that my own experiences will help prepare the next generation to pledge their hearts, minds, and strength to Christ and serve Him through and by whatever means He makes available to them. Because, afterall, until you serve Christ you *cannot* serve man (neither can you serve *a man* ladies).

Today, I have so many wonderful Bible heroes: 1) the woman with the issue of blood who persevered; 2) David who was able to lead others even when he himself was at a loss; 3) Noah who worked faithfully and diligently on his own assignment, and probably looked as foolish as I have all these years announcing, "The book is coming! The book is coming!" 4) Jeremiah who cried for the lost; and, now, 5) John the Baptist.

John the Baptist was the voice of one crying out in the wilderness. So, it has become apparent to me that all I really needed to do was accept my call, or what I've recently defined as my *life's challenge [from God],* to advocate for children and let my writing be the conviction (make straight the way of the Lord). I get to touch hearts and change lives *one voice* at a time. That's it. No bells and whistles; no jumping through hoops. Am I afraid? Well, just because I have never liked public speaking, and I know I cannot do it in my own strength. But, that's how the Lord works. If I could do it on my own, I wouldn't need Him. He called me voice of power, so I *must* be voice of power—capable of living it out only in Him.

The interesting thing in all of this is that it started with a car wreck and ended with a car wreck. And, right smack in the middle of both crashes, God was preparing me for the fight of my life… the original dream (you're going into battle). Who knew all the years of going to court, fighting lawsuits, etc. were grooming me to fight for children's rights. *Me, a children's advocate?* That was the *real* mindblower! I fought that entire process which, by the way, had absolutely nothing to do with what I was fighting anyway. It was just one more thing working for my good; yet, not knowing the ultimate plan

I didn't make the connection. Oh, but how great a gift from where I now stand!

I felt like I'd lost the world. Instead, God gave me more than I ever could have imagined possible; things I could never buy. He gave me new life... *more abundantly* (see John 10:10). He gave me a purpose, a promise, and a pen—with an anointing! All of which the enemy sought to steal, kill, and destroy.

Like me, everyone has a call, life challenge, purpose, destiny—or whatever you choose to recognize it as. And, now, I firmly believe our goal should be nothing short of setting out to find whatever it is, daily. God created each of us for something *far* greater than ourselves, and He wants to show us what. I'm not saying to you, "Quit your job," but I am suggesting that you ask yourself the "hard" questions in life. For instance, is power greater than purpose? Is wealth more desirable than willingness? Then again, what do I know? Except whom I am and what I'm supposed to be doing in this life. In the end, isn't that what really matters?

for Personal Reflection

"He is like a shepherd: He gathers the lambs in his arms and carries them close to his heart." Isaiah 40:11

_____'s

(Insert your name)

Testimony of Trials and Triumphs

Daily Prayer:

Good morning Lord, today, help me to trust You unconditionally to fulfill the plans You have for my life, and to serve You consistently as they fully manifest. For You know the plans You have for me, plans to give me a future and hope—for my success and not my demise—in Jesus' name, amen.

Brokenness:
The Trials

He leads me.
I am dependent on Him to build my trust.

Brokenness (adj.)
Subdued totally; humbled: a broken spirit.

"Those who sow in tears will reap with songs of joy. He who goes out weeping, carrying seed to sow, will return with songs of joy, carrying sheaves with him." (Psalm 126:5-6)

Brokenness symbolizes spiritual dependence. It is because dependent people need others to get what they want and/or need. Likewise, we are to depend on our Shepherd to give us what we want, realizing that He depends on us to trust Him to give us what we need. Dependent people cannot choose to become spiritually interdependent *with* God, without choosing to be faithfully independent *in* God first. They don't have the individuality to *do* it, one; and they don't possess enough of themselves to *be* it, two.

Prayer

You, oh Lord, are close to the broken-hearted and You save those who are crushed in spirit. Hear me now and give me a clean heart, renewing in me a right spirit that I may overcome by the blood of the Lamb and the word of my testimony, in Jesus' name, amen.

Part One

We must first and foremost understand that God is the Shepherd, and no matter what we do as sheep we are His; we are saved. We must now strive to trust Him to take care of both our natural and spiritual needs. Like any good parent, at this level we can at least expect Him to provide the basic necessities of food, clothing, and shelter. It is His job as our Heavenly Father.

I once heard it said, "When you're saved, expect necessities, but when you're blessed, expect abundance." God told Moses, in Exodus 6:2-8, He wants everyone to know Him as Lord (Jehovah), not God [of wrath] as Abraham, Isaac, and Jacob had. Decide today to move out of the "God's going to get you" zone and into the "Lord, My Provider" arena. Start getting to know Him as your Shepherd. If not, there will be consequences.

As we see in Psalm 23:2, the Lord, who is our Shepherd, makes us lie down in green pastures. That lets me know sometimes God goes to extremes just to get closer to us. It's either take a break (as in make time), or be broken and have to take time [off].

When a sheep starts a pattern of wandering off, oftentimes the shepherd willingly breaks its leg so it will become helplessly dependent upon him. During this experience, the shepherd carries the broken sheep on his shoulders, or in his arms, in order to discipline it and teach it to stay near. The sheep, through this process of brokenness, becomes solely dependent upon the shepherd and gets comfortable in the presence of its lord. It will then grow closer to the shepherd and learn that the safest place is near him or simply in his presence.

In the area of spiritual dependence:

1. How do you personally define brokenness?

_____
_____
_____

2. Based on your answer, are you able to recognize brokenness in your own life and/or in the lives of those around you? Why, or why not?

_____
_____
_____

3. If so, what part did/has brokenness play(ed) in your salvation and/or spiritual growth?

_____
_____
_____

4. Having been broken (be it your health, heart, finances, circumstances, pride, etc.), Your Lord will then place you on the path of righteousness. It is at that time when He will begin to lead you in an area that seems to be life-threatening, in your opinion, but safest in His, as He attempts to increase your faith and build your trust. God will, in a sense, allow you to "limp" after Him as He shows you that He only bothers to train those who are in His pasture. Then, He will lead you beside still water, or with the Holy Spirit, on the path to righteousness because the Holy Spirit is a constant keeper, or Guardian.

5. In which of the following areas are you able to identify with brokenness? Explain if applicable.

   a. Emotionally (example: depressed; unfulfilled life)

_____
_____

b. Financially (example: lack of finances; poor steward)

c. Physically (example: weak; ill)

d. Mentally (example: stress: worry; tired)

6. What circumstances in your life can you contribute to brokenness in any given area? (Example: relationship demise, job termination, death of a loved one) How did you handle the situation?

   After being broken and having gained a new perspective in your Shepherd's leading, only then can your soul be restored. It is during this process where you can begin to fully heal and be renewed physically, mentally, emotionally, financially, and spiritually as well. It is then that you are made completely whole.
   Now that you have been restored unto the Father, He can continuously lead. You will then be able to continually follow in a righteous way of living for His glory. A righteous way of living does not mean you won't *look* back, but that you will not *go* back. The

people around you will be able to see the change and know you are the righteousness of God. This is all done to the glory of the Father, so that He can get the praise for what He has done in your life. Simply put, "Drastic times call for drastic measures," as someone once said. Yes, it was necessary for Him to take this route. It was needed in order for you to heal and to grow, in hopes that you may one day lead others. Remember, in order to lead, one must first follow.

7. Following the leading of the Holy Spirit, what were you able to learn in your last storm? What are you able to share with others regarding the experience?

_____
_____
_____

8. What can you apply as a life lesson? Give a scenario.

_____
_____
_____
_____
_____

Blessedness: The Triumphs

He walks with me.
I look to Him, in my independence, to increase my faith.

Blessed (adj.)
Held in admiration; valued.

"Know that the LORD has set apart the godly for himself; the LORD will hear when I call to him." (Psalm 4:3)

Blessed(ness) symbolizes spiritual independence. Able to independently make trustworthy decisions regarding taking care of ourselves, spiritually independent people can get what they want through their own faith effort, because they are able to make mature faith-based decisions that God will honor. True independence of spiritual personality empowers us to act *with* God, rather than be acted upon *by the enemy*. It frees us from our dependence on circumstances and other people, but is not the ultimate goal in spiritually effective living.

Prayer

Father, I recognize that after I have suffered for a little while You, the God of all grace who has called me to Your eternal glory in Christ Jesus, will Yourself complete me and make me what I ought to be, establishing and grounding me securely, as well as strengthening and settling me, amen.

Part Two

Now, you should be at a point where God can use you greatly. The road on which you are presently traveling isn't necessarily one you'd call safe, due to your brokenness, but you are not afraid because you have learned He is with you always; not so much in your visual sight, but in your spiritual sight. He is there in your restored soul, and you are now able to discern for yourself the difference between the good, bad, best, or worst path. Just the presence of God in your spirit keeps you from fear, and in essence keeps you from falling.

The Bible says in Proverbs 9:10, *"The fear of the Lord is the beginning of wisdom, and knowledge of the Holy One is understanding."* You are wise to have trusted Him. This truly is the blessing, to know Him as you now do. Arise in holy boldness and allow your steps to be ordered. The Lord, *your God*, is with you!

In the area of spiritual independence:

1. How do you personally define "being blessed"? What role has it played in your growth or sanctification?

_____
_____
_____

2. Based on your answers, are you able to recognize the blessings in your own life and the lives of those around you? Why, or why not?

_____
_____
_____

3. Now that you know what to look for, can you recall a

season of brokenness in your own life? If so, in which areas do you now recognize your blessings? Explain how or why?

___

___

___

    The rod and staff are typically used for guidance and protection. Instead of regretting chastisement, we are to accept it. It is because with the straight end the Shepherd lovingly directs, and with the hooked end He equally guards. The Bible says in Proverbs 13:24 *"Spare the rod, spoil the child."* We typically quote this passage; however, it is usually mis-quoted. *Help me, Lord!*

    This scripture tells us that, as Christians, we are not to spare the righteous guidance and protection of a child, simply put. Because failure to reprimand—not always whip—means failure to *lead*; and therefore, *the lack of guidance or spiritual direction* will ruin, mess up, damage—if not devastate and destroy—a child (natural or spiritual). Not the lack of *beating*, but the lack of *blessing. Deliver us, Jesus!*

    As Christian parents, grandparents, guardians, and so on, we are spiritual leaders who should be in the habit of blessing our children from generation to generation, which is the gem in all of this. I realized this one day after I had whipped Emahn. I don't remember the event which led to the action I opted to take, but I felt seriously convicted afterwards. This was not the first time it had happened either. In fact, it was more like the last three or four times I had whipped her. I felt like there had to be a better way. So, uncomfortable about the situation, I prayed. I said, *"Lord, show me how You want me to treat your child. How do you expect me to parent?"*

    It was about a week later when I'd dropped her off at Pre-K and was heading home, that He dropped the words "discipline does not equal whipping" into my spirit. I cried. I knew what I was feeling wasn't anything I had made up. I got whipped; my sister got whipped; my friends got whipped. Whipping was all I knew, but God was showing me a better way because I asked Him for one. I decided then to parent His child, His way... by treating her as a disciple, as opposed to acting as a disciplinarian.

When I picked Emahn up from school, I apologized to her. Yep, you read right. I apologized to my three-year-old daughter for handling her in the "tradition" of parenting and not the "spirit" of parenting. I could actually see a change in her demeanor. It's like a burden was lifted from her shoulders right before my eyes. I saw a spiritual transformation take place in her, because I said I'd only whip her if the Spirit told me it was time for a leg breakin', which meant I had to remain spiritually connected in order to hear Him. Ever since then, I have tried to lead my girls as my Shepherd leads me; oftentimes, we are all surprised.

4. Name some instances in which you have been unexpectedly or surprisingly blessed in the midst of a trial. What did the experience teach you?

_____
_____
_____

5. How have you been able to encourage others, possibly even unawares?

_____
_____
_____

Having lived the 23rd Psalm, a new relationship with your Shepherd allows you the blessed opportunity to see Him do unnatural things in the eye-sight of your enemies. All you have to do is come and sit at the table. Now, your Shepherd will prepare a feast of life for you in the presence of those who watched others, or maybe even sought to destroy you themselves. Prepare for your feast and give thanks. Your rebirth is near!

6. Understanding all that you now know, how will you find contentment with what the Lord has already given?

_____

_____

_____

7. What can you presently give thanks for in being where He now has you?

_____

_____

_____

8. What do you think God was trying to teach you all along?

_____

_____

_____

_____

_____

Dwelling:
The Testimony

He resides with me.
I believe in Him, in my interdependence, to sustain my assurance of Him.

Dwelling (n.)
A place to live in; an abode.

"I am the Vine; you are the branches. Whoever lives in Me and I in him bears much (abundant) fruit. However, apart from Me [cut off from vital union with Me] you can do nothing." (John 15:5, Amplified)

Dwelling symbolizes spiritual interdependence with God. Spiritually interdependent people combine their own efforts with the efforts of their Shepherd to achieve their greatest success. Spiritually independent people, who do not have the maturity to think and act interdependently with God, may be good individual producers (single and satisfied), but they won't be good leaders or team players (married and miserable). They haven't reached a mode of interdependence, with their Shepherd, that is necessary to succeed in marriage, family, or organizational reality (i.e. ministry or sports).

Interdependence is a far more mature and more advanced spiritual concept. We must realize that God and us working together can accomplish far more than even our best efforts could accomplish alone. As interdependent people, we have the opportunity to share ourselves deeply and meaningfully with others, and we also have access to the vast resources and potential of other spiritual beings around us. Spiritual interdependence is a choice only spiritually independent people can make. Only when we become truly self-sufficient *in Christ* will we have the foundation for effective interdependence *with God*. Understanding how what we are impacts every spiritually interdependent inter-action will help us to focus our efforts sequentially, in harmony, with the spiritual laws of growth.

Prayer

Lord God, help me to remember that before I call, You hear me, and before I ask, You answer. Teach me to be mindful that You know the plans You have for me; plans that are to prosper and not harm me, to give me hope and a future. In remembering that, help me to daily press on toward the goal to win the prize for which You have called me heavenward in Christ Jesus, my Lord, in Jesus' name, amen.

Part Three

Are you now ready to be used by God for *His* glory? If so, decide today to become the vessel you were divinely designed, delivered, and destined to be! Make every effort not to stray again. This time you've got far too much to lose if you should fall prey to the enemy and choose to turn back. At this point, not only are you following your Shepherd, but others are following you. If you fall, so might they. God now holds you accountable to, or responsible for, everything you have learned, so keep in mind that *you must go through.*

In the area of spiritual interdependence:

1. What are you naturally able to do, even if not-so-well? List as many things as possible. (Example: run, sing, dance, style hair, cook, etc.)

_____
_____

2. Of the previously compiled list, write all of the items that you are *specifically* talented at. (Example: Something others speak highly of you for always doing well.) List all that apply.

_____
_____

3. Of the second list, which activity(ies) do you really enjoy? List those items you would do even if you were never paid to do so.

_____
_____

4. Which item(s) on the remaining list is/are something you'd like to do for the rest of your life? When you currently use it, is it to God's glory? (In other words, if it's singing can you visualize God clapping His hands to it?)

_____
_____

If you've narrowed your list to include all of the items you do one, exceptionally well; two, to the glory of God, and three, would do free of charge, then chances are you are operating in your gift in at least one area. However, if you aren't certain about where you are, please revisit your previous lists and zero in on those things that cover all three. It may be something as simple as babysitting.

God has specifically gifted each of us to serve Him directly, or to serve Him indirectly through serving others. You may find that you have been called to a children's ministry, to be a Sunday School teacher, etc. When you discover your calling, pray *over it* and use it *selflessly*. However, if you do not discover your calling, pray *about it* and let God use you *selfishly* in the meantime. Either way, I want to hear about it!

In His Love,

Shaundale

Bibliography

Baxter, Mary K. *A Divine Revelation of Hell*. New Kingston: Lowery Ministries International, 1993. Pg. 69.

"blessed." Lexico Publishing Group. 2006. http:/www.dictionary.reference.com. (18 February 2006).

"brokenness." Lexico Publishing Group. 2006. http:/www.dictionary.reference.com. (18 February 2006).

"dwelling." Lexico Publishing Group. 2006. http:/www.dictionary.reference.com. (18 February 2006).

Eastman, Dick. *The Hour that Changes the World*. Michigan: Baker Book House, 1978. Pg. 90.

Smith, Amanda Jane Berry. *An Autobiography of the Story of the Lord's Dealings with Mrs. Amanda Smith the Colored Evangelist; Containing an Account of Her Life Work of Faith and Her Travels in America, England, Ireland, Scotland, India, and Africa, as an Independent Missionary 1837-1915*. Chicago: Meyer & Brother, 1893. Pp. iii, 143-144, 444-445, 505-506.

Troxel, Steve. *Living in the Presence of God... The Works and Life of Brother Lawrence with Devotions by Steve Troxel*. San Antonio: God's Daily Word Ministries, 2002. Pp. 70-71.

Snell, Jay. *How to Claim the Abrahamic Covenant*. Jay Snell Evangelistic Association, 1995.

Stanley, Charles. *How to Listen to God*. Nashville: Thomas Nelson, Inc. 1985.

Book Club
Discussion Questions

1. Surrounded by bad news on every side, how would you have responded differently?
2. Have you ever been stuck-on-stupid regarding a relationship? Career? Lifestyle? Explain.
3. Do you believe in coincidences? Why or why not?
4. Could you relate to the underlying issues of depression, displacement, and detainment to name a few?
5. What would have been your greatest moment(s) of despair?
6. Do you look/listen for the Lord in general, everyday occurrences? Why or why not? If so, has it been beneficial to you in any similar ways mentioned in this book? Explain.
7. Has reading this book personally helped you in your faith? If so, please share how or why.
8. Did you learn anything new about yourself? If so, what can you tell us?
9. Did you learn anything new about God? If so, what was it?
10. Can you think of anyone else who would benefit from reading this book? Are you willing to carry them? Why or why not?

AUTHOR BIO

A native of Bunkie, Louisiana Shaundale Hornes Johnson has been married ten years and is the mother of two. She helps to rebuild communities from the inside out under the leadership and vision of Dr. Anthony (Tony) Evans, Senior Pastor of Oak Cliff Bible Fellowship in Dallas, Texas, as the Adult Programs Coordinator of the Technology Institute/Project Turn.*Around.*

Founder and president of Journey to Journal Publishing, LLC in Cedar Hill, Texas, Johnson has a whole new outlook on and appreciation for the road she has traveled from brokenness to blessedness. Having gone through the fire, she has emerged believing her own allusion: dreams are God's way of reminding us that we have a purpose greater than ourselves, and nightmares are the enemy's confirmation of it. Now, fully awake, she acts on behalf of abused and neglected children as a *Court Appointed Special Advocate (CASA) for Children* in Dallas County.

Comfortable and confident in her calling, Johnson has accepted her life challenge and makes it her personal mission to "save the children." She currently partners/volunteers with numerous organizations whenever possible and continues to work on future manuscripts, as she lets her writing be the conviction. Making her debut as an Inspirational Author, Community Activist and Children's Advocate, Johnson looks forward to touching hearts and changing lives *one voice* at a time.

"ONCE BROKEN, NOW BLESSED"
Book Order Form

Name: _____

Address:
_____
_____
_____

Phone: _____

Email: _____

Number of books requested: _____

Autographed ( ) Yes ( ) No   If so, to whom:

_____

Please mail this form, along with a cashier's check or money order for $14.95 (plus $3 shipping), to:
Journey to Journal Publishing, LLC
P.O. Box 4474
Cedar Hill, Texas 75106-4474

Or, order online at:
http://www.shaundalejohnson.com.

10 % of all orders placed with this form will be donated to Dallas Court Appointed Special Advocates (CASA) for Children.